Educating
the
Human
Brain

Educating
the
Human
Brain

Michael I. Posner and Mary K. Rothbart

American Psychological Association • Washington, DC

First Printing, September 2006
Second Printing, July 2007
Third Printing, November 2007

Published by
American Psychological Association
750 First Street, NE
Washington, DC 20002
www.apa.org

To order
APA Order Department
P.O. Box 92984
Washington, DC 20090-2984
Tel: (800) 374-2721
Direct: (202) 336-5510
Fax: (202) 336-5502
TDD/TTY: (202) 336-6123
Online: www.apa.org/books/
E-mail: order@apa.org

In the U.K., Europe, Africa, and the Middle East, copies may be ordered from
American Psychological Association
3 Henrietta Street
Covent Garden, London
WC2E 8LU England

Typeset in Goudy by World Composition Services, Inc., Sterling, VA

Printer: Data Reproductions, Auburn Hills, MI
Cover Designer: Naylor Design, Washington, DC
Technical/Production Editors: Genevieve Gill and Harriet Kaplan

The opinions and statements published are the responsibility of the authors, and such opinions and statements do not necessarily represent the policies of the American Psychological Association.

Library of Congress Cataloging-in-Publication Data

Posner, Michael I.
    Educating the human brain / by Michael I. Posner and Mary K. Rothbart.—1st ed.
        p. ; cm.
    Includes bibliographical references and index.
    ISBN-13: 978-1-59147-381-7
    ISBN-10: 1-59147-381-0
    1. Brain. 2. Brain—Growth. 3. Child development. 4. Attention.
  I. Rothbart, Mary Klevjord. II. Title.
    [DNLM: 1. Attention. 2. Brain—growth & development.
3. Child Development. 4. Child. 5. Infant. WS 105.5.C7 P855e
2007]

    QP376.P67   2007
    612.8′2—dc22
                                                 2006009971

British Library Cataloguing-in-Publication Data
A CIP record is available from the British Library.

Printed in the United States of America
First Edition

CONTENTS

List of Tables and Figures .... *vii*

Preface .... *xi*

Overview 3

Chapter 1.   Education, Psychology, and the Brain 7

Chapter 2.   Relating Brain and Mind 25

Chapter 3.   Learning to Look 55

Chapter 4.   A Mind of One's Own 79

Chapter 5.   Genes and Environment 99

Chapter 6.   Temperament and Learning 121

Chapter 7.   Literacy 147

Chapter 8.   Numeracy 173

Chapter 9.   Expertise 189

Chapter 10.   Preparing for School 209

References 217

Author Index 245

Subject Index 253

About the Authors 263

LIST OF TABLES AND FIGURES

TABLES

Table 3.1. Brain Area and Chemical Modulators for Three
Attentional Networks 60
Table 4.1. Reaction Time and Time to Resolve Conflict 93
Table 5.1. The Effects of Training in Comparison
With Age Effects 114

FIGURES

Figure 1.1. Neuroimaging Before and After Practice 8
Figure 1.2. Brain Networks Revealed by Neuroimaging Studies 9
Figure 2.1. Areas of Brain Activation in Neuroimaging Study 31
Figure 2.2. Network of Cortical Areas Involved in
Word Reading 34
Figure 2.3. Electrodes Used to Measure Brain Electrical Activity 37
Figure 2.4. Event-Related Potentials Recorded From a
Single Electrode Site 38
Figure 2.5. Tracing of Connections Between Hemispheres
by Diffusion Tensor Imaging 40
Figure 2.6. Role of Effortful Control in Modulating Personality
in Two Cultures 47
Figure 2.7. A Schematic of the Attention Network Test 49
Figure 2.8. Brain Areas Active for Three Attentional Networks 51
Figure 3.1. Measuring Visual Acuity in Infants 56
Figure 3.2. Development of Orienting Function During Infancy 57
Figure 3.3. Network of Cortical Areas Involved in Orienting
to Sensory Stimuli 61
Figure 3.4. Development of Inhibition of Return in Infancy 66

Figure 3.5.   Soothing by Orienting of Attention 72
Figure 3.6.   Apparatus Used to Examine Learning in Infants
               and Young Children 75
Figure 4.1.   The Interaction of the Anterior Cingulate With
               Other Brain Areas 81
Figure 4.2.   Cognitive and Affective Division of the Cingulate 83
Figure 4.3.   Conflict-Related Tasks for Young Children 84
Figure 5.1.   A Network of Areas Involved in Schizophrenia 104
Figure 5.2.   Attention Network Test Results for Patients
               With Chronic Schizophrenia 105
Figure 5.3.   Imaging of Brain Areas During the Attention
               Network Test for Different Genetic Alleles 108
Figure 5.4.   Comparison of Human and Primate Conflict
               Resolution Scores 111
Figure 5.5.   Examples of Exercises for Training Attention
               in Young Children 113
Figure 5.6.   Scalp Electrical Activity With and Without
               Attention Training 116
Figure 6.1.   A Model of Mechanisms for the Influence
               of Temperament on Subjective Experience in
               School Situations 142
Figure 7.1.   Model of Operations Involved in Reading 149
Figure 7.2.   Areas of the Cortex Critical to Fluent
               Reading Acquisition 150
Figure 7.3.   A Time Line for the Activation of Different Forms of
               Information and Process During Word Reading 157
Figure 7.4.   Transfer of Information Between Brain Areas During
               Semantic Analysis 160
Figure 7.5.   Improvement in Reading Resulting From Training 167
Figure 7.6.   Brain Activity During Reading Before and
               After Training 168
Figure 8.1.   The Distance Effect in Number Processing 175
Figure 8.2.   Reaction Time as a Function of Notation, Distance,
               and Responding Hand 177
Figure 8.3.   The Anatomical Locations Involved in
               Number Comparison 179
Figure 8.4.   Development of Number Comparison 180
Figure 8.5.   Paradigm for Exact Calculation and for Approximation
               for Simple Arithmetic Problems 184
Figure 9.1.   Studying Performance in Expert and Novice
               Chess Players 190
Figure 9.2.   Electrical Signs of Individual Differences
               in Working Memory 196

Figure 9.3.   Hippocampal Activation During a Memory Task 198
Figure 9.4.   Development of Sequence-Learning Skill 200
Figure 9.5.   Comparison of Brain Areas Involved in
              Perception and Imagination 206

PREFACE

Parents, philosophers, psychologists, and educators have for centuries struggled with questions about learning in the young child. Questions about learning have been referred to general ideas about what it means to be human, and how the human brain might constrain what the child is capable of learning. Nevertheless, until recent years, the brain has remained much of a mystery, allowing each thinker to endow it with the properties that best fit their conclusions. This situation has now changed dramatically with advances in our understanding of the human brain. It is now possible to image the normal brain during thought (Posner & Raichle, 1994; Toga & Mazziotta, 1997).

During the past 10 years, we have run a joint laboratory of attention and temperament at the University of Oregon. We have based much of our work on the results of model tasks based on imaging of adult cognitive and emotional processes. We began the study of development of attentional networks in infancy by examining anticipatory eye movements toward objects presented at predictable positions. Infants were able to orient their attention to predictable positions but encountered troubles when there were conflicting cues about where the next event would occur. It was not until they were 2 to 3 years old that the ability to resolve conflict developed. In our work with adults, this ability was related to the activation of a high-level attentional network that regulates cognitions, and development of this network appeared to be a crucial step in the ability of children to regulate their behaviors. We also found large individual differences in both toddlers and adults in the ability to resolve conflict, with these differences related to temperament and to different forms of the genes associated with dopamine and other chemicals that modulated the attention network. This finding led us to wonder whether we could influence executive attention by training during its development.

At about the same time this research was developing, we began to collaborate with the Organisation for Economic Co-operation and Development (OECD), a group of more than 22 developed countries that arose out of the U.S. Marshall Plan following World War II. OECD wished to hold a number of meetings to engage educators, scientists, and policy planners in understanding the significance of brain research for educating the world's children. We were involved in a number of meetings and, with the help of OECD, developed networks to work on early childhood literacy and numeracy. This work has led to the design of a Web site (http://www.teach-the-brain.org) that allows teachers interested in brain research to find out more about this research and to contribute their insights. This Web site is actively engaging teachers.

We believe these efforts merit the attention of educators and others interested in the early education of children. The ability to control attention can be important in the child's adaptation to school and ability to acquire the important skills of schooling. In this volume, we relate our current knowledge of the developing brain to issues of teaching and learning within various domains. The volume emphasizes methods of research in the development of attentional networks, and it is meant primarily for teachers, researchers, and students interested in the development of brain systems underlying attention, and for those who work with caregivers. In this volume, we suggest potential application of these findings to education, while recognizing that educational design is a complex and sophisticated art. We offer to those interested in carrying out educational designs our understanding of relevant brain research, with the hope that it may form a basis for future dialogue between scientists, educators, and parents.

To begin, we propose a few general caveats. First, there is likely to be no single set of rules appropriate for teaching all forms of skilled learning. Some skills may be taught to the very young, but other skills rest on the achievement of more advanced stages of development. In addition, research rarely establishes a simple educational idea as all right or all wrong. Rather, it allows us to see how individual cases may relate to general principles.

Second, much of the research that forms the basis of this volume is as yet incomplete or has yet to be attempted. Thus, this book contains no final answers but tries instead to point the way toward new discovery. Third, we examine some information about how children differ in their response to home and school environments. Parents and teachers need to be sensitive to the wide range of individuality. Brains differ dramatically from one person to another, and we are only at the beginning of understanding how such differences are related to home and classroom behavior, and to the development of cognitive and emotional skills. Finally, even a detailed answer based on new methods of brain imaging may not answer the kinds of questions parents and teachers most want to know. It may be that even when we understand exactly what happens as we read, that understanding will have only a small bearing on how to teach reading. However, at the least, if scholars and practitioners communicate with and provide parents and teachers with information based on research in this volume, parents and teachers may be able to resist overly simple solutions to their problems. They may also ask for the right kinds of documentation of evidence and be guided in directions of their own toward solving problems that arise as children develop and learn.

We are grateful to the many students who have participated in our research and to all those whose work is cited in this volume. Our joint efforts have had support from the National Institute of Mental Health, the James S. McDonnell Foundation through a 21st Century Award, and the Dana Foundation Consortium on the Arts. We gratefully acknowledge support from the Sackler Institute at Weill Medical College of Cornell University, made possible through a donation from Mortimer Sackler and his family. We also thank Vonda Evans, Penny Moore, and Jesse Springer for their work on production of the narrative and figures for this volume. Lansing Hays and Susan Herman and their associates in the Books Department of the American Psychological Association have been helpful and patient as we have put together this volume.

Educating
the
Human
Brain

OVERVIEW

This volume traces development of the human brain from infancy through middle childhood from the perspective of cognitive and affective neuroscience. We view the brain in terms of networks of neural areas that can be shown to be active when adults orient their attention or resolve conflict between competing thoughts or emotions. We ask how these networks develop and what their consequences are for the developing child and the adults with whom they interact. Because formal schooling plays such an important role in this development, we are particularly concerned with networks involved in processing the written word and in carrying out numerical computations.

We recognize that knowledge about the brain alone cannot provide a blueprint for how to educate. Information about brain development can assist only in educational design, which is no less a creative act than is the design of a bridge or a new factory. In their work, engineers and architects base their designs on constraints imposed by materials and the needs of a structure in relation to its site. In the same way, parents, educational researchers, and curriculum designers need to be able to think about the nature of minds and the characteristics of the individual child.

The first part of this volume (chaps. 1 and 2) provides a background for relating new developments to past ideas about the brain and education. In chapter 1, we lay a foundation for this work by describing how new methods of neuroscience relate to the early development of attention and the child's preparation for schooling and learning of school subjects. In chapter 1 we also discuss the history of the formal disciplines and examine how attentional networks constitute the new formal discipline. Chapter 2 provides a brief tutorial on methods that can be used to examine the brain networks underlying attention. Though imaging studies are mostly done with adults, they provide the background for examining how attentional networks develop and how their efficiency differs among individuals.

The second part of this volume deals with the development of attention networks in infants and young children. Chapter 3 examines the development of sensory orienting in young infants. We review how infants develop the ability to direct their attention at 3 to 4 months and examine how developing brain networks provide for this ability and for its earlier limitations. We discuss the use of orienting in soothing the infant's distress. Chapter 4 examines the network that underlies the later developing ability of children to regulate their thoughts and emotions. Though all children develop this network, there are large individual differences in control of attention and other aspects of temperament. Chapter 5 provides a background on how specific training builds on genetic differences to shape the network underlying self-regulation. We also introduce a method for training attention at 4 and 6 years of age, showing that interventions can influence the network's development. Differences in self-regulation are critical for adapting to the school environment, and studies related to temperamental differences are examined in chapter 6. We expect that the success of the training methods will depend on the child's temperament and the influence of the child's environment.

The third part of the volume deals with what is known about brain changes during the learning of individual school subjects. Chapter 7 deals with the most frequently studied such topic, learning to read. Elements of the network involved in reading depend critically on the method followed and the skills developed as the child learns to read. Imaging is an ideal method for identifying the brain areas influenced by each method. The processing of number is dealt with in chapter 8. The ability to comprehend the analog representation of small numbers (the number line) develops surprisingly early, and this skill proves to be of major importance in the child's ability to deal with elementary school arithmetic. Chapter 9 deals with the role of attention and memory in school subjects that rely on the acquisition and utilization of conceptual knowledge. The distributed nature of the brain networks underlying complex knowledge is outlined and used to evaluate instruction. Finally, in chapter 10 we discuss how the design of preschool work could be informed by some of the new findings related to the study of attention and learning in the brain.

It is our belief that the studies discussed in this volume provide a novel perspective on the acquisition of school subjects. The ability to learn literacy and numeracy appears to rest on specific brain networks involved in these subjects and also on attention networks, all of which are partly present prior to the start of formal schooling. Although in recent years parents and teachers have learned about the general importance of the first few years of life, they may not have realized the extent of specific learning about language, number, and attention that takes place. A combination of psychological and brain science studies have given us a window on the shaping of this knowledge early in life.

Our view suggests that education should begin in infancy and involve a continuous cooperative enterprise between home and school in shaping the neural networks involved in school subjects. Parental knowledge of what is happening in the brains of their children can serve as the basis for enlisting a new level of involvement, at least from those parents most likely to be concerned with school achievement.

1

EDUCATION, PSYCHOLOGY, AND THE BRAIN

The ability to see things has always had a dramatic impact in science. The microscope, for example, allowed people to see things too small to be observed by the senses. At the beginning of the 20th century, Santiago Ramon y Cajal was able to observe individual nerve cells under magnification, and during the century's last 2 decades, neuroimaging technology allowed scientists to observe the human brain in operation. For the first time, it was possible to view the areas of the brain that are active during thinking (Posner & Raichle, 1994). A second major 20th-century development stemmed from the epic discovery of the role of DNA as the basis for the gene (Crick & Watson, 1954). By century's end we had a complete map of the human genome (Venter et al., 2001).

Although aspects of neuroimaging technologies had been developing over a long period, only in the late 1980s did it become clear that a new era of direct observation of human brain activity had arrived. The ability to see into the human brain depends on the operation of the nerve cells originally observed by Cajal. When neurons are active, they change their own local blood supply, which makes it possible to trace areas of the brain that are active during cognitive processes by measuring local changes in the brain's blood supply.

It is now possible to look inside the human brain as it thinks. Dramatic pictures can be taken of brain activity tasks such as those involved in

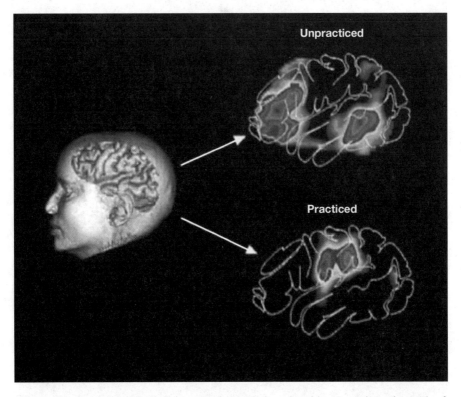

Figure 1.1. Neuroimaging before and after practice. A subject practices the task of generating the use of words such as *hammer* (e.g., *pound*) while his brain is scanned. When he goes through the list the first time, his responses are slow and effortful and a network of brain areas including left frontal and parietal areas is active. After a few minutes of practice, the task is effortless, previously active areas are now quiet, and a new more automatic route to output becomes active. From "Practice-Related Changes in the Human Brain: Functional Anatomy During Nonmotor Learning," by M. E. Raichle, J. A. Fiez, T. O. Videen, A. M. K. McCleod, J. V. Pardo, P. T. Fox, and S. E. Petersen, 1994, *Cerebral Cortex, 4,* p. 14. Copyright 1994 by Oxford University Press. Adapted with permission.

practicing the retrieval of word associations shown in Figure 1.1. Within a few minutes of practice, the brain networks involved change radically. Seeing the brain in action provides information on how brain networks adapt to learning. Figure 1.2 shows the results of a number of such studies and illustrates that particular brain areas can become active in studies of reading, attention, and perception. These results provide a whole new perspective on how the brain responds to common events and tasks.

Over a decade has now passed following the discovery of a method for the active imaging of the mind. During this period, much has been learned about the anatomical areas that underlie many human skills, includ-

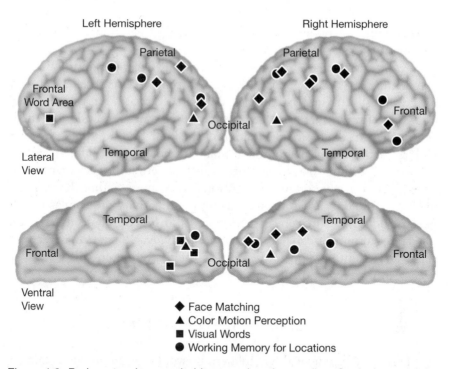

Left Hemisphere   Right Hemisphere

Figure 1.2. Brain networks revealed by neuroimaging studies. Cortical area of the side (lateral view) and midline (ventral view) during a number of common tasks involving passive perception of colors and motions (triangles), the visual word form (squares), working memory for locations (circles), and face matching (diamonds). In all of these a number of discrete areas often widely separated are involved. Adapted from "Functional Brain Imaging Studies of Cortical Mechanisms for Memory," by L. G. Ungerleider, 1995, *Science, 27,* p. 771. In the public domain.

ing aspects of language, face perception, the control of attention, reading, and arithmetic. These studies have generally involved adults, but researchers have also sought to understand skills important to the learning of infants and children. In this volume, we address the significance of these observations. For parents and teachers these new findings will allow for a degree of understanding of human development not available to any other generation. To take best advantage of this new knowledge, educators and parents will need to understand the strengths and limitations of these methods, and researchers will need to understand how to use these methods to identify new lines of inquiry.

Attention has been one of the most important areas for imaging studies (Posner, 2004). It has been possible to image brain networks related to orienting to sensory information, obtaining the alert state and mediating conflict between possible behaviors. Because attentional networks are central to the ability of infants and children to regulate their emotions and behavior, they are at the heart of our volume.

As mentioned earlier, the second major development during the late 20th century was the mapping of the human genome (Venter et al., 2001). It is now possible to understand that some of the variation in the efficiency of neural networks might be due to the form of genes the child inherited. Genes lay down the basic organization of the brain and the time course for the birth and death of neurons, and influence how people differ. Together with experience, they play a substantial role in determining the organization of neural networks important to attention and memory. Although the genes involved in coding structures underlying brain activity are similar for all humans, differences in gene structure are also found. These differences, called polymorphisms, can help account for individual differences in temperament and attention, and relate to how different children will react to a given learning environment.

LEARNING AND EDUCATION

Parents have taught their children, by word or example, since human life appeared. In addition, the professions of teaching and research have gradually added more formal guidance to children's instruction. Educators and researchers have traditionally been concerned about what can be taught and why. Without understanding how experience influences the brain systems of children, however, there has been a wide range of speculation about education and the brain.

Current views range from the belief that education can serve only to select mechanisms that have been already built into the brain (selectionism), to the belief that there is no limit to the skills any person can acquire with practice (constructivism). In his book, *Nature's Mind*, Michael Gazzaniga (1994) put forward a selectionist view of the development of the mind. In this view education is mostly about finding specific skills, the capacity for which is built into the brain. This view holds that genetic determination of what can be learned is so complete that it is foolish to attempt development of skills for which a person is not inclined. Taking a very different view, the late Herbert Simon (Chase & Simon, 1973) argued that we can all become experts, given time and effort. An expert in Simon's view is anyone who spends 50,000 hours acquiring a high-level skill. Simon knew that the brain was involved in such learning, but he did not regard it as limiting what can be achieved in any important way. When two brilliant scholars of mental function hold such opposing views about what education can achieve, it is clear that a further look is needed to reach some kind of consensus about the brain and education.

Cognitive Development

Controversies about education are by no means new, and psychology has often played a central role in them. The psychologist Edward Thorndike developed an approach based on association of ideas (Thorndike & Woodworth, 1901). According to Thorndike, associations between an external stimulus (e.g., a question posed by the teacher) and a response (e.g., the student's correct answer) are the central goal of learning. Specific associations differ from one domain of study to another, and the likelihood that one idea would activate another depended on their similarity. Thorndike argued that any transfer from one field of study to another needed to be based on common elements between the things to be learned. According to his analysis, identical elements between English and Latin or Greek, rather than any general increase in capacity from having learned the classical grammars, made for good transfer.

Association

Thorndike's associationist view of learning was carried further by the students of behaviorism in the early to mid-20th century. Research conducted at the beginning of the century by the Russian physiologist I. P. Pavlov provided a physical basis for association. Pavlov showed that pairing a new stimulus with a stimulus that elicited a reflex led the new stimulus to produce the reflex response. In the classic example, a bell paired with food powder came to elicit salivation. Thus, experience could lead to the acquisition of new associations. This experiment, termed *classical conditioning,* provided a physical basis for the association of ideas.

B. F. Skinner (1968) generalized the reflex ideas of Pavlov, proposing that the association between a response and a subsequent reward could also be strengthened (*instrumental conditioning*). The effect of repeated pairings of response and reward would increase the probability that the rewarded response would occur. Skinner argued that experience worked in much the same way as did evolution: Experience selected the responses that led to a reward, just as evolution selected the genes underlying responses that led to survival. In the educational situation, students make the responses, and rewards most often come from the teacher. Skinner's educational goal was to analyze the mastery of any subject, breaking it down into component steps that would allow the student to easily perform a correct response, receive a positive reward, and thereby have the association increased in strength. As each new correct answer was given in the presence of the appropriate question, it formed the basis for still higher level questions, leading inevitably to mastery of the subject.

The teaching machines and programmed learning that followed from Skinner's analysis assumed that the student can learn best if an environment is created in which no errors occur (Terrace, 1963). Continuous positive reinforcement would gradually shape the response. In one sense, Skinner's view was very optimistic. He, like Simon, felt there were few limitations on what any human might learn. In Skinner's view, the capacity for learning was present in each individual; it was up to the teacher to provide the structure and rewards that fostered learning of the specific associations needed to master a field.

The principle of association of ideas was further developed and related to the brain. The idea was that one thought led to another based on (a) the similarity of the two or (b) their having been previously active at the same time. The idea of association was also transferred to a model of brain function by the Canadian neuropsychologist D. O. Hebb (1949), who later laid out mechanisms by which experience would allow nerve cells to be organized into new assemblies. He argued that when neurons were active at nearly the same time, a physical change occurred that increased their ability to activate each other. The acquisition of a skill required neurons to improve in their ability to communicate by increasing the likelihood that one cell would activate the others. As a skill develops, the assembly of neurons begins to act as a unit or cell assembly (Hebb, 1949).

Cognition

For nearly 40 years in the mid-20th century, the ideas of Jean Piaget dominated psychological thinking about how the mind develops (Flavell, 1963). Piaget produced a detailed and sophisticated treatment describing how the initial genetic endowment of human infants matures in a series of stages into the formal operations of the thinking adult. Piaget placed relatively little emphasis on the ability of education to alter or speed these changes, and his views were used to support the idea that subjects should be introduced only when the child's stage of mental development was ready.

Jerome Bruner (1960) took a different view. He argued, based on a cognitive perspective, that when properly analyzed, any subject can be introduced in some legitimate form to students at any age. Bruner, like Piaget, marveled at the intellectual accomplishments of the infant. Bruner was not arguing that there were critical periods for learning, that is, times when a certain kind of learning must occur or it never will. Instead, he was suggesting that the achievement of mental potential might be based on experiences appropriately provided for the very young. The basic issue is whether the new learning can influence the maturing brain. We examine this issue with respect to attention in chapters 3, 4, and 9 (this volume), and suggest evidence in accord with Bruner's view.

Arguments like those of Skinner, Bruner, and Simon about using psychology to influence educational design were not concerned with any particular model of the brain. In fact, most of the psychologists mentioned earlier, while regarding brain activity as basic to learning in some theoretical sense, believed we could discover all the principles of psychology needed for learning without any reference to brain activity. Although B. F. Skinner was the leading figure in American behaviorism, and Herbert Simon was the founder of the opposing approach of cognitive science, both held similar beliefs about learning and skill development: By studying the student's environment and knowing the relatively simple principles by which organisms learned, it would be possible to guide the educational process. In Skinner's case, the principles were mainly motivational and concerned the optimal use of rewards. In practice this meant having such a detailed knowledge of the subject matter to be taught that it could be broken down into tiny steps, allowing mastery without error. Students would be rewarded at every step.

Simon also argued that the environment must be understood, because it was responsible for the diversity of human behavior. Different environments require different kinds of expertise. Depending on the situation, a person might become more skilled in one but not in another domain, just as the memory of a skilled chess player is merely ordinary when he or she is taken away from the context of a master-level chess game. Simon saw the common internal mechanisms of people as relatively simple and quite uniform, whereas the contents of semantic memory differed because individuals were exposed to varied environments. Though Piaget held to a much more complex theory of cognitive development, in which each stage provides a readiness to learn in particular ways, he, like Simon, did not try to indicate how the maturing brain supported each of the stages.

Transfer of Training and Expertise

At the turn of the 20th century, a view of formal disciplines was dominant in the schools. The basic idea was that the brain's general capacity could be exercised like a healthy muscle, and that certain areas of learning, such as logic, mathematics, Latin, and Greek, were better sources of brain exercise than were other areas. Schools required students to learn these subjects, partly in hopes that they would be able to transfer the increased mental power and motivational discipline acquired from the formal disciplines to whatever else they needed to learn.

As schooling expanded to involve more and more of the population, with the goal of preparing children for work, questions were raised about the usefulness of the formal disciplines. Thorndike's ideas on association of ideas (Thorndike & Woodworth, 1901) were used as the justification for turning away from the notion that formal discipline training would transfer to all other school subjects. In her historical essay on education in America, Diane Ravitch (2000) put the challenge raised by Thorndike in this way:

> The issue of transfer of training became crucial to the viability of the academic curriculum, and the implications for the schools were mind-boggling. Some educational psychologists, citing Thorndike and Woodworth, insisted that nothing learned in one situation could be applied to any other. (p. 65)

Pedagogues quickly realized that Thorndike's experiments had undermined the rationale for the traditional curriculum and that it was up to them to create a new education, one that would train students for the real world of work.

Cognitive Science and Transfer of Training

Much later support for the specificity of training came from applications of cognitive science to skill learning. As computers developed, there was an effort within psychology and cognitive science to produce models of mental processes in the form of computer programs. An early example was the General Problem Solver (Newell, Shaw, & Simon, 1958). This program was able to produce proofs of the basic theorems of mathematics, and it had a powerful influence on the psychology of the time. It was the first clear demonstration that truly complex problem solving could be carried out by a purely electromechanical system like a computer, suggesting that even the highest forms of human thought might be based on computations that could be specified and simulated in a digital computer. The General Problem Solver demonstrated that relatively few basic principles could be used to produce a program capable of proving a broad range of mathematical theorems.

Many followers of this effort believed that the General Problem Solver simulation of the human mind indicated that humans needed to acquire only a very few general principles to solve a wide range of complex problems. This viewpoint was more favorable to the idea of transfer of higher level concepts than were the studies of Thorndike and Woodworth (1901). There then followed an effort to develop computers that could perform many of the tasks of thinking and problem solving that up to then were seen as the exclusive province of human thought. This research on artificial intelligence, however, led away from the idea that only a few general principles were needed. Instead, it was revealed that a great deal of information about the specific domain of application was needed for problem solution within that domain. Duda and Shortliffe (1983) summarized this realization as follows:

> The early hope that a relatively small number of powerful general mechanisms would be sufficient to generate intelligent behavior gradu-

ally waned. When significant problems were addressed, it was often discovered that problem independent, heuristic methods alone were incapable of handling the sheer, combinatorial complexity that was encountered. (p. 261)

When applied to humans, this view led to the concept of expertise based on a large amount of domain-specific learning, acquired with practice and stored in semantic memory (Chi, Glaser, & Farr, 1988). Research on human chess masters led Herbert Simon (1969) to conclude that their skills were based entirely on knowledge about chess and not on any general ability, either innate or learned. Chess masters can reproduce the positions of up to 30 pieces on the chessboard of a master-level game after a brief view of the board, whereas average chess players can reproduce only about 7 pieces. The chess master needs to know nothing about the particular game to do so. However, chess masters' performance on this task falls to that of the average player when pieces are placed in random order or when any other memory test is used. The chess master seems not to have a generally large memory capacity, but only a highly developed memory for meaningful organizations of the chessboard. On the basis of his analyses of chess masters, Simon reasoned that up to 50,000 hours of training was necessary to develop the semantic memory of chess that allowed the master to do so well in remembering positions on the chessboard.

Perhaps the most persuasive evidence of the power of expertise was in the training of several students to exhibit a memory span of up to 100 digits (Ericsson & Chase, 1982). Normally, humans can report only about seven digits in correct order after listening to a random list of digits delivered at a rate of about one per second. However, after months of learning a coding scheme in which each successive triple set of digits was associated with the running times for various track events, students could correctly repeat back 100 digits. When they were switched to remembering letters, their memory span fell back to the usual seven (Ericsson & Chase, 1982).

Psychological ideas about how well skills in one domain can be transferred to another have served to influence how society views the process of teaching the young about the world in which they live. Universities now teach Latin and logic almost entirely to a relatively small group of students specializing in classics and philosophy, and vast numbers of courses present specific knowledge about almost every subject to the general university student.

Attention: The New Formal Discipline?

The controversy between whether humans learn through improvements in general capacities or whether we learn only through domain-specific knowledge has been addressed in the study of the brain. Everywhere in cognitive neuroscience, specific brain networks seem to underlie performance. However, some of those networks have the important property of being able to modify the activity in other networks. For example, much presented in this volume rests on discoveries made in cognition and cognitive neuroscience under the topic of attention. From a psychological view, attention includes changes from sleepiness to high alertness, from focused orienting to a single object to unfocused awareness of the general scene, from responsiveness to external events to responses driven by the achievement of a particular goal.

As we show in this volume, attention involves specific networks of the brain that mature from infancy (see chap. 3) well into childhood (see chap. 4). However, attention also involves regulation of the activity of other networks, thus improving the prospects of acquiring an unlimited number of skills. Attentional networks interact with other brain systems to establish priorities in perception and action. This ability to regulate brain function makes attention relevant to all domains of learning. In chapters 3 through 5 we examine how attention networks develop from infancy to late childhood. We also argue that increases in attentional efficiency can influence progress in a wide range of school subjects (see chaps. 7, 8, and 9). In this sense, attention serves as a different kind of formal discipline that can influence the efficiency of operations of a wide range of cognitive and emotional networks.

INDIVIDUAL DIFFERENCES

Another major contribution to the contact between schools and psychology has been in the study of individual differences in mental ability and in the ability of children to adjust their emotions, activity level, and attention to the demands of the classroom environment. The study of mental ability has taken place largely under the topic of intelligence, whereas individual differences in the emotions, activity, and attention have been examined in the study of children's temperament. In both of these areas there have been efforts to relate the dimensions thought to underlie differences in cognition, emotion, and personality to underlying neural systems.

Intelligence

Prediction of School Performance

The study of intelligence deals with individual differences in cognitive ability predictive of performance in school subjects. A major impetus for the development of intelligence tests by Alfred Binet at the turn of the past century was the beginning of compulsory education in Europe and the United States. As Leona Tyler (1976) put it, "Obviously what the legislation [for compulsory education] did was to assemble in one place, probably for the first time in human history, almost the full range of human intellects, and to make it necessary for educators to struggle with this diversity" (p. 14).

Binet's unique contribution to this effort was to short-circuit philosophical and intellectual problems involved in the definition and measurement of intelligence. Binet based his tests on two important principles that have held up over the long history of intelligence testing. The first was to select test items similar to the skills the test was designed to predict—in this case, school performance. Items on Binet's tests dealt with memory, mental imagery, imagination, attentiveness, mechanical and verbal comprehension, and aesthetic appreciation, relatively specific skills likely to be useful in school. The second principle was to use age equivalence as the measure of intelligence. The intelligence of a child was judged by comparing his or her performance with the performance typical for a child of that age. The *intelligence quotient*, or IQ, was the ratio of a child's score on the test to the average score at the child's age, multiplied by 100 to make the average score for a given age 100. Performance on intelligence test items improved over the life span of the child, and Binet chose to test functions that showed this increase over age in scores, but he then normalized the test for each age group. By basing the tests on the mental functions that grew with age, Binet avoided the problem of defining intelligence. Tests based on these principles have grown in precision over years of refinement, with powerful statistical methods and large numbers of subjects needed to provide accurate norms.

Binet's method was successful in producing a technology for the measurement of intelligence. However, its success was based on avoiding the fundamental question of the nature of intelligence. Intelligence came to mean whatever was measured by intelligence tests. During the 1960s, people began to question whether what was measured by intelligence tests gave a good account of intelligence as manifested in daily life. Measurement of individual differences in intelligence had been isolated from the study of the mechanisms likely to bring about these differences. To determine how differences in intelligence come about, one must relate intelligence to a theory of cognition.

The General Factor "g"

There is a strong historical basis for relating intelligence to a theory of cognition. Even prior to the work of Binet (Tyler, 1976), Francis Galton (1907) attempted to study individual differences in intelligence by examining what he considered to be fundamental human capacities such as the acuteness of the senses and the speed of responses. However, efforts by Galton to find correlations between these predictors and later achievement were not particularly successful. Nor was there any agreed-upon set of basic mental operations that might be thought to be fundamental to thought processes.

The efforts of Galton and Binet represent two distinct approaches to the problem of intelligence. Galton looked for fundamental differences among people of the type that might be explained by brain mechanisms. Binet, however, took on the more practical task of examining problems that required skills similar to those used in school. Though the Binet approach has been widely applied in school to predict success, it has provided no real information as to how individual differences emerge from neural mechanisms, or to what degree learning may change them. Another question pursued throughout the history of work on intelligence testing concerns the degree of relationship across different domains of intelligence. Are there general factors in intelligence or is intelligence domain specific? This issue is quite similar to the one discussed earlier on general versus specific influences on the behavioral and cognitive analysis of learning.

Spearman (1904) used the intercorrelations between scores on simple mental tasks as the basis for concluding that there was a universal intellectual capacity, which he labeled g for general intelligence, along with a number of more minor special capacities. Not all investigators in mental testing, however, have believed that g was as important as Spearman proposed. Thurstone (1924), for example, subdivided Spearman's general factor into a set of primary mental abilities (spatial visualization, perceptual ability, verbal comprehension, numerical ability, memory, word fluency, and reasoning). As more factors emerged as primary mental abilities, a desire grew to develop an organizing framework to support this analysis of individual differences in intellectual skill. One such scheme, represented by the work of Vernon (1961), viewed factors as different levels within a hierarchy. At the bottom are specific factors developed from individual items of tests; at the highest level of the hierarchy is the general intelligence factor g. The hierarchical models represent a loose but nonetheless helpful way of organizing a large number of different factors, while still preserving a general common core to the notion of intelligence.

Guilford (1967) developed a different structural analysis of intellect using a three-dimensional array rather than a hierarchy to organize relations among tests. The three major dimensions of his tests correspond to the content of the mind's representation (e.g., visual imagery, words), the product (e.g., classification), and the mental operation involved (e.g., combining information, comparing). Content corresponds to the domain of representation, whereas operation and product correspond roughly to the type of mental operations seen as fundamental to thought processes.

Multiple Intelligences

A more sophisticated approach to intelligence was stimulated by neuropsychology and has recently proved important for education. Howard Gardner's book *Frames of Mind* (1983) broke new ground. Gardner did not base his analysis of multiple intelligences on scores obtained from tests. Instead, he sought to connect intelligence with general features of brain systems emerging from studies of patients and individual differences in these abilities among normal people. He argued that one could identify at least seven forms of intelligence: linguistic, mathematical, musical, spatial, kinesthetic, and inter- and intrapersonal. Educators adapted his ideas to the design of special curricula that attempted to provide education in each of these domains of intelligence. Gardner's views placed intelligence testing more in line with the neural systems approach of this volume, and his theory has been influential in some public and private schools, giving support to brain-based thinking about curricula. We regard the new brain imaging methods discussed in chapter 2 (this volume) as providing a deeper and more differentiated view of how cognitive tasks are performed by the brain, allowing for new conceptualizations of the nature of individual differences in intelligence (Posner, 2003).

Temperament

Although education typically focuses on individual differences in cognitive skills, learning also depends on children's goals, values, motivation, and their ability to cooperate with others and to regulate both positive and negative emotions. To do an effective job of teaching, one must take the child's emotional and attentional characteristics into account, and these characteristics are studied within the domain of temperament. We define *temperament* as constitutionally based individual differences in reactivity and self-regulation, as observed within children's emotions, motor activity, and attention (Rothbart & Derryberry, 1981). By *reactivity* we mean characteristics of the individual's responsiveness to changes in stimulation. By *self-regulation*, we mean processes modulating this reactivity, including behavioral approach, avoidance, inhibition, and attentional self-regulation. In our view, individual differences in temperament constitute the earliest expression of personality and the substrate from which later personality develops.

In early infancy the caregiver provides much of the regulative control for the child, but mechanisms of self-regulation undergo strong development in the 3rd year of life and beyond (see chap. 4, this volume). So that the processes of education can be better understood, we now trace the development of temperament and the adaptations it supports across different periods of the life span.

History of Temperament

Unlike the study of individual differences in intelligence, the study of temperament had its roots in centuries-old efforts to link individual characteristics to variation in physiological structure. The fourfold typology of the sanguine (positive and outgoing), choleric (irritable), melancholic (sad and fearful), and phlegmatic (low emotionality) types of persons based on the bodily humors goes back to ancient Greek and Roman physicians and persisted throughout the Middle Ages and Renaissance. More modern views of individual differences in temperament, stemming from the studies of Pavlov, were related to the brain. Pavlov, for example, believed that organisms differed in the strength of their nervous systems so that they differed in the degree to which they would be able to withstand high levels of stimulation. It has recently also become possible to relate some of these temperamental differences to genes that vary among people (see chap. 5, this volume). As more is understood about how genes and experience shape brain networks, psychologists will be increasingly able to study educational environments in terms of their overall influence and their effects on different temperaments.

An early British tradition in the study of temperament emphasized self-report measures and the extraction of broad factors from temperament and personality items and scales rather than ties to the brain. However, beginning in the 1950s, Hans Eysenck attempted to relate how the temperament dimensions obtained from self-report scales, particularly extraversion–introversion and neuroticism, were linked to ideas stemming from the Russian reflex tradition. Eysenck's efforts were carried over and modified by Gray into what he called the Behavioral Approach system and the Behavioral Inhibition System. These two systems provided a fundamental basis for thinking about individual differences in behavior.

The application of temperament to child study has been relatively recent (see review in Rothbart & Bates, 2006). In the great normative studies of the 1920s and 1930s, Gesell (1928) and Shirley (1933) identified what Shirley called the early core of personality. Shirley argued that although children's emotional reactions change with development (e.g., children decrease in their expressed negative emotion with age), children's individuality can nevertheless be observed in their disposition toward such reactions as timidity, positive affect, and irritability.

Gesell (1928) noted that for any set of temperamental characteristics, many possibilities for development would exist, depending on the child's social experiences. To illustrate this principle, he used the case of C. D.,

> who had maintained her tendencies to the positive emotions from observations as early as nine months: She is now five years of age, and in spite of a varied experience in boarding homes and institutions she has not lost these engaging characteristics. They are part and parcel of her makeup. . . . It can be predicted with much certainty that she will retain her present emotional equipment when she is an adolescent and an adult. But more than this cannot be predicted in the field of personality. For whether she becomes a delinquent, and she is potentially one, will depend upon her subsequent training, conditioning, and supervision. She is potentially, also, a willing, helpful, and productive worker. (Gesell, 1928, pp. 372–373)

These ideas from the temperament area provide an important bridge to thinking about links between individual differences and educational outcomes. In Gesell's (1928) example, one set of emotional equipment can, depending on the nature of the child's life experience, be related to two quite different possible outcomes (Cicchetti [Cicchetti & Rogosch, 1996] has called this the principle of multifinality). In addition, different sets of emotional equipment can, through different pathways, lead to similar outcomes (the principle of equifinality). Kochanska (1995) has established evidence for different trajectories in more fearful and more extraverted children's pathways to conscience, with the fearful children's conscience more related to the caregiver's gentle punishment and extraverted children's conscience to shared positive emotion with the caregiver. Considered more generally, these ideas provide a helpful way of thinking about how nervous system constraints may operate in development.

Dimensions of Temperament

The researchers who have had the greatest impact on studies of temperament in childhood are Stella Chess and Alexander Thomas and their colleagues in the New York Longitudinal Study (NYLS; Thomas & Chess, 1977; Thomas, Chess, Birch, Hertzig, & Korn, 1963). The NYLS researchers carried out a content analysis of mothers' reports of their children's behavior during the first 6 months of life, identifying nine dimensions of temperamental variability. The proposed temperament dimensions, later applied to all ages, included children's activity level, threshold for reaction, rhythmicity of eating, sleeping and bowel habits, intensity of response, approach versus withdrawal to new situations, general mood, adaptability to change, distractibility, and attention span–persistence. Recent research, however, suggests the need to revise this list of temperamental dimensions (Rothbart & Bates, 2006). We discuss these revisions in chapter 6 (this volume).

In part, revisions may be required because temperament develops, whereas the NYLS content analysis was based only on individual variability in young infants. The dimensions thus identified characterize children only early in life; later developing dimensions were not considered. Although temperament researchers had originally believed that temperament systems would be in place very early in development and change little over time (e.g., Buss & Plomin, 1984), we have since learned that temperament systems follow a developmental course (Rothbart, 1989b; Rothbart & Bates, 2006). Children's tendencies to experience and express negative and positive emotions and their responsivity to events in the environment can be observed very early in life, but children's self-regulatory capacities develop later in the toddler to preschool periods, and continue to develop throughout the early school years.

One major area of development during the early years is children's effortful control (Rothbart & Rueda, 2005). A major aspect of our research links this temperamental dimension with the neural network underlying executive attention as outlined in chapter 4 (this volume). The orienting and distractibility observed in young infants' early months of life are chiefly reactive and automatic. Beginning late in the 1st year and developing through the grade school years, however, executive attentional control allows increasing self-regulation of behavior and emotion (Posner & Rothbart, 1998).

Only recently have researchers considered how ideas of temperament can be applied to the school environment (Keogh, 1989, 2003; Martin, 1989; Rothbart & Jones, 1999). Because children differ in the speed and intensity of their emotional reactions, the same stimulus does not have the same effects for all. Children differ in how easily and intensely they become fearful, frustrated, or positively excited and they also differ in their capacities for attentional self-regulation. Because attentional control involves the regulation of emotions, some schoolchildren will be lacking in controls of emotion and action that other children can demonstrate with ease. By the time of school entry, temperament affects the nature of children's adjustment to the requirements and challenges of the educational setting. Experiences of success and failure in turn influence children's views and evaluations of themselves, their school, and their teachers and peers.

Brain research on the emotions and temperament has been revived by relating animal studies of brain circuitry underlying many emotions, particularly fear (LeDoux, 1987; Panksepp, 1998). These methods have been complemented by studies of emotional responses of patients with specific brain lesions (Damasio, 1994), as well as by studies using the methods of neuroimaging (R. J. Davidson, 2000). The brain systems underlying temperamental self-regulation have also been studied. In this volume we examine some of the mechanisms that allow regulation of emotion by caregivers (see chap. 3) and by the developing child (see chap. 4). Mechanisms of self-regulation play a critical role in the child's adaptation to the school setting.

Alternatives to Temperament

Social Learning and Cognitive Approaches

Behaviorists and social learning theorists of the 20th century emphasized the importance of socialization in the development of individual differences. Temperament differences were not considered; instead, there was an emphasis on the social learning of the child. It was believed that learning in school would be motivated by rewards (social reinforcers, prizes, tokens, and high grades) and sometimes punishments (low grades) from the external environment. The possibility that children might differ in their sensitivity to rewards and punishments was developed in later temperament work (Rothbart, Ahadi, & Hershey, 1994; Rothbart & Jones, 1998).

Social learning theories were subsequently refined by cognitive, social, and behavioral theorists, including Bandura (1989), Dweck (1991), and Eccles (1983). These approaches emphasized cognition by stressing the importance of children's goals, thoughts, and beliefs. The idea was that children's motivation is based on their school-related self-concepts (beliefs about their abilities, competencies, self-worth), expectations for success and failure, and feelings that emerge from anticipated and experienced success and failure. These approaches, especially Harter's (1998), could be easily supplemented by temperament ideas about susceptibility to reward and punishment, but in general, they were not.

Motivation

In more recent times, theorists have stressed the importance of intrinsic motivation, that is, the internal processes that generate interest and approach in subjects of attention. This approach has also focused on children's development of learning goals (Clifford, 1984; Nicholls, 1984) and children's beliefs that what they are doing has meaning. Connell and Wellborn (1991) have also stressed the importance of children's involvement in deciding what they would like to learn and do, giving them feelings of autonomy and control. Again, individual differences in children's reward- and punishment-related temperament characteristics and their related feelings of need for control will be important in revising these theorists' approaches.

SUMMARY

In this chapter we considered some of the connections between psychological ideas about the basis of learning and the educational process. Sometimes, as in the case of the rejection of formal discipline, the use of intelligence tests, and programmed learning, these efforts have had profound and long-lasting effects on what is taught and the methods applied to teaching. These connections have generally not been based on ideas about how the brain functioned. We perceive a new opportunity for making connections between the study of brain mechanisms and education based on improved methods for studying the brain and advances in the understanding of individual differences. Much of this opportunity rests on our improved understanding of the child's ability to regulate cognitive and emotional networks through the temperamental dimensions of effortful control. Effortful control is related to attention, and together they allow a link between the control systems of the classroom and brain networks. These new and more detailed methods for making connections between brain and education should be subject to careful scrutiny in light of the prior history of often unfortunate attempts to base education on psychological concepts.

2

RELATING BRAIN AND MIND

New methods of examining brain activity are transforming researchers' ability to understand the development of the human brain, with implications for the education of children. Our goal in this chapter is to provide the reader with sufficient information about these methods and the methods for assessing temperament to appreciate current findings and those likely to occur in the near future.

The first section of this chapter deals with methods that allow the imaging of specific brain areas that become active during mental activity (and exciting recent findings on the localization of mental operations). We then outline methods for tracing networks of brain areas in real time as mental tasks are performed, examining the transfer of information from one node to another (tracing neural circuits). Finally, we consider methods for obtaining information on individual differences in cognition and temperament, and methods for separating genetic and environmental influences on the development of brain networks. Overall, this chapter should provide the reader with what is needed to understand the chapters in this volume on development of attention networks in early childhood (see chaps. 3 through 5) and on brain changes in the study of school subjects (see chaps. 7 through 9).

LOCALIZATION OF MENTAL OPERATIONS

Historically, psychologists have kept the study of complex learning, such as that which takes place in schools, separate from research on brain mechanisms. The reasons are simple; there are few ways to examine what takes place in the brain as people learn. One major issue that arises when the brain is considered is whether local areas of the brain are to be identified with specific psychological functions.

History of Localization of Function

One reason many psychologists have been skeptical about brain research may have been the earlier popular acceptance and subsequent failure of phrenology as a brain theory. Those who practiced phrenology supposed that the bumps on the head would reveal the size and the importance of the brain tissue underlying them. The bumps could then be used as a basis for predicting cognitive skill and personality.

Of course there was no real basis for relating the anatomy of the skull to any function. The failure of phrenology to predict function and the clear commercial motivation of some who practiced it led to a very general rejection of the enterprise. To some degree, the failure of phrenology also led to a more general rejection of the idea that higher functions were localized in the human brain. The lesson of the failure of phrenology is still being used as an argument against taking too seriously the local activations found in modern brain imaging studies such as those shown in Figure 1.2 (Uttal, 2001). However, in the case of imaging there is a theory relating the areas of activation to underlying brain mechanisms. Moreover, as we show later, imaging has moved well beyond localization. It now provides an approach to the development of specific neural networks related to a wide variety of thoughts and emotions.

A later and stronger blow to localization came from studies by Karl Lashley (1929). Lashley studied the ability of rats to learn mazes after he systematically created lesions in various parts of the rat brain. He found that the amount of cortical tissue removed, rather than any specific areas of the brain, best predicted decrements in learning to run mazes. His studies led him to conclude that the memory trace that recorded the way the rat had learned to navigate the maze was not stored in any particular location, but depended on the total mass of brain tissue available to the rat. Modern studies based on brain imaging tell quite a different story about localization and also help explain why the maze skill might not be stored in any particular area.

Localization of functions in the human brain drew some research support from the findings of Broca (1861) and other neurologists indicating that specific cognitive functions, such as those involved in language, might reside in specific brain areas. The study of patients with damage to parts of the brain has been an important aspect of neuropsychology throughout the 20th century.

Split Brains

Roger Sperry received a Nobel prize in medicine for his studies of patients whose cerebral hemispheres had been separated to stop otherwise uncontrolled seizures. This work demonstrated the different complex capabilities of each separated hemisphere; the left hemisphere appeared dominant for language, the right for spatial processes related to attention and navigation and to aspects of emotion.

Research on split-brain patients led to a renewal of interest in the problem of localization of function, even though localization in this case was confined to the hemisphere involved, because the split brain only allowed isolation of each individual hemisphere. The split-brain research also had a profound influence on a generation of psychologists whose studies examined specializations that might be present in the right and left hemisphere of the normal person (Hugdahl & Davidson, 2002). As in the case of phrenology, there was wide public interest in this research, which often overdramatized the separate contributions of the two hemispheres in normal function. Training models for the right and left hemisphere became fashionable and the description of people or institutions as either left or right brained passed into everyday language. Studies of the processing capacity of the two hemispheres came to dominate neuropsychology so much as to almost define the content of the field.

There is no question that the split-brain studies have done a great deal to awaken interest in the neurology of higher mental processes and to offer hope for the development of an understanding of how cognitive and emotional processes are carried out by the brain. In normal persons, however, there is always very strong interaction between the hemispheres, and the relatively few split-brain patients studied had intractable cases of epilepsy in their childhood, making it difficult to arrive at firm conclusions about normal function. These problems made it hard to establish an agenda of research that could counter the very simplified views of hemispheric function that became the basis of popular understanding.

Psychologists who entered the field in the mid-20th century thus learned that it was impossible to localize higher mental functions. Two pieces of evidence were often cited. The first was that studies of maze learning in rats showed that the amount rather than the location of tissue removed correlated best with the deficit in ability to learn (Lashley, 1929). A second argument was from the effects of frontal lesions in humans. It was argued that frontal lesions did not reduce intelligence, suggesting that the frontal tissue was unrelated to specific mental operations.

These conclusions were developed in the absence of the understanding that has arisen from cognitive studies of mental tasks. To be able to take the most advantage of studies of brain imaging, mental processes must be viewed in terms of constituent mental operations, sometimes also called computations or subroutines. Mental operations appear to be local, but because even simple tasks involve networks of widely separated neural areas that often occupy much of the brain, these findings tend to reconcile ideas of localization of function with those of activity of the whole brain.

SPEED OF MENTAL OPERATIONS

In these days of high-speed computers, it is commonplace to think of human thoughts and actions as relatively slow. However, this was not always the accepted view. Until 1850, the speed of neural conduction was believed to be at least as fast as the speed of light. Johannes Mueller, a famous German physiologist of the mid-19th century, asserted that the speed of neural conduction would never be measured. Whereas scientists had the whole heavens in which to measure the speed of light, he argued, physiologists had only animal bodies of limited size in which to measure the speed of neural conduction. However, a few years later his student Hermann von Helmholtz measured the time of neural conduction in humans, and showed that the nerve impulse took a measurable time (about 20 milliseconds, or 0.02 seconds) to travel from the foot to the head, with an estimated rate of about 100 meters a second. This speed is only an order of magnitude faster than the speed of a sprinter running a 100-meter race.

Subtractive Method

Helmholtz measured nerve conduction, a concrete physical phenomenon. One might correctly expect that measuring the speed of thought would be much trickier, yet surprisingly, a method for doing so did not take long to appear. Soon after Helmholtz's discovery, the Dutch physiologist F. C. Donders proposed a general method for measuring internal thought processes by the time it takes to perform them, a method that has become known as *mental chronometry* (Donders, 1868; Posner, 1978). He used a very simple subtractive logic. Suppose you are asked to press a key as quickly as possible in response to a flash of light. This task involves a kind of instructed reflex. Once the instruction has been given, the flash of light evokes pressing the key in much the same way as a simple reflex makes the hand withdraw from heat or the eye blink in response to an air puff.

Next, suppose you are presented with two flashing lights and are asked to respond to Light 1 but not to Light 2. For this task, you must discriminate which light appears before making the response. Subtracting the time required for the reflexive task alone from the time required for this new task yields a measure of the time required to discriminate between the two lights. Donders found that such subtractions yielded a mean value of about 50 milliseconds for the discrimination he studied. Now suppose there are two keys as well as two lights. When Light 1 appears you must press Key 1, and when Light 2 appears, Key 2. Before you can make a response, you must not only discriminate which light has appeared but also choose the correct key. Subtracting the time established for the discrimination task from the time needed to accomplish this new task yields a time for the mental operation of choosing between responses.

The success of Donders's method was an important early demonstration that mental processes could be isolated and measured. It opened up the possibility of defining mental processes in a quite precise way, thereby giving scientists a key element they needed to begin devising a scientific strategy for relating the complexity of thought to the intricate neural actions of the brain.

Moreover, the subtractive method has been effectively applied to neuroimaging, where its use has become one of the main ways of localizing mental operations. The subtractive method proposed by Donders was not without critics, however. Nothing could guarantee that any subtraction made would cleanly isolate a single mental operation. Perhaps more than one additional process had to be carried out in going from the instructed reflex to the discrimination. Even more important, the whole method by which a person performed the task might change when new elements were added.

Additive Factors

To circumvent these criticisms, Sternberg (1969) presented the additive factors approach, which provides another way to view the isolation of mental operations. A cognitive task is viewed as a series of additive stages, which sum to the overall reaction time. This serial view is plausible when each stage must be completed prior to being able to do the next operation. In the case of serial stages, any two variables that influence separate stages will be additive. For example, if increasing the intensity of a stimulus influences a different stage than does increasing the difficulty of a response, the influence of intensity on overall reaction time will be the same regardless of whether the response is a difficult or easy one. If intensity has the same influence irrespective of response difficulty and vice versa, the two factors are additive and they influence different stages. If the effect of intensity on reaction time is different according to response difficulty, the two variables interact and must then influence a common stage.

Independent Manipulation

Even the additive factors method required analysis of the task into a set of exhaustive and mutually exclusive operations. When mental operations take place in parallel one can still examine the degree to which they are independent (Posner, 1978; Sternberg, 2004). If methods can be found to manipulate one operation without affecting another operation and vice versa, the two have a kind of independence. Take the task of matching two simultaneous letters to determine if they have the same name. If one letter is red and the other is blue, it will take longer to match them provided they are in the same case (e.g., AA); however, color has no effect on matching letters in different cases (e.g., Aa). Opposite-case letters are influenced by interference from holding letter names in store, but this has no effect on matching same-case letters. This type of evidence has been used to argue that the matching of the same-case pair involves a visual system operation whereas matching cross-case pairs involves the letter names and is done in a phonological code (Posner, 1978).

The subtractive method, additive factors, and independent manipulation can provide tools for identifying mental operations that might be suitable candidates for localizing in the human brain, and they can and have been applied to imaging data (Posner & Raichle, 1994; Price, Moore, & Friston, 1997; Sternberg, 2004). Tasks such as reading, mental imagery, shifting attention, and processing numbers have all been analyzed in detail by these methods. In many cases, the identification of mental operations allowed specific predictions about the nature of brain lesions in acquired dyslexia, acalculia, and attentional disorders. The advent of neuroimaging provided an opportunity to examine whether the methods for isolating operations in cognitive psychology could help in understanding the operations of areas in the normal adult brain.

IMAGING OF HUMAN BRAIN FUNCTION

By *neuroimaging*, we refer to a wide variety of methods designed to sense activity within large populations of neurons in humans from outside the skull (Posner & Raichle, 1994; Toga & Mazziotta, 1997). To understand the specific areas of the brain involved in mental processes, we use positron emission tomography (PET) and functional magnetic resonance imaging (fMRI) methods that involve the study of changes in blood circulation. To study the circuitry involved in task performance, we examine the time course of activation of the specific anatomical areas found active in fMRI studies by use of high-density electrical recording (Posner & Raichle, 1994; Toga & Mazziotta, 1997).

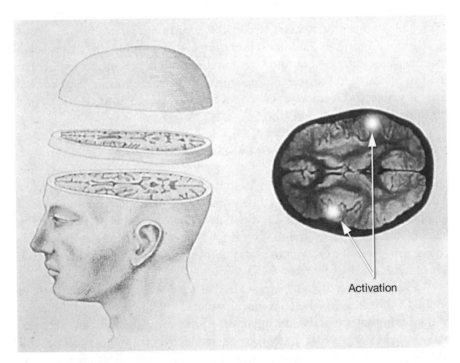

Figure 2.1. Areas of brain activation in neuroimaging study. The left picture illustrates how the computer can image the brain to show areas that are active during tasks. The right picture shows a magnetic resonance image illustrating the anatomy of one slice with two areas of activation, one in each hemisphere. From *Images of Mind* (p. 19), by M. I. Posner and M. E. Raichle, 1994, New York: Scientific American Books. Copyright 1994 by W. H. Freeman & Co. Reprinted with permission.

When neurons are active, they change their own local blood supply. Exactly how or why this occurs we don't know, but this change can be sensed from outside the head. The two most prominent methods for doing so are PET and fMRI (see Figure 2.1).

Positron Emission Tomography

PET uses a radionucleide that is injected into the bloodstream and emits positively charged particles (positrons). The positrons are annihilated after moving short distances and exit the skull as photons. These hit opposite sides of the detectors that have been arrayed around the head. The fact that these radioactive events are simultaneous shows they come from the brain and not from some external source. Because the radioactivity is delivered by the blood, the number of radioactive events can be related to the rate of blood flow through particular brain regions.

The most commonly used PET method for studying perceptual and cognitive processes is to examine blood flow with the isotope of oxygen,

O15. This isotope is very short-lived, and pictures can be taken of sustained activation of less than a minute's duration. Other possible PET approaches include using isotopes that allow examination of glucose utilization or that bind to various receptors (e.g., dopamine). Thus PET can be used to deal with a whole spectrum of questions related to localization of the neural transmitters.

Functional Magnetic Resonance Imaging

In fMRI, the participant is placed in a tube on which a large magnetic field is imposed. When increased neuronal activity changes the local blood supply, the oxygen content of the blood changes as well. Because the hemoglobin that carries the oxygen is paramagnetic, it is possible to sense changes in levels of oxygen and display them as images of local brain activity. This method is used by most fMRI studies.

Magnetic resonance imaging (MRI) is a general medical tool that can be used to image both the anatomical structure of the brain and the areas of the brain that are active during a task. The natural connection between images of blood oxygenation (fMRI) and images of brain anatomy (structural MRI) allow one to examine both the anatomy of a particular area (e.g., its size) and its activity during the task. In addition, the noninvasive method used in MRI allows the investigator to collect a sufficiently large amount of data on an individual subject to be sure the results are reliable for that person. Thus fMRI has become the method of choice for most cognitive studies of brain function. However, the ability of PET to easily image the whole brain and to use radioactive isotopes that bind to a wide variety of chemicals ensures a continued role for PET.

These two major methods, PET and fMRI, are fully complementary and have usually provided converging evidence when they have been applied to cognitive studies. The resolution of imaging has also improved to such a degree that functional activations can be localized to within about a cubic millimeter. Both of these methods have now been widely used to image discrete areas of increased neural activity during the performance of many tasks (Posner & Raichle, 1998). In most cases, two experimental conditions that are thought to differ in only a small number of cognitive operations are compared. For example, when the viewing of a stationary object is compared with viewing the same object placed in motion, there is activity in brain areas specifically related to motion, while the common effects of color and form are subtracted. These neuroimaging studies have almost universally found networks of cortical and subcortical areas that are altered between the two conditions, and the goal then is to relate this neural anatomy to the component operations or computations required by the task.

Design of Brain Imaging Studies

Brain imaging reveals changes in the brain as people change what they are doing. The most frequently used design for brain imaging studies involves comparing an experimental and a control condition within the same persons. The data obtained in the control condition can be subtracted from the experimental condition with the goal of determining what brain areas differ between the two. Consider the task of passive viewing of words. If passive viewing of consonant strings is subtracted from passive viewing of words, we ought to see areas unique to processing words. In fact, we find that both posterior and anterior areas of the left hemisphere are active, including an area of the posterior left hemisphere related to the operation of chunking the letters into a unit (visual word form) and a frontal area that increases with activation when semantic tasks (such as naming the use of a word) are used. This design has been quite successful in localizing areas of the visual system related to motion, color, and form (see Figure 1.2 and also Posner & Raichle, 1994). A quite different design uses the same stimulus in all conditions but requires the subject to attend to different aspects of the stimulus. Attention to motion has been shown to activate pretty much the same areas as passive viewing, but when the stimulus is attended to, the area of activation tends to be somewhat larger than that found for passive viewing (Posner & Raichle, 1994).

Things become more complicated when higher level cognitive processes are studied. It is certainly not possible to say that most experimental and control tasks differ in only one way. For example, consider a task in which one wishes to understand how a word association is generated (see Figure 1.1). If the experimental condition involves asking the subject to generate the use of a word (e.g., *pound* for *hammer*), and the control condition involves merely reading the word aloud, a subtraction might eliminate the sensory and motor components but leave intact a number of operations related to differences in the attention and effort required by the task and also aspects of semantic processing. This issue has sometimes been called the problem of pure insertion. It is very similar to what we discussed earlier for reaction-time data, and it is generally agreed that it is not possible to guarantee successful control of all but one operation. However, in reaction-time studies the subtraction yields only a single number that represents the difference in reaction time between conditions.

In imaging studies one can examine the differences in activity in the whole brain. For example, it may be known that the activity in a particular area is related to increased attention or to emotions that might be evoked by task difficulty. Thus even if the more complex tasks involve several differences from the simpler task, it may be possible to work out exactly what these differences are by the brain areas they activate. Moreover, it is

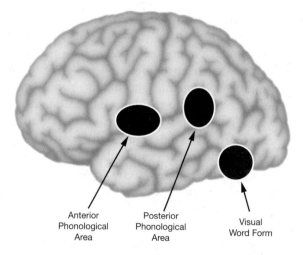

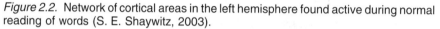

Anterior	Posterior	
Phonological	Phonological	Visual
Area	Area	Word Form

Figure 2.2. Network of cortical areas in the left hemisphere found active during normal reading of words (S. E. Shaywitz, 2003).

possible to subtract in both directions. Sometimes a simpler condition will activate areas not present in the more complex condition. For example, if one subtracts the data of generating uses from the data of reading the word aloud, one finds activity in a brain area known to be active when familiar words are read but not active when word associations are developed (Raichle et al., 1994). In fact, lesions in this area (Dronkers, 1996) produce a specific deficit in vocalization of words.

Other Imaging Designs

The subtractive method has proven that it is possible to determine the specific operation of a large number of brain areas involved in specific tasks (see Figures 1.2 and 2.2). It is fortunate that the subtractive method is also not the only strategy for analyzing functional imaging data. Conjunction designs (e.g., Friston, Holmes, Price, Buchel, & Worsley, 1999) attempt to target the same brain area with more than one task that would capture the same mental operation. For example, visual motion areas may be targeted either by comparing a moving and a stationary stimulus or by comparing an instruction to attend to motion with one in which the subject attends to another dimension. Sometimes it has proved useful to use several levels of the same variable (Smith, Jonides, Marshuetz, & Koeppe, 1998). For example, studies of working memory have manipulated the number of items held in memory store. People are given a series of visually presented words, some of which are repeated. They press one key if the word has not been previously presented and another key if it was repeated N (e.g., 1 or 3) items before. As the number increases, there are systematic increases in the strength of activation of brain areas related to storage load.

The additive factors method previously discussed has also been applied to imaging data (Sternberg, 2004). There is thus a whole toolkit of methods that can help us understand where mental operations are localized. A surprising number of familiar human tasks have now been analyzed in this way and there is a great deal of agreement on their localization. Among the best examples are reading words, comparing numbers, and shifting attention.

For example, in reading words, many neuroimaging studies have indicated three important localized areas of activity (S. E. Shaywitz, 2003). These are illustrated in Figure 2.2. One area is in the left hemisphere visual system and seems important for chunking letters into a visual unit. A second posterior area is in the left temporal occipital boundary near the location of the auditory system. It is involved in providing a name for the visually presented string. A third area in the frontal lobe seems to become active when one needs to provide a meaning for the word. These brain areas are described in more detail in chapter 7 (this volume), but they show that a degree of localization of function can be obtained even in complex tasks by neuroimaging. Moreover, they illustrate that the overall task of reading is orchestrated by a brain network, often involving both anterior and posterior brain areas, not by a single area.

When a person is generating the use of a visually or orally presented word (e.g., *hammer* and *pound*, *bell* and *ring*), it turns out that a network of areas is more strongly activated than when reading the same word aloud (see Figure 1.1, unpracticed). These areas of increased activity include a left temporoparietal area, thought to be related to aspects of finding the information needed to generate the word use, and frontal areas related to attention to the word meaning.

Effect of Practice on Brain Activity

It is possible to show how a brief period of learning influences the computation taking place within each area. If one practices generating uses with the same list of words for a few minutes, the activations that involve the frontal circuit related to generating word association are lost; instead, there is more activity in the more automatic route to output that is usually active in reading words (Raichle et al., 1994). The thinking needed to generate word use involves a brain network that is not involved when a skilled person simply reads a word or has very recently practiced generating the word's associated use. Within the time limit of a brief school lesson, brain circuits thus adapt and change dramatically. The ability to examine how brain areas change with specific learning opens up the opportunity to associate specific lessons with the brain changes they cause.

Distributed Brain Networks

During the past 10 years, many tasks have been analyzed by brain imaging, and the processing always seems to be done by a distributed network of often widely separated brain areas as shown in Figure 2.1. In some cases, experiments have been successful in providing information on what occurs in each brain area. In a few cases that have good animal models, much more detailed analysis within an area has been done by electrical recording of the activity of individual neural cells from cells in the area. For example, rhesus monkeys, like humans, orient to visual objects by moving their eyes or by shifting attention covertly without an eye movement. In both humans and monkeys, one brain area involved in this shift is the superior parietal lobe. Monkey work as described in chapter 3 (this volume) has shown that separate transmitters within the lateral intraparietal sulcus carry out the mental operations of alerting and shifting. Once these areas have been identified, it is possible to study the detailed circuitry involved by use of implanted electrodes. Other efforts to validate localization by fMRI have used data from patients with specific brain lesions (Posner & Raichle, 1994). It is also possible to use brief magnetic pulses delivered outside the skull—transcranial magnetic stimulation (TMS)—to disrupt the circuitry momentarily. TMS has been used to test whether interrupting a specific brain area disrupts performance in the way predicted (Ro, Farné, & Chang, 2003).

The results of many brain imaging experiments suggest that mental operations appear to be local, but because even simple tasks involve networks of neural areas that often occupy much of the brain, these findings tend to reconcile ideas of localization of function with those of mass action.

Timing Activity in Brain Networks

One of the nearly universal findings from imaging studies is that any given task activates a network of areas, including both frontal and posterior cortical areas as well as subcortical areas. How can we study the time course of these events? The temporal resolution of methods based on change in blood flow is relatively poor because it takes seconds for the neurons to change their blood supply. However, cognitive studies of these same mental operations have shown clearly that the operations involved occur in tens to hundreds of milliseconds.

In the study of how networks of brain areas become active in real time, electrical activity from the scalp that is time-locked to stimulus events is recorded (the event-related potential [ERP] method). The ERP is a technique long used in chronometric studies in psychology (Posner, 1978). Figure 2.3 shows two people, each wearing a geodesic sensor net that allows recording from large sets of electrodes.

Figure 2.3. Electrodes used to measure brain electrical activity. A large number of electrodes are placed on the head to measure the electrical activity time-locked to the presentation of a stimulus. The resulting event-related potential can then be related to generators from imaging studies.

Electrical activity following the presentation of a stimulus (e.g., a word) is recorded at each electrode site. If a word is presented a number of times and the electrical activity at each electrode site is averaged, one can obtain a picture of the electrical activity time-locked to a stimulus over the whole surface of the head (see Figure 2.4). Thus the effect of the stimulus can be seen millisecond by millisecond. The recording at the bottom of Figure 2.4 is the average ERP for the presentation of the stimulus.

Combining Electrical and Functional Images

Efforts to determine the location of information in the brain as measured from electrodes on the scalp have changed dramatically with the new neuroimaging techniques because they can be linked to PET and fMRI data. The use of fMRI has provided precise information on the location of the areas of activation that are the putative sources for the recorded scalp electrical activity. Because there is now specific information based on PET and fMRI about where in the brain the electrical generators are located in a given task, that information can be used to constrain the task of inferring the location of the brain activity from scalp-recorded electrical activity,

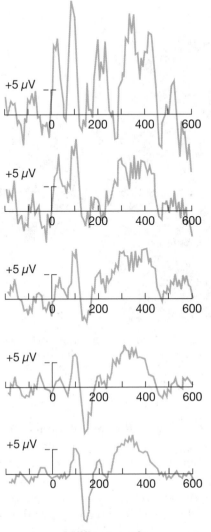

Milliseconds

Figure 2.4. Event-related potentials (ERPs) recorded from a single electrode site after (from top to bottom) 1, 2, 4, 8, or 16 trials averaged together. The various positive and negative deflections are called components of the ERP.

which will have been distorted by tissue between it and the electrode. In adapting the ERP method to fit with imaging data, it has been useful to use the constraints provided by the fMRI to predict the areas of activation on the surface of the scalp (scalp signature) to be expected in a given task. These predictions can then be compared with the obtained scalp signatures to test whether the area of the brain activated is consistent with the distribution of electrical activity on the scalp. A number of efforts to compare fMRI and ERP methods using similar tasks have been successful. Some of the most interesting studies involve mapping the visual system (Clark & Hillyard, 1996). For example, the known relation between the position on the retina and the location of neuronal activity in the brain was first used to validate PET blood flow studies and has now been used to show that the distribution of electrical activity from scalp electrodes also fit with this model (Clark & Hillyard, 1996). In a similar way, ERP signals to moving stimuli from scalp electrodes have been localized to brain areas similar to those previously found active with PET (Ffytche, Guy, & Zeki, 1995). In more complex cognitive tasks, including the processing of words (Abdullaev & Posner, 1998) and number (Dehaene, 1996), these methods have successfully allowed researchers to work out the time course of the anatomy underlying the task.

One study of brain activation in visual attention that employed both PET and ERP methods used the same subjects and the same task (Heinze et al., 1994). Subjects were asked to report targets in one visual field (to either the left or right of the visual fixation) while a series of visual stimuli occurred in both fields. Attending to stimuli in one visual field formed the experimental condition whereas stimuli in that same field when attending to the opposite field served as the control. Both PET and ERP data suggested areas of activation in the fusiform gyrus (a part of the visual system) of the hemisphere opposite the attended visual field. However, the generators localized by the two methodologies were about a centimeter apart. Some of this difference might arise because the two methods are measuring different aspects of the neural activity, or it may also suggest inherent error in the two methods. Though exact correspondence between measures cannot be expected, the two should localize to approximately the same area of the brain (e.g., within a centimeter or so).

The study of higher level tasks critical to human skill has generally employed the same subtractive method used with PET and fMRI and the same task structure. These studies are reviewed in detail in chapter 7 (this volume). They have consistently shown it possible to find evidence of each generator in the scalp activity and have proposed a particular time course for each of them. Sometimes these time-course data are critical to understanding how the task is performed. For example, when a word association is made, the extra attention required in comparison with reading words aloud seems to activate frontal attention areas at about 150 to 200 milliseconds, well before the temporoparietal activation at 450 milliseconds, when areas that store information about the semantics of words are active. This finding suggests that attention constrains the semantic search. We rely on time-course data particularly in understanding tasks such as reading (see chap. 7, this volume) and number processing (see chap. 8, this volume).

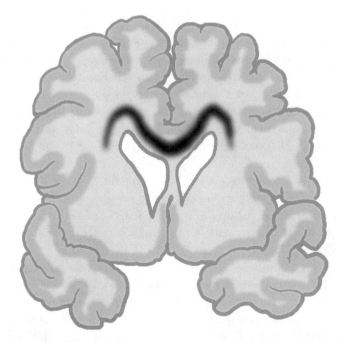

Figure 2.5. Tracing of connections (dark lines) between hemispheres by diffusion tensor imaging. The dark lines show the corpus callosum, the fiber tract that holds together the two cerebral hemispheres. From "Tracking Neuronal Fiber Pathways in the Living Human Brain," by T. E. Conturo, N. F. Lori, T. S. Cull, E. Akbudak, A. Z. Snyder, J. S. Shimony, et al., 1999, *Proceedings of the National Academy of Sciences of the USA, 96*, p. 10423. Copyright 1999 by National Academy of Sciences, USA. Reprinted with permission.

Measuring the time course of mental processing helps in understanding the underlying circuitry by providing the order of operations involved. It is possible, however, to further this understanding by carefully examining the correlation between active brain areas. Although adjacent electrodes may be correlated as a result of volume conduction through the skull, correlation between more distant electrodes is more likely to represent the transfer of information between these areas. Both fMRI and electrical data have been used to study such correlations and to attempt to infer which brain areas are in contact and when.

In some cases, it is possible to examine the white-matter connections between brain areas directly by use of diffusion tensor imaging. This imaging method uses MRI but examines the diffusion of water molecules, which normally follow the white-matter tracts, allowing organization of these tracts to be imaged (see Figure 2.5). For developmental studies, one might bring together a combination of diffusion tensor imaging and high-density electrical activity to examine when white-matter tracts between distant brain sites are first formed and when they become operational during actual tasks.

BRAIN DEVELOPMENT

Changes in behavior during early development are obvious to all observers. Young infants seem so dependent on their caregivers for stimulation, but within the first 3 years they gain a strong measure of independence and develop an agenda of their own. What are the reasons for these changes in behavior?

A number of clear developments in the brain could be responsible for them. Analysis of the brains of infants and children who have died young has indicated that the first few years of life bring dramatic changes in their brains. At birth, the upper layers of the cortex are only sparsely settled by cells, and during the 1st year cells migrate into these upper layers, allowing increased performance. These events have been studied most carefully in relation to eye movements and orienting and are discussed in chapter 3 (this volume).

Synaptic Exuberance

If knowledge of the two cerebral hemispheres was insufficient to establish an agenda for educating the brain, perhaps it would be possible to use knowledge of developmental neurobiology to support an educational agenda. This seemed a real possibility when findings based on cellular studies of animals suggested an overexpression of the structures responsible for connections between nerve cells (synapses) between birth and about 3 years (Rakic, Bourgeois, Eckenhoff, Zecevic, & Goldman-Rakic, 1986). At about 3 years of age, synapses appeared to be abruptly pruned to occur at less dense adult levels. If one reasoned that having more synapses meant enlarged opportunity to make new connections, then it followed that the first 3 years of life must be the crucial time for learning. In this view, the period from birth to 3 was identified as a critical period in which learning had to occur or the opportunity to influence the brain's networks would be lost (Bruer, 1999).

However, it was quickly discovered that much of the pruning actually took place after puberty (Huttenlocher & Dabholkar, 1997). Moreover, there was not a clear link between an abundance of synapses and the ability to learn. Indeed, there has been accumulating evidence from neuroscience that the opportunity for rewiring of even primary sensory systems extends into adulthood (Merzenich & Jenkins, 1995). The idea that birth to 3 was the one critical period for learning could not survive this kind of evidence. This is not to say that early experience is of little importance (note the arguments of Bruner discussed earlier), but only that attempts to link the brain to education must not rely on making broad connections between some form of change at the cellular level and particular educational consequences. Instead, methods are needed that will support systematic research connecting learning in the area of interest to the brain mechanisms that can be shown to support it.

One source of changes in behavior, at least following puberty, may be the pruning back of neurons and synapses that do not seem needed. It has been thought, for example, that there is much greater connection between different sensory systems in children, with these connections tending to be lost by adulthood (Maurer & Maurer, 1988).

Longitudinal MRI Studies

Though there have not been good methods for tracing cellular events in living humans, longitudinal MRI results have suggested a thickening of cortical structures during childhood (see the *Intelligence and Efficiency* subsection). Structural MRI of children has also shown increases in white matter during childhood. These increases are generally thought to be due to the fact that the fibers that connect distant brain areas are developing the myelin sheath that improves conductivity of electrical activity along these tracts.

With the method of diffusion tensor MRI, it will be possible to observe these changes in brain connections throughout childhood and thus understand their role in the changes in behavior so obvious in infants and young children. By combining diffusion tensor images with scalp recording of electrical activity, we may be able to know when areas of the brain involved in specific tasks first become connected. This knowledge might allow development of a better theory of when specific skills can be most effectively taught to children.

The methods of functional neuroimaging have not often been applied at very young ages. PET involves radiation and is forbidden for use in those under 18 in most cases. Although fMRI can and has been used safely even with infants (Dehaene-Lambertz, Dehaene, & Hertz-Pannier, 2002), there must be careful control of movement to study activation tasks, which has proven difficult with children before the age of 6 or 7. As newer scanning environments become available, it will be increasingly possible to apply them to younger children. At present, however, only recording from scalp electrodes has been systematically applied to young children.

Behavioral and Electrical Recording Studies

Studies that have been done reveal some important aspects of developments in brain systems that are often hidden from direct observations of behavior. For example, infants as young as 6 months who do not systematically use language nevertheless show that they are learning implicitly very important aspects of their language (Kuhl, Tsao, & Liu, 2003). Infants come into the world with the ability to discriminate the basic speech sounds (phonemes) in all of the world's languages. This can be shown by changes in their behavior. If the same speech sound is played over and over, they will adapt to it as measured by their no longer looking at the source of the sound or by their continuing to suck on a pacifier in its presence. If the sound is altered, the infant's renewed orienting or an interruption in sucking indicates that the child has noticed or discriminated the change. Very young infants can discriminate changes in languages other than their own that an adult speaker of their own language might not recognize. Studies using electrical recording from outside the skull have shown that by 6 months infants discriminate the sounds of their own language more easily than they do those not in their own language. Studies using infant habituation methods have also shown that the infant enters the world with core knowledge about the nature of objects and their solidity and number, as well as some knowledge about the intentions of people (Premack & Premack, 2003; Spelke, 2004). Although it is difficult to study infant behavior with fMRI, one study examined infant phoneme perception at 3 months and found evidence of similar neural systems to those that would be active in adults (Dehaene-Lambertz et al., 2002).

Marker Tasks

When it is not possible to perform direct imaging of the infant or young child, marker tasks allow researchers to study development. Marker tasks are simple behavioral tasks that have been shown in adults to involve particular brain systems and even particular portions of these systems. Studying the ability to perform different marker tasks with increasing age makes it possible to make inferences about the developmental course of these systems and networks.

One example is Adele Diamond's work involving the "A not B" task and the reaching task. These two marker tasks involve inhibition of an action that is strongly elicited by the situation. In the "A not B" task, the experimenter shifts the location of a hidden object from Location A to Location B, after the infant's retrieving from Location A has been reinforced as correct in the previous trials (Diamond, 1991). In the reaching task, visual information about the correct route to a toy is put in conflict with the cues that normally guide reaching. A toy is placed under a transparent box. The opening of the box is on the side (it can be the front side, the back side, etc.), and the infant can reach it only if the tendency to reach directly along the line of sight through the transparent top of the box is inhibited. Important changes in the performance of these tasks are observed from 6 to 12 months. Comparison of performance between monkeys with brain lesions and human infants on the same marker tasks suggests that the tasks are sensitive to the development of the prefrontal cortex, and maturation of this brain area seems to be critical for the development of this form of inhibition. This approach is examined in more detail in chapters 3 and 4 (this volume).

Individual Differences in Brain Structure and Function

The study of the generalized mind and the study of individual differences in functioning are usually the province of two different areas of psychology. However, because people differ from birth, it is important to have methods to study both the general features of the neural networks developing and how they might differ. New methods have been accumulating to deal with these differences between people.

Morphometry

This methodology began with the use of X-rays, but current images are based on magnetic resonance of hydrogen molecules present in abundance throughout the body in the form of water. Magnetic resonance images can give exquisite pictures of individual brain structures, allowing neurologists to trace changes in the brain resulting from stroke, tumor, or atrophy. They also allow scientists to see the structure of the individual brain. Although human brains are all rather similar in overall structure, each brain, even of identical twins, differs in detail. Morphometry allows one to capture these details and to attempt to relate differences in overall brain size, or the size or shape of each structure, to conceptions about how individuals differ. In fact it has been something of a surprise that despite such anatomical variability, the higher mental processes are executed sufficiently similarly among individuals that it is possible to specify a general anatomy and circuitry. Apparently for many tasks, humans tend to use their brain in somewhat similar ways. Morphometry also allows the examination of the effects of changes with age or of specific experiences on brain structures.

Intelligence and Efficiency

Differences among individuals can indicate something about their relative abilities. For example, as discussed in chapter 1 (this volume), intelligence measures provide some information about the ability of children to do well in school. For that reason, scientists have expected to find evidence of these differences in the brain. The use of MRI has allowed careful measurements of the size and shape of different brain areas, which can then be normalized to the total brain size.

In one study of 100 normal children from ages 5 to 17, overall size of the gray matter remained rather constant while, presumably as a result of myelination, white-matter volume increased during this period (Giedd et al., 1999). When the total volume of the brain was related to IQ, a curvilinear relation was found. There was a sharp rise in IQ at the smaller volume, reaching a plateau at moderately large brain size. If only the frontal areas were considered, the stronger linear correlation of about .45 predicted about 20% of the total variance in IQ.

These findings and others suggest that the extent of brain devoted to a process may have relevance for how well one performs tasks that require use of that brain area. Studies of long continued practice in monkeys have shown that the amount of tissue devoted to a particular sensory surface (e.g., one particular finger) can be altered by extensive experience given to that finger (Merzenich & Jenkins, 1995). In the other direction, the loss of brain tissue from stroke or lesion influences the efficiency of the processes performed in that brain area. Animals with an enriched environment also tend to show expanded cerebral cortex. There have also been reports that long practice, such as playing the violin, may lead to an expansion of the amount of brain tissue related to that function (Elbert, Pantev, Wienbruch, Rockstroh, & Taub, 1995). These are hints that under some conditions the relative size of brain areas could be important.

However, it will require additional research to understand how important the size of particular brain areas in development will be. Perhaps size will prove of less importance than other variables, such as the interconnection between one brain area or another and the cellular structure or branching within a brain area.

Genetics

The development of neural networks underlying behavior depends on both genes and experience. Genes themselves do not produce behavior. Behavior is an interaction between the neural networks we have been discussing and the environment. However, genes do determine the basic structure of neural networks by specifying the proteins out of which the various components of the nervous system are constructed. Genetic instructions are contained in the chromosomes constituting an individual's genetic makeup. The genetic instructions are not altered during the lifetime of a person, but aspects of the environment can influence the expression of genes within particular neural networks.

Although the sets of genes for all humans are highly similar, detailed differences can influence, for example, the amount of activity of particular neuromodulators such as norepinephrine or dopamine, which in turn can influence the characteristic behavior of an individual. The genome of any given individual can be assayed from a small amount of DNA contained in blood or other tissue by standard methods of molecular biology (Fossella & Posner, 2004). The field of cognitive genetics is at the very beginning of attempts to understand differences among individuals in intelligence or temperament in terms of variation in genes. However, both animal and human studies have already suggested that important differences among people in adapting to different environments can be illuminated by an understanding of genetic variation.

Temperament

Temperament refers to individual differences in reactivity and self-regulation assumed to have a constitutional basis (Rothbart & Derryberry, 1981). *Constitution* is

> the relatively enduring biological makeup of the organism, influenced over time by heredity, maturation, and experience. Reactivity refers to the excitability, responsivity, or arousability of the behavioral and physiological systems of the organism, whereas self-regulation refers to neural and behavioral processes functioning to modulate this underlying reactivity. (Rothbart & Derryberry, 1981, p. 40)

Each infant comes into the world with a prepared set of reactions to their environment. As parents often recognize, infants can be very different in their early reactions to events. One infant is easily frustrated, has only a brief attention span, and cries with even moderate levels of stimulating play, whereas another may tolerate even very rough play and seek out exciting events. These constitutionally based reactions to the environment, together with the mechanisms that regulate them, constitute infant temperament. As experience accumulates, temperament becomes the basis for individual differences in personality in the older child and adult. A short list of temperament dimensions includes fear, anger–frustration, positive affect–approach (extraversion), activity level, perceptual sensitivity, and attentional focusing. These dimensions, along with soothability, offer broad characterization of early temperament.

Temperament arises from a person's genetic endowment, but it both influences and is influenced by the experience of each individual. Figure 2.6 deals with three broad dimensions of temperament in childhood and their interrelations within two cultures. Extraversion and negative affect are early developing dimensions of temperament that are generally present across different cultures. Effortful control is a later developing dimension

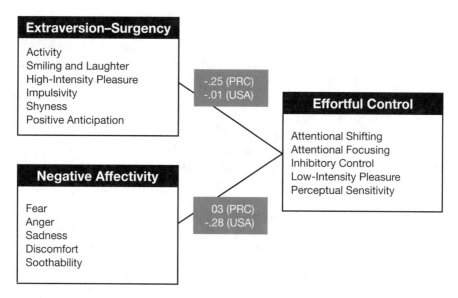

Figure 2.6. Role of effortful control in modulating personality in two cultures. Effortful control is used to reduce negative affect in the United States (USA), but in China (PRC) it is used to reduce positive affect (extraversion). This diagram illustrates common mechanisms used differently in two cultures (Ahadi, Rothbart, & Ye, 1993).

that also appears within all cultures (see chap. 4, this volume) and is important in the development of self-regulation. However, there are likely cultural differences in how this regulation takes place. Within most Western societies like the United States, extraversion is highly valued, and effortful control is associated with a lower amount of negative affect. In China, however, effortful control seems to relate more to the regulation of extraversion, perhaps in accord with that culture's traditional emphasis on reserve. An important goal of temperament research has been to specify processes at the levels of biology that may be linked through social development to later expression in the adult.

Temperament itself develops—that is, emotions and components of emotions appear at different ages (Rothbart & Bates, 2006), as do aspects of motor functioning, arousal systems, and systems of attention (Posner & Raichle, 1994). To some degree the young infant is chiefly reactive, and early development involves the adding of self-regulatory capacities to this reactivity (Rothbart & Derryberry, 1981). The fear system includes behavioral inhibition and appears in the 1st year of life (see chap. 6, this volume). Effortful control emerges later, in the 2nd year of life, along with the executive attention system (see chap. 4). Effortful control seems to be largely self-regulatory, with important implications for the developing personality (Kochanska & Knaack, 2003).

A major problem in the temperament area, and one that has also affected personality research, is the tendency for each researcher to rename temperament variables, even when the content of the construct studied is quite similar. This tendency produces an apparent lack of agreement about the subject matter of temperament. Variability in labels sometimes reflects real differences across studies, but there is substantial agreement across a number of studies of temperament (Rothbart & Bates, 2006), and there are similarities between temperamental scales and the most common personality traits, often called the Big Five personality factors (Extraversion, Agreeableness, Conscientiousness, Neuroticism, Intellect or Openness), observed in adult personality.

Temperament research will be of increasing importance as attempts are made to identify, through studies involving morphometry, the brain structures and genes (see chaps. 5 and 6, this volume) that might be related to different aspects of temperament. There has been wide agreement about the importance of the amygdala in fear responses, mostly from animal research on fear conditioning, but it is also true that frightening faces activate the amygdala in adult imaging studies. There have been efforts to tie dimensions of temperament and personality to genes. For example, the dopamine-4 receptor (DRD4) gene has been related to sensation seeking (see chap. 5). The ties between genes, regional brain areas, and behavior are an important direction for research on individual differences, to which we now turn.

Efficiency of Neural Networks

It is possible to examine individual differences in the efficiency of networks that are thought to underlie important temperamental differences. This examination involves the use of marker tasks, and attention offers a good opportunity for carrying out this examination. Figure 2.7 illustrates a method for studying the efficiency of three quite different attentional networks within one experiment, the Attention Network Test (ANT). The task of the person is to determine as quickly as possible whether the middle target arrow points to the left or to the right. Sometimes the arrow is presented alone so that no conflicting information is introduced, but on other trials it is surrounded by flanking arrows that point either in the same direction (congruent) or in the opposite direction (incongruent). The incongruent arrows require the resolution of a conflict in tendencies to move toward the left or right, provided they are close enough to the target. The extra time needed to resolve this conflict becomes one measure of the efficiency of an attention network related to the resolution of conflict.

Conflict resolution, even in this simple task, turns out to be related to effortful control during childhood. Although questionnaires use the wide experience of the caregiver to report on this ability, they do not provide a

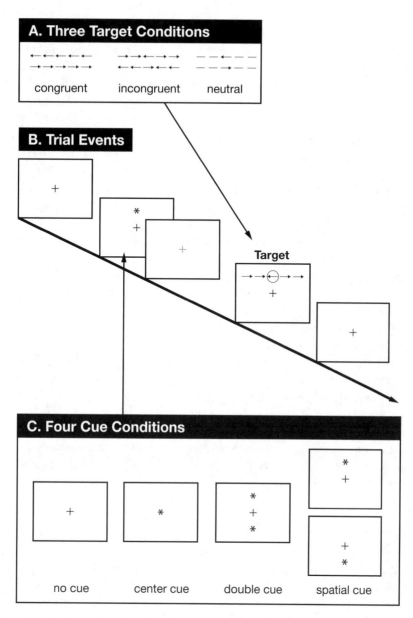

Figure 2.7. A schematic of the Attention Network Test. The task requires a left keypress when the central arrow points left and a right keypress when it points right. The arrow is surrounded by flankers pointing in the same (congruent) or opposite direction (incongruent). Before the target appears, cues inform the person of when and where a target will appear. From "Testing the Efficiency and Independence of Attentional Networks," by J. Fan, B. D. McCandliss, T. Sommer, M. Raz, and M. I. Posner, 2002, *Journal of Cognitive Neuroscience, 14,* p. 341. Copyright 2002 by the Massachusetts Institute of Technology. Adapted with permission.

method for examining the neural networks or genes involved. The link between questionnaire responses and this simple marker task provides a connection between everyday life behavior and the neural networks that underlie it. This connection is discussed in chapters 4, 5, and 6 (this volume).

The ANT also measures the efficiency of alerting and orienting. Before the target occurs, cues are used to warn the person that the target is about to occur. The presentation of a warning leads to a change of state called alerting. By subtracting the speed of processing during warned trials that present a cue above and below the target from the speed of processing during trials that do not present a cue, one gets a measure of the improvement in reaction time resulting from alerting. Finally, a cue may be presented at the position of the target, which is always presented either above or below the center of the screen, or in the center. If reaction times for presentation of the cue at the location of the target are subtracted from reaction times when the cue occurs at fixation, we get a measure of the savings in reaction time when attention is directed to the target. This subtraction provides a score for the efficiency of orienting.

The ANT is one example of an experimental marker task that can measure efficiency of attentional systems, which in turn can be linked to an fMRI study. Figure 2.8 shows the neural areas involved for each of the three attention networks measured. The study requires subjects to carry out the ANT while being scanned. By use of the same subtraction discussed above, each of the networks can be depicted as images. Moreover, prior studies with related tasks in both primates and rodents have confirmed the location of many of the brain areas shown in each of the networks, providing strong evidence of the connection between the ANT and the underlying neural systems, and validating use of the ANT as a marker task.

Temperament and Behavioral Genetics

The heritability of animal temperament has been long recognized; in fact, many animal lines have been bred for various individual traits, especially fearfulness (Broadhurst, 1975; Brush, Gendron, & Isaacson, 1999). It is also true, however, that even after breeding for a specific behavior, that behavior may still be significantly altered by experience.

Methods of molecular genetics have shown it is possible for single genes to exert an influence on complex behaviors (Gerlai, 1996; Kieffer, 1999; Wahlsten, 1999). Young and colleagues (Young, Nilsen, Waymire, MacGregor, & Insel, 1999) reported the genetic transformation of a comparatively unsocial strain of field mouse into a more gregarious temperament. They achieved this by a transgenic manipulation that elevated the number of vasopressin receptors in the brains of the rather unsocial mountain voles to more closely resemble those of their highly social relatives, the prairie voles.

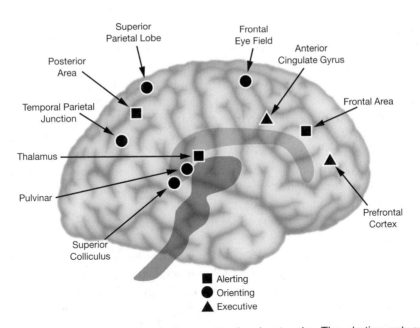

Figure 2.8. Brain areas active for three attentional networks. The alerting network (squares) includes thalamic and cortical sites related to the brain's norepinephrine system. The orienting network (circles) is centered on parietal sites (discussed in the text), and the executive network (triangles) includes the anterior cingulate and other frontal areas.

Another psychosocial change was achieved by deleting a single gene (in this case, the oncogene fosB) from female mice. These mice, when they became mothers, exhibited a dramatic reduction in their nurturant tendencies (Brown, Ye, Bronson, Dikkes, & Greenberg, 1996). It is also possible to stop sexual urges almost completely by eliminating the estrogen receptor from an animal's genome (Pfaff, 1999). A difficulty with many of these mouse models is that the emerging behavioral changes may be due to compensatory effects occurring during earlier phases of development (these animals have been missing the single deleted gene in all their cells throughout their lives). It is becoming increasingly possible, however, to introduce the gene deletion on a contingent basis at any point in development and thus avoid some of these problems (Lobe & Nagy, 1998).

Human Genetics

Human behavior genetics has been dominated by studies of disorders (e.g., developmental dyslexia, schizophrenia, attention-deficit/hyperactivity disorder [ADHD]), and in many cases the definition of the disorder has included a wide range of behavior. Nonetheless, family and twin studies have established high heritability of a number of disorders. Heritability estimates are also substantial for intelligence and for such temperamental characteristics as shyness, extraversion, and fear.

Sometimes the same genetic variation has been associated on the one hand with a disorder and on the other hand with normal temperament. An example is the association of the DRD4 gene. This gene has a polymorphism in which various numbers of 48 base pairs are repeated. The 7-repeat version has been associated both with the childhood disorder of inattention and hyperactivity (ADHD) and with sensation seeking as a normal temperamental variation of extraversion. Furthering an understanding of the connections between a gene and an abnormality requires an understanding of the genetics of normal attention.

The individual differences found in the ANT form an ideal way to make this connection. The logic is simple. The neuromodulator associated with the executive attention network appears to be dopamine. Thus genes that influence this modulator would be candidates for showing differences that can be related to network efficiency. To test this idea, we can take DNA from people who are performing the ANT and determine whether, for example, the DRD4 gene involved in ADHD is related to the conflict scores as found in the ANT. This test has been done for several candidate genes and the results form much of the material in chapter 5 (this volume).

SUMMARY

The ability to see the brain in action means a great deal for the development of educational methods. Though it is not possible to use neuroimaging to study each individual child to determine which parts of the brain are performing normally in reading, writing, or arithmetic, studies with selected groups can identify the common networks in tasks studied in school. They can also indicate what activation is usually lacking in people who fail the task. Imaging can then be used to see which types of training are most effective in improving the activity in given brain areas. This general methodology can be used for discovering and integrating the best parts of different methods developed for improving performance.

In this chapter, we have summarized new methods designed to shed light on the neural networks involved in cognition and emotion. Adult studies have relied on the use of fMRI and PET to image areas of the human brain that are active during tasks. These studies have provided localization of mental operations with considerable precision. In many studies these local activations in the brain have been connected with the component computations found in human cognition.

Use of high-density electrical recording allows researchers to obtain the time course of these anatomically restricted activations and thus begin to outline the specific circuitry of the tasks. These putative circuits can be tested through animal models, through the study of patients with specific lesions that may include parts of the circuitry, or by disruption of the circuitry by magnetic stimulations. In subsequent chapters of this volume, we discuss how we have used these methods to examine how neural networks develop in the brains of infants and young children. In chapters 3 and 4 (this volume) we focus on networks underlying attention, and in chapters 7 through 9 we consider networks related to school subjects.

In psychology the experimental and individual differences approaches to the study of mental processes related to cognition and emotion have been kept quite separate. One has concerned general properties of the mind related to cognitive and emotional functions. The second is the study of individual differences related to these same functions. The new methods provide a means of synthesizing these two approaches through the examination of the development of neural networks. This developmental process is mediated through genes and experience. Genes are responsible for the strong commonalities found between neural networks among human beings. We all share the same genes. However, genes also contribute to differences among us in the efficiency of operation of these networks. These genetic differences or polymorphisms between genes can help account for individual differences in brains and in the neural networks that they support. In addition, human individual behavior is also influenced by the experiences that differ among children during the socialization process. In chapter 5 (this volume) we summarize the data on how genes and experience shape attentional networks.

3

LEARNING TO LOOK

Many social skills of daily life rely on the direction and duration of gaze. The direction of gaze indicates where one's interest is directed, often reflects patterns of social dominance and submission, and suggests where important information is most likely to be gathered. As human beings, we use our gaze to regulate our emotions when we look away from a disturbing sight and to regulate our cognitive state when we look away from possible distractions as we think. Even as adults we are usually unaware of these influences, but they can be brought to awareness when different rules apply, as can happen when we move to a different culture. These facts make it unsurprising that training where to attend by infant and caregiver is of importance in early infancy.

Infants come into the world with only the deepest layers of the cortex developed. Over the first year of life, cells migrate into the more superficial layers, setting the stage for the completion of new pathways linking vision to other functions. In addition, the boundaries between vision, audition, and other modalities are not finally or firmly set (Maurer & Maurer, 1988). During the first year of life, the visual system undergoes remarkable development, with increasing visual acuity (Gwaizda, Bauer, & Held, 1989), the ability to voluntarily control where to look and for how long, and other aspects of attention related to taking in sensory information (Johnson, Posner, & Rothbart, 1991). The infant also shows recognition of faces and other visual objects. In this chapter, we discuss the early development of orienting in the infant.

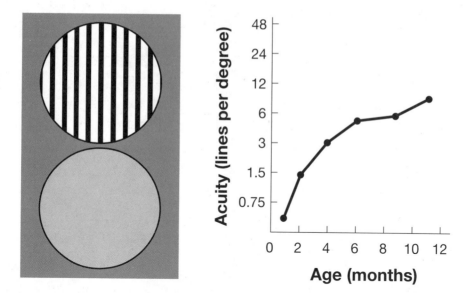

Figure 3.1. Measuring visual acuity in infants. The top left side of this figure shows a grating. As the lines become finer and finer (higher frequency), the ability of the infant to discriminate the grating from a uniform gray (below) declines. The right side of the figure shows how this grating acuity increases over the months to reach nearly adult levels at about 1 year. From "From Visual Acuity to Hyperacuity: A 10-Year Update," by J. Gwaizda, J. Bauer, and R. Held, 1989, *Canadian Journal of Psychology, 43,* p. 112. Copyright 1989 by the Canadian Psychological Association. Adapted with permission.

VISUAL ACUITY

Figure 3.1 illustrates the month-by-month improvement in visual acuity (the ability to detect small differences) during the 1st year of life. One form of acuity (grating acuity) indicates how well the infant can discriminate very fine black stripes. If given a choice between black stripes and a uniform gray, infants prefer to look at stripes. The infant's eyes are generally attracted to stimuli that have higher spatial frequency (more stripes per unit area), and this preference can be used to study the infant's visual acuity. In a study of this kind, the stripes are made narrower and narrower. As the stripes become narrower they begin to fuse so that the infant cannot discriminate the stripes from plain gray. The infant now shows no preference for the stripes over the uniform gray. When looking preferences disappear, it is assumed that the infant can no longer see the individual stripes. Just below this point is taken as the infant's threshold for discriminating a thin stripe from the background. The results illustrated in Figure 3.1 show how detailed and precise measurement of infant visual abilities can be.

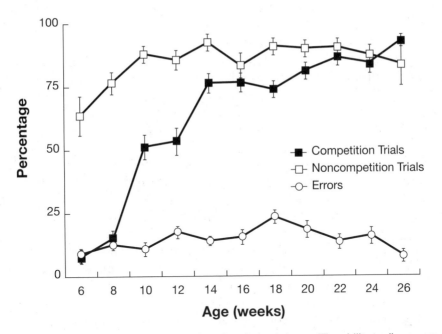

Figure 3.2. Development of orienting function during infancy. The ability to disengage (percentage) and move the eyes toward a visual object in the presence of a distractor develops slowly over the first few months of life. From "Infants' Shifts of Gaze From a Central to a Peripheral Stimulus: A Longitudinal Study of Development Between 6 and 26 Weeks," by P. R. Butcher, A. F. Kalverboer, and R. H. Geuze, 2000, *Infant Behavior and Development, 23,* p. 11. Copyright 2000 by Elsevier. Adapted with permission.

EYE MOVEMENTS IN CHILDREN

When one examines an object, one's head and eyes orient in its direction. This visual orienting has long provided a key to the study of attention (Ruff & Rothbart, 1996). One usually looks where one is attending, although it is well known that in adults attention can be separated from fixation, as when one looks out of the corner of one's eyes. Eye movements are present even before birth, and at birth, infants demonstrate that they can follow the movement of objects. However, as previously noted, their acuity is limited, and thus their ability to discriminate objects is rather poor. It is also difficult to attract infants' eye movements toward peripheral objects because the extent of their visual field is limited. However, orienting to attend to peripheral objects undergoes very rapid development between 2 and 4 months as shown in Figure 3.2.

The newborn infant is not very responsive to visual events. Although the infant's gaze may be captured by a slowly moving object, eye movements are jerky and may undershoot the target. Even at 2 months, when the infant is orienting for longer periods, the child may focus on an edge or corner of the stimulus, and attention does not seem to be under voluntary control. Emde and his associates (Emde, Gaensbauer, & Harmon, 1976) have described a shift in behavior due to underlying brain changes between 2 and 3 months of age. They note that whereas previously much of the infant's reaction seemed reflexive and exogenously driven, the 2- to 3-month-old seems to be actively seeking stimulation, often smiling in response to it.

Whereas previously the major communication of the infant to the caregiver had been crying or distress, which the caregiver tried to alleviate, the 2- to 3-month-old infant showed, through positive affect and patterns of looking, and even through swiping the hand at objects presented, patterns of behavior that seemed endogenously driven or voluntary. Interactions had moved beyond a sequence of distress–soothe–sleep–distress to longer waking and alert periods along with evidence of interest and pleasure, including pleasure in the caregiver.

Caregivers frequently use the presence of interesting visual objects to distract and soothe their children. By 4 months of age, infants look from place to place to explore their visual environment, and through looking they learn much about their physical world. The long process of development of self-control has begun, even though much of their stimulation still rests in the hands of others. What is seen in these infants' behavior reflects a remarkable development of brain systems that underlie the ability to orient to sensory events. In this chapter we describe the use of marker tasks to trace the hidden developments that lie behind the observable change in voluntary orienting during the early life of the infant.

EARLY BRAIN DEVELOPMENT

Although much of the nervous system develops prior to birth, for primates and particularly for humans, a long period of postnatal development is needed to complete the basic formation of the brain. Some aspects of development continue throughout life. A great deal has been learned about changes in the distribution of neurons and the formation of synapses during early development (Johnson, 2002).

The explosion of new connections between neurons (synapses) that begins well before birth continues at a rapid pace in the months after birth. In some brain areas, there follows a long period of stable synaptic density and a substantial loss following puberty (Huttenlocher & Dabholkar, 1997). However, in some areas of the brain there is continual development through adolescence, and new cells can be developed in some areas even in adulthood

(Hastings, Tanapat, & Gould, 2001). There has been much speculation that the density of synapses during childhood might be responsible for increased learning capability in this period, but the connection between synaptic density and learning is yet to be established.

There is also a steady change in white matter as nerves become covered by myelin sheaths that make long-scale communication between brain areas faster. The formation of myelin goes on throughout childhood (Giedd et al., 1999). It is likely that many of the long connections between neural areas needed to carry out complex cognitive tasks (see chaps. 4, 6, 7, and 8, this volume) depend on the development of these connections.

These important changes in the brain are accompanied by equally impressive evidence of changes in behavior. During the first few years of life, infants and toddlers gain control of their behavior and mental state, so that as older children and adults they can exercise a degree of central regulation over their emotions, thoughts, and action. We call the brain system through which this control is exercised the *attention system*. The development of attention is essential to understanding how the interaction between infant and caregiver can lead to the impressive self-control needed for schooling and is the central topic of chapters 4, 5, and 6 (this volume).

Although it is not fully known how cellular events such as cell migration, increased synaptic density, and myelination relate in detail to the achievements of self-regulation, there is enough information to make intelligent connections between precisely specified attentional mechanisms of attention and some of the underlying neural events. These connections are sure to grow with new research.

THE ATTENTION SYSTEM OF THE HUMAN BRAIN

Chapter 2 provided a method for measuring the efficiency of the three attentional networks shown in Figure 2.8 by use of the Attention Network Test (ANT). Many people have thought that attention is a single thing. If it were, performance in all of the networks should be highly correlated and they should have a similar or perhaps identical anatomy. In fact, for the most part, performance in the three networks is not correlated, and differing locations of networks have been identified. However, the networks certainly communicate in carrying out the many tasks that involve attention.

The attention system has been explored extensively in adult neuroimaging studies and includes several distinct networks of brain areas that perform the functions of acquiring the alert state (alerting network), orienting to sensory events (orienting network), and maintaining continuity of

TABLE 3.1

Brain Area and Chemical Modulators for Three Attentional Networks

Function	Sources	Modulator
Alerting	Locus coeruleus Frontal and parietal cortex	Norepinephrine
Orienting	Superior parietal Temporal parietal junction Frontal eye fields Superior colliculus Pulvinar	Acetylcholine
Executive attention	Anterior cingulate Lateral prefrontal Basal ganglia	Dopamine

behavior in accordance with goals when conflicting responses could be called for (executive network). Brain areas involved in three of these networks are illustrated in Table 3.1. The areas are the sources of attentional effects that might have their influence in all areas of the brain.

We are all familiar with changes in our level of alertness as it varies from sleep through an alert state that is highly prepared for and efficient in processing information. The alerting network is involved in achieving and maintaining the alert state. Each new stimulus has an impact on the overall tuning or arousal level of the cerebral cortex (Hebb, 1949). In the absence of external stimulation the organism may lose vigilance or lapse into a sleep state. The alerting network arises in the midbrain and activates frontal and parietal areas.

The *alerting network* arises in an area of the midbrain called the *locus coeruleus*, which is the source of the neuromodulator norepinephrine. When vigilance must be sustained over long periods of time (tonic alertness), the right cerebral hemisphere is most heavily involved (see Posner & Petersen, 1990, for a review). Levels of alertness can also be manipulated by placing a warning signal prior to a target to which the participant responds. The warning signal enhances the speed of responding to the target.

A second network, the *orienting network*, is involved in orienting to sensory events, and key cortical parts of this network are illustrated in Figure 3.3. A new event produces orienting of attention through either (a) shifts of the eye or head position to bring the event on the fovea and align the sensory processors or (b) covert shifts of spatial attention that also increase sensory perception and activation within the appropriate sensory system, but in the absence of any overt eye or head adjustment. Most of the studies of the orienting system involve visual events, but very

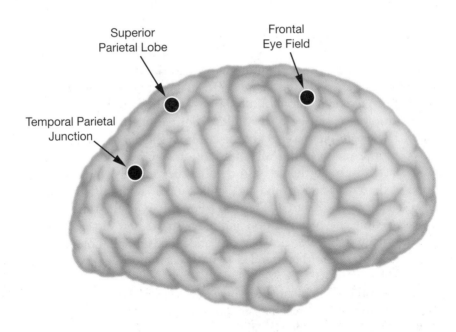

Figure 3.3. Network of cortical areas involved in orienting to sensory stimuli. This figure illustrates how studies of alert monkeys and of human neuroimaging converge on the superior parietal lobe and the temporal parietal junction and frontal eye fields as key areas in orienting of attention (Corbetta & Shulman, 2002).

similar mechanisms are found with other sensory stimuli and with objects that involve multiple senses. The orienting network involves two quite separate areas of the parietal lobe that work in conjunction with specific frontal, thalamic, and midbrain areas, many of them closely related to eye movements. Together, these areas are responsible for the ability to align attention to a sensory stimulus of interest.

The third network, which we call the *executive network*, provides the basis for voluntary behavior. A typical means of activating this network in adults is creating conflict between two possible responses to an event. For example, in the classic Stroop task a word is presented in an ink color that is either the same or different from the word name. The subject's task is to avoid saying the word and instead respond to the ink color. Because word reading is so automatic in adults, there is a strong tendency to read the word (e.g., red) rather than identify its color (e.g., blue). This quite difficult task activates brain areas that are important for voluntary control. The executive network is the major subject of interest in chapter 4 (this volume), where its development is discussed in more detail. In the current chapter, the infant's control of orienting is considered.

THE ORIENTING NETWORK

Many studies of visual orienting have used the spatial orienting task that is a part of the ANT (see Figure 2.7). A cue at the location where the target will be presented automatically brings attention to that location, or a control arrow cue can be used to allow the person to voluntarily shift attention. By separating the effect of the cue from the target one can isolate those operations involved in shifts of attention from target identification. One can actually go further by using valid cues reliably, indicating the position of the target and invalid cues indicating a location that could be a target but is not on this trial. This task allows study of the time required to disengage from the cued location and move to the new target. Reaction time, sensory threshold, electrical activity, and blood flow all show enhancement of the signal from the attended (valid) location in comparison with unattended locations.

The network of neural areas involved (see Figure 3.3) and even some of the cellular and synaptic mechanisms have also been identified. Recordings from microelectrodes in alert monkeys (Wurtz, Goldberg, & Robinson, 1980), studies of stroke patients (Posner & Raichle, 1994), and neuroimaging studies (Corbetta & Shulman, 2002) all show the importance of portions of the parietal lobe in orchestrating shifts of orienting. Of particular importance are areas of the superior parietal lobe (area LIP [lateral intraparietal] in monkeys). This brain area is particularly active following the cue. A quite separate area of the parietal lobe (the temporal parietal junction) is particularly active when an invalid target requires a shift from attending to one location to attending to another location. The temporal parietal junction appears to serve as a means of orienting to unexpected stimuli. The localization of these areas is shown in Figure 3.3. Although these two areas work in conjunction with other brain areas, the two areas are sufficient to illustrate the critical operations involved in orienting to new events. Studies using neuroimaging during the ANT have suggested that warning signals that influence phasic alertness operate most strongly through the left cerebral hemisphere (Fan, McCandliss, Fossella, Flombaum, & Posner, 2005).

Lesions of cells in the parietal lobe, whether from stroke, tumor, magnetic stimulation, or closed head injury, interfere with the ability to shift attention from a cue toward a target on the opposite side of the visual field that projects directly to the lesioned hemisphere. In particular, lesions of the temporal parietal junction appear to cause the difficulty stroke patients have in orienting to stimuli opposite the lesion. If these patients have an intact superior parietal lobe and if they can anticipate the target, they are sometimes able to compensate.

In normal visual behavior, orienting of attention occurs when a novel stimulus is presented prior to an eye movement. Orienting of attention helps to select areas of the visual field that should be fixated. When the target is important, eye movements usually result, and if attention must be sustained the alerting network also becomes involved. Once attention is summoned away from the target there is a bias called *inhibition of return* (IOR) that favors orienting to novel locations in the visual field over those already attended.

FUNCTIONS OF ORIENTING

What happens in the brain when one orients to a source of sensory information? Adult imaging studies offer a provisional answer. When subjects were asked to orient their attention to stimuli arising in one visual field, blood flow in the areas of the visual system processing this event increased. Scalp electrical activity was also enhanced in these areas about 100 milliseconds after the target was presented. When a person was asked to attend particularly to the color, form, or motion of the stimulus, just those areas of brain that process these attributes showed increased blood flow (Corbetta & Shulman, 2002).

In the same adult studies, if a target occurs to which attention is directed, responses will be fast and accurate. If instead a target occurs in another location, response times will be delayed. These same behavioral effects are seen in infants of 4 months. A cue to attend to a stimulus in one field too brief to elicit an eye movement will enhance the speed of a subsequent movement of the eyes (saccade) to the same field. Because the behavioral cuing effects are so similar in infants and adults, one might expect the underlying brain mechanism to be the same. Infants, like adults, can direct attention toward target events and when they do so the subsequent stimulus produces a response as though it were more salient or had a higher priority. Orienting thus operates by increasing the effective signal of a target that occurs at an attended location.

VISUAL ATTENTION IN INFANCY

The visual system is the best understood of the sensory systems. Visual experience is critically important for the normal maturation of the visual system. For example, if one eye of a cat is closed so that it receives no pattern vision in the early months, the cortical representation of that eye within the primary visual system is greatly reduced (Hubel & Wiesel, 1977). Human infants who undergo unilateral removal of cataracts show clear reduction of acuity due to the early period of deprivation and also the extent of the visual world to which they will orient (Maurer & Lewis, 2001). Thus, the genetic plan for development of the visual system includes a critical role for exposure to the visual world.

We first describe how it is possible to explore the capacities of this system in early infancy, and then show how orienting of attention relates to these capacities. Recent studies have fundamentally altered the conception of the infant's capabilities. In the 1950s it was thought that in the early months of life, infants were without substantial cognitive capacity. Although there is still a dispute about the way to conceptualize the knowledge infants have, it is clear that infants, through their looking behavior, demonstrate substantial sensory and cognitive abilities that would have previously been thought impossible. Moreover, infant research also makes it clear that psychologists have the tools to trace the development of these abilities.

Detecting Novel Events

To what are infants most likely to attend? In this section we consider the involvement of orienting with the detection of novel events, with the reduction of distress, and with learning to orient to anticipate objects in their absence. All three of these functions are crucial to later development of the more voluntary mechanisms of attention discussed in chapter 4 (this volume). Infants of 3 months appear to be virtually helpless. They cannot yet talk and are unable to locomote. Yet having the ability to control where they look and to what they attend is of more importance than might at first be apparent. This ability allows infants to enter into their own education by selecting aspects of the environment that are of interest to them. It also allows the caregiver a means of interacting with them. Even from birth, a caregiver whose gaze is on the infant is more likely to attract the infant's looking.

Evidence that there are cultural differences in orienting comes from a study of eye movements of American and Chinese viewers of complex scenes. Americans tended to fixate on objects and move their eyes from one object to another more quickly. Chinese viewers made more saccades to the background events, showing clear differences in the distribution of attention to the scenes (Chua, Boland, & Nisbett, 2005).

The basic mechanisms of attention are developing from 3 to 6 months, but we know that by 18 months, the infant will be able to use the attention of the caregiver for his or her own education and thus to associate new words with objects in the direction of the speaker's attention (Baldwin, 1991). In this section, we show the mechanisms by which novelty directs the orienting of the infant. We discuss IOR as a preference for novel locations and object novelty preference.

Inhibition of Return

A principle of infant development is that subcortical visual mechanisms tend to develop before cortical mechanisms do. In adults, orienting away from just-attended locations reduces the probability of returning attention to that location. This phenomenon, called *inhibition of return* (IOR), was first demonstrated in reaction time studies with normal adults (Posner & Cohen, 1984).

IOR seems to reflect one of many preferences favoring novelty. In vision it favors searching and looking toward new locations rather than ones already examined. Studies with patient populations showed that lesions of a midbrain eye movement structure, the superior colliculus, but not of various other cortical structures interfered with this preference for a novel location. In addition, studies of normal subjects showed that IOR was more likely to occur when stimuli were presented in the temporal visual field rather than the nasal visual field. As the temporal field is closely connected to the colliculus, while nasal field stimuli go directly to the cortex, this finding was thought to suggest that IOR is due to the colliculus. A recent case of a unilateral collicular lesion (Sapir, Soroker, Berger, & Henik, 1999) showed interference with IOR on the side of the field opposite the lesion, confirming the idea of a collicular basis for IOR.

Adult data were consistent in showing that IOR was related to the superior colliculus, which is relatively well developed at birth. We developed a marker task (see chap. 2, this volume) to study the development of the colliculus by studying IOR in infancy. Obviously we could not use instructions so our method had infants orient to a peripheral stimulus and then back to the center. This was followed by a double target to determine if they oriented to the previously cued side or to the uncued novel side. We expected IOR to be present at the earliest ages, but instead we found it to develop between 4 and 6 months of age (Clohessy, Posner, Rothbart, & Vicera, 1991). These findings were replicated and extended by Butcher and colleagues (1999) as shown in Figure 3.4.

Our original studies used targets 30 degrees from fixation, and we observed that 3-month-olds, but not older infants, tended to make several eye movements before reaching the target. It often took more than a second for the infant to reach the 30 degrees. Adult studies (Rafal, Calabresi, Brennan, & Sciolto, 1989) have argued that the necessary and sufficient conditions for observing IOR in adults were the programming of an eye movement. We reasoned that if IOR required programming of eye movements, the infants who required many saccades might not be showing IOR because they were not programming their eye movements directly to the target but rather searching for the target. As most 3-month-olds moved

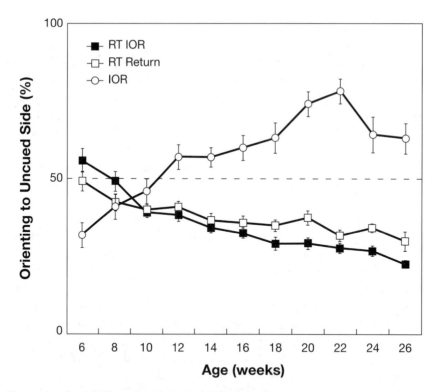

Figure 3.4. Development of inhibition of return in infancy. Inhibition of return, which is a preference for novelty dependent on subcortical structures, develops over the early life of the infant. RT = reaction time; IOR = inhibition of return. From "Inhibition of Return in Very Young Infants: A Longitudinal Study," by P. R. Butcher, A. F. Kalverboer, and R. H. Geuze, 1999, *Infant Behavior and Development, 22,* p. 311. Adapted with permission.

their eyes directly to 10-degree targets, by this logic they should show IOR at 10 degrees. Harman, Posner, Rothbart, and Thomas-Thrapp (1994) studied IOR for stimuli at 10 degrees and found it to be fully present at 3 months.

Subsequent studies showed that IOR can be present in newborn infants, presumably reflecting how the relatively early maturation of the midbrain superior colliculus makes it dominant at birth (Valenza, Simion, & Umilta, 1994). When these infants oriented directly to 30-degree targets they showed clear evidence of IOR. This finding, taken with our results at 10 degrees, suggests that the basic computations for IOR are present at birth. We are not sure what factors produce so many eye movements that fall short of the target in infants of 3 months and block the expression of IOR for longer movements at this age. However, these may be related to maturation of the cortical systems (e.g., parietal lobe, frontal eye fields), which appears to occur about this time.

It is not at all unusual to find functions present very early in infancy, based on a subcortical system, that seem to go away at about 2 months only to return later with cortical maturation. For example, infants at birth favor a real face over a scrambled face (Johnson & Morton, 1991). This difference is thought to be based on a primitive midbrain mechanism, but the preference later disappears only to return at 4 months with more adult-like properties.

Preference for Novel Objects Versus Locations

Presenting targets at 10 degrees allowed us to begin to compare the development of preference for novel locations (IOR) with preferences for novel objects (Harman et al., 1994). Adults have separate mechanisms involved in orienting to objects and to locations. As we have noted, IOR, a process related to locations, is a property of the midbrain collicular system, but this system does not have information on the identity of objects. Visual object identification depends on cortical systems of the inferior temporal lobe.

We compared novelty preference for location with novelty preference for objects. To study orienting to novel objects, we exposed a single object to allow fixation. After the single object was removed from fixation, it was shown at 10 degrees to the left or right of fixation together with a novel object at the same distance on the opposite side.

Infants of 3 and 6 months showed strong novelty preference when a novel target was shown at a novel location. When object and location preferences were put in competition, however, 3-month-olds no longer showed an object novelty preference, orienting instead to the novel location. Even at 6 months, we found preference for a novel object only when the infants examined the first object for 3 seconds or more, not when they oriented to it for only 1 second. The time of exposure necessary to show an object preference in our 6-month-old infants was similar to that reported for infant monkeys (Gunderson & Swartz, 1986). Location preference, however, was established even when the duration of orienting was as brief as we could make it.

We extended these studies to show directly that the two forms of novelty preference were independent at 6 months (Posner, Rothbart, Thomas-Thrapp, & Gerardi, 1998). We compared the same 40 six-month-old infants in single-trial paradigms. These paradigms involved exposure either to a single object or to a single location, followed by choice between two objects or two locations. Both forms of novelty preference were demonstrated, but data indicated that they were not related. The form of novelty preference called IOR is closely related to eye movements, is exhibited only when the infant is able to program his or her eyes to move toward objects, and is present in some form at birth. Preference for novel objects seems to arise along with important development in the visual pathways related to object recognition occurring at about 4 months.

Novel objects have three distinct effects on attention. First, they lead to faster and more reliable orienting. Second, they activate alerting systems that lead to increased alertness via the norepinephrine system, and third, they lead to an effort to develop a new object file that will code the novel event. Adult studies have shown that all three of these processes may be influenced by a very brief flash of a novel object. These studies also show that presentation of a novel object cues the initial orienting, but the sustained attention that follows begins to involve more complex executive functions (Posner, Rothbart, & DiGirolamo, 1999). This finding may explain why it has been hard to find consistent results on whether infants look longer at familiar or novel objects, because the looking preference may depend on much more than just the orienting tendency.

DEVELOPING CONTROL OF FIXATION

At birth, infants do not seem to have fixation under their voluntary control. By the end of the first month, however, the development of a brain pathway from the basal ganglia, which lays below the frontal cortex, to the superior colliculus, a midbrain structure strongly involved in eye movement, appears to usher in a period in which infants maintain fixation for long periods (Posner & Raichle, 1994).

Obligatory Looking

According to the work of Haith (1980), infants' eyes at this age are attracted to stimuli that, like a checkerboard, have a very large number of repetitive edges (and high spatial frequency). This tendency to look at edges makes sense for infants learning about the visual world because edges mark the boundaries of objects and can also provide strong activation of cells in the primary visual cortex. If infants 1 to 3 months old orient toward a checkerboard pattern, their eyes can be caught on it and they may remain fixated for long periods. The checkerboard has a very strong stimulating effect on the infant's visual system and this orienting can lead the infant into distress. If adults orient to the stripes in Figure 3.1, they also might find it slightly distressing because of its regular pattern. There is a period of 2 to 3 months when the infant's eyes do get caught on such stimuli. This effect is sometimes called *obligatory looking* and seems to occur between the time the infant begins to have some control of fixation and the time the maturation of the parietal lobe of the cerebral cortex provides improved ability to disengage from a visual stimulus.

This period of extended orienting is important to the child's early communication of love to the caregiver. During the period of obligatory looking, infants will also gaze into the caregiver's eyes for extended periods, which lays the basis for the strong bonds that develop between them (Bowlby, 1969). The caregiver is likely to use this opportunity to provide pleasurable stimuli to the infant, allowing a far different behavioral response than to the checkerboard. Nonetheless, the internal mechanisms underlying the initial orienting at this age appear to be the same.

Disengaging From Stimuli

Development of orienting can be documented by marker tasks that measure the infant's ability to disengage from a location. In our method (Johnson, Posner, & Rothbart, 1991), infants' attention is brought to a powerful central visual attractor that either looms or spirals on the screen. At 2 months, even strong peripheral stimuli will not be sufficient to cause the infant to disengage from fixation and shift to the new object. The situation changes very dramatically between 2 and 4 months, when the ability to disengage from a central event develops very rapidly (see Figure 3.2). At about 4 months, there is a major change in the social interaction between infant and caregiver. Whereas before, the child was mainly engaging visually face-to-face with the caregiver, there are now visual interests beyond the caregiver, and infants have a control over orienting that allows this exploration. Caregivers often adjust to this change by facing the child away from the adult's face and toward the outside world.

Habituation

As we have seen, the infant nervous system is strongly attracted toward novel events that produce change in their sensory world. However, if the same stimulus is presented for a long period or introduced again and again, there is a reduction of sustained orienting toward that event that we call *habituation*. Habituation has been very effective in tracing the sensory and language abilities of infants. It has also been applied effectively to access an infant's cognitive processes. In this method infants are shown a stimulus many times in a row until they begin to look at it only briefly. The infants appear bored with the stimulus and are said to have habituated to looking at it. On the next trial either the old stimulus is repeated or a new stimulus that differs from the old in some critical way is shown. If looking time lengthens to the new stimulus, one concludes that the infant discriminates the new stimulus from the old. By this and related methods it has been shown that infants have the ability to discriminate between the phonemes of their own and other languages, that they have an appreciation of objects even in their absence, and that they can understand the concept of number if the numbers are small and can even do addition of small numbers (for an overview of this work, see Spelke, 2004). Aspects of the infant's visual orienting, such as habituation of looking, can also be used to predict intelligence score in childhood (Slater, 1995).

When sensory thresholds are traced by a behavioral method such as habituation or preferential looking times (Figure 3.1), it is possible to know something about the brain mechanisms involved, because the neural basis of sensory acuity is partly understood. However, when habituation and preferential looking have been applied to cognitive issues, the brain areas involved have been unknown.

This has led to a great deal of dispute as to what is indicated when infants show increased looking times. A good example of this problem is in the work of Wynn (1992). She showed an infant one object and then hid it from view. The infant then observed a second object placed next to the hidden object. When the objects were revealed, looking times were longer when there was only a single object than when two objects were present. Wynn argued that this indicates that infants expect the one object plus a second object to yield a total of two, and when shown that there is only one, they are surprised. Brain studies (Berger, Tzur, & Posner, in press) have shown that infants of 7 months activate areas of the dorsal anterior cingulate in the error condition that has frequently been related to the detection of error in adults (see chap. 4, this volume, for more details). Error detection is part of the executive attention system so important in voluntary control and these findings suggest that infants as young as 7 months have some recognition of error with their brains responding to it as adults do.

Conclusion on Control of Fixation

So far we have briefly reviewed a number of infant studies designed to examine the infant's tendency to orient to novelty. We have found that orienting arises in close correspondence with the eye movement system, and that elements of orienting are present from birth. The course of development appears to reflect the general maturation of cortical visual systems during the 1st year of life. Thus IOR is present at birth, yet may not be observed at around 3 months. Only later does the ability to voluntarily disengage from a fixation show strong development. The development we see between 2 and 4 months is probably a consequence of maturation of parietal systems.

Novelty preference for objects appears to develop strongly from 4 to 6 months and is probably driven by maturation of the ventral prestriate structures involved in object identification. The independence of novelty preference for objects and locations fits well with the view emerging from adult data that suggests location- and object-based attention involve different mechanisms. Orienting as directed by peripheral and central cues appear to develop together, supporting the lesion evidence and the strong involvement of the parietal lobe in both forms of orienting. The ability of 4-month-old infants to use central cues to direct anticipation toward an upcoming target suggests that a form of implicit learning is exhibited by the eye movement system at this age. We discuss this development further in the section on learning.

SOOTHING

The early life of the infant is concerned with the regulation of state, including distress. During the 1st year of life, attention appears important in developing this form of control. Caregivers provide a hint of how attention is used to regulate the state of the infant. Earlier than 3 months, caregivers usually report themselves as using holding and rocking as the main means of quieting their infant. However, at about 3 months, many caregivers, especially in Western cultures, attempt to distract their infant by bringing his or her attention to other stimuli. As infants attend, they are often quieted, and their distress appears to diminish.

We have conducted a systematic study of attention and soothing in 3- to 6-month-old infants (Harman, Rothbart, & Posner, 1997). Infants first became distressed as a result of overstimulation from lights and sounds but then strongly oriented to interesting visual and auditory events when these were presented. While the infants orient, their facial and vocal signs of distress disappear. However, as soon as the orienting stops, as when the new object is removed, the infant distress returns to almost exactly the levels shown prior to presentation of the object (see Figure 3.5). The loss of overt signs of distress apparently is not always accompanied by a genuine loss of distress. Instead, some internal system, which we have termed the *distress keeper*, appears to hold the initial level of distress and it returns if the infant's orientation to the novel event is lost. In our later studies we quieted infants by distraction for as long as 1 minute without changing the eventual level of distress reached once orienting was ended. The effectiveness of a repeated stimulus in achieving soothing in the infant also appeared to be reduced at 6 months over its influence at 3 to 4 months. Our results also suggest that brain states related to distress may be maintained over a period even while the person is attending to another event.

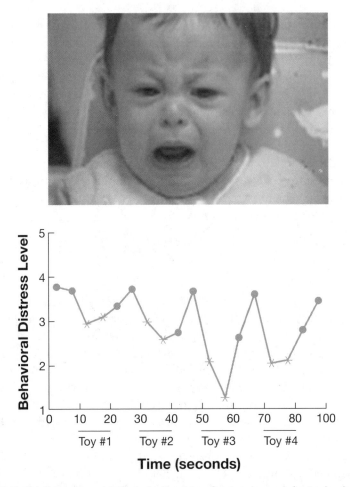

Figure 3.5. Soothing by orienting of attention. On top is an infant who has been distressed by overexposure to sound and lights. On the bottom is a composite graph showing the distress score before and after the introduction of different stimuli to which the infant oriented. During orienting, the distress level dropped, but when orienting was broken it returned to about the same level as prior to the stimulus. From "Distress and Attention Interactions in Early Infancy," by C. Harman, M. K. Rothbart, and M. I. Posner, 1997, *Motivation and Emotion, 21,* p. 31. Copyright 1997 by Springer Science and Business Media. Reprinted with permission.

For infants, the control of orienting is partly in the hands of the caregiver's presentation of relevant information. However, the infant is clearly also involved in soliciting attention from the adults. During the first years of life, more direct control of attention passes from caregiver to infant. It seems likely that the same mechanisms used to cope with early self-regulation of emotion are then transferred to issues of control of cognition during later infancy and childhood. For young infants, the control of orienting is at first largely in the hands of caregiver presentations. By 4 months, as we have indicated, infants have gained considerable control over disengaging their gaze from one visual location and moving it to another, and greater orienting skill in the laboratory has been associated with lower parent-reported negative affect and greater soothability (Johnson et al., 1991). A related phenomenon of looking away to control negative affect appears to be present in infancy and continues through adulthood, and it provides an important aspect of self-regulation. Adults and adolescents who report themselves as having good ability to focus and shift attention also say they experience less negative affect (Derryberry & Rothbart, 1988). Indeed, many of the ideas of both modern cognitive therapy and Eastern methods for controlling the mind are based on using attention to reduce the intrusive influence of negative information.

We observed a number of changes in emotion regulation across longitudinal observation of infants between 3 and 13 months (Rothbart, Ziaie, & O'Boyle, 1992). First, older infants increasingly looked to their mothers during presentation of arousing stimuli such as masks and unpredictable mechanical toys. Infants' disengagement of attention from arousing stimuli was also related to lower levels of negative emotion displayed in the laboratory at 13 months. Stability from 10 to 13 months was found in infants' use of attentional disengagement, mouthing, hand to mouth (e.g., thumb sucking), approach, and withdrawing the hand, suggesting that some of the infants' self-regulation strategies were becoming habitual. Over the period of 3 to 13 months, passive self-soothing decreased, and more active approach, attack, and body self-stimulation increased. Infants who showed the greatest distress at 3 months, however, tended to persist in a very early form of regulation, self-soothing. Once a mechanism for emotion regulation develops, it may persist because it has brought relief, even though more sophisticated emotion regulation mechanisms are now available, an important consideration in developmental approaches to clinical problems.

More recent studies have found direct links between infants' self-regulated disengagement of attention and decreases in their concurrent negative affect (Stifter & Braungart, 1995), and there is also support for the idea that early mechanisms for coping with negative emotion may later be transferred to the control of cognition and behavior, as suggested by Posner and Rothbart (1998). Correlations have been found, for example, between infants' use of self-regulation in anger-inducing situations and their preschool ability to delay responses (Calkins & Williford, 2003). In research by Mischel and his colleagues (Sethi, Mischel, Aber, Shoda, & Rodriguez, 2000), toddlers' use of distraction strategies in an arousing situation was also positively related to their later delay of gratification at age 5. In the next chapter we return to the mechanisms of self-regulation. First, however, it is important to establish some of the first skills the infant develops in controlling orienting responses.

LEARNING

How and when do infants learn where to put their eyes? We believe this is one of the earliest forms of skill learning exhibited by infants. It is also a form of learning that can be examined over the life span to compare aspects of adult and infant learning. It is important for a society to instruct the young on where to attend, and many social conventions depend on such learning. Infants at 18 months, for example, use the direction of adult orienting to guide the association between an object and its name (Baldwin, 1991), and infants 12 to 18 months old check to see where a speaker is looking when uttering a word that is new to the infant.

Anticipating Targets

Infants of 4 months showed that they were also able to learn to use a central cue to reorient attention (Johnson et al., 1991). When we associated one attractor (e.g., the spiral) with a subsequent stimulus to the right and another with a target to the left, the infants learned to anticipate the target by moving their eyes in the direction indicated by the cue before the stimulus appeared. This ability to direct the eyes toward a target based on an arbitrary association was present at 4 months, but not at 2 months. By 4 months, the shift of attention can also be entirely covert, that is, without any eye movement. To show this, we presented a brief flash at a peripheral location that captures the infant's attention, but does not cause an eye movement. A covert movement of attention is confirmed if the infant then shows a high probability and reduced latency in moving the eyes to subsequent targets at the previously cued location, in comparison with a target at a similar distance on the opposite side. Like adults, infants at this age can have attention influenced by a cue without actually executing an eye movement to it. The development of the control of eye movements and covert orienting by peripheral and central cues seems to reflect the common parietal mechanism shown to be involved in attention shifts in adults by both lesion and PET studies. Next, we examine the infant's ability to anticipate the location of a target.

Sequence Learning

We studied the ability of 4-, 10-, and 18-month-old infants and adults to learn to anticipate at which of three locations a target might occur (Clohessy, Posner, & Rothbart, 2001). Earlier work had used reaction times to show clearly the ability of infants by 4 months to learn to anticipate visual objects (Haith, Hazan, & Goodman, 1988). We used three monitors

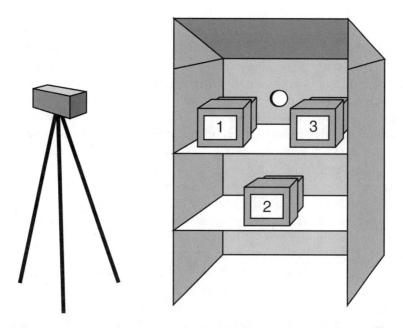

Figure 3.6. Apparatus used to examine learning to anticipate the location of a stimulus by infants and young children. A camera aimed through the hole between the monitors is used to film the infant's face, the camera shown at the left of the figure films the stimuli on the monitors, and the two films are superimposed electronically and used to code the latency and direction of head and eye movements toward the stimulus locations. The digits shown did not actually appear on the screen. They refer to the order of appearance in the two sequences, 1-2-3 and 1-2-1-3, described in the text.

attached to a computer (see Figure 3.6) and taught two types of sequences. In a simple sequence, the target moved from one location to another around the triangle (e.g., 1-2-3). For complex sequences, the targets moved in a sequence such as 1-2-1-3. One of the locations (e.g., Location 1 in the latter sequence) occurred unambiguously following an event at 2 or 3. The other two locations could not be predicted unless one knew where in the sequence one was or when one had last gone to that location.

By 4 months, infants showed they were able to know the location of a new visual input in the first quarter of a second after input. This ability can be shown by examining how long after an event occurs that a location dominates as a target for a saccade. By this measure, 4-month-olds had gained enough information about the location of the target by 250 milliseconds that they moved their eyes directly to the correct target more than 80% of the time (chance would be 50%). The speed of registering the location of the input changed very little over development (adults were about 100 milliseconds faster), but the time to initiate the eye movement dropped by 50% between infants and adults.

At 4 months of age infants learned to anticipate the location of a new target in the simple sequence well enough to be correct about 70% of the time. This performance was excellent. In fact, adults, who learned the sequence without being aware that there was a sequence, were correct about the same proportion of the time. However, the 4-month-olds were not able to learn the ambiguous sequence. They did go back to 1 following 2 or 3 more than would be expected by chance, but they were at chance in deciding to go to 2 or 3 following being at 1. By 18 months, they seemed to acquire the ambiguous sequence, but it took quite a lot of training for them to accomplish this. Later we showed it was not until 24 to 30 months that infants could do well on the ambiguous trials. At this age there was a correlation between their ability to learn the ambiguous sequence and performance on the conflict tasks (Rothbart, Ellis, Rueda, & Posner, 2003). This finding led us to believe that important developments might be taking place in higher level attention mechanisms by about 30 months of age. In chapter 4 (this volume) we discuss this issue further.

Using percent correct anticipation as a measure proved to be useful, particularly in work with young infants and in cases where learning was compared across age groups. A distinct advantage of the anticipatory eye movement measure is that the response is elicited within a few trials, and significant differences in accuracy can be seen after as few as 18 trials. The small number of presentations required to demonstrate expectations with anticipatory eye movements makes it a valuable tool for assessing infants, who often do not tolerate long testing periods. In addition, the measure of percent correct anticipation gives a consistent metric to compare across ages, where reaction times differ greatly.

Recall that simple unambiguous sequences were learned well at 4 months of age, whereas the ambiguous events were not learned until about 30 months. In fact, 4-month-olds showed about 70% correct anticipations in our study, which was not very different for the 69% found by adults who showed little awareness of the sequence after learning. Learning without awareness of the sequence (implicit learning), was very similar from infancy to adulthood. There are vast differences in the ability of young children and adults to take advantage of knowledge of the sequence when it is explicitly provided to them. In chapter 9 we discuss how explicit knowledge of a sequence improves learning of sequences greatly for adults and 10-year-olds but not for younger children (see chap. 9, this volume, for more details).

Imaging studies of adult sequence learning (Grafton, Hazeltine, & Ivry, 1995) found that implicit learning, without any awareness of the sequence, involved subcortical (basal ganglia) and parietal structures. Both of these areas develop early in life. However, explicit learning seemed to depend on frontal structures, which have a much later developmental course.

SUMMARY

Socialization builds on the natural tendency of infants to examine novel objects. It allows the caregiver, as a representative of the culture, to provide instruction on where to look. These early unconscious learned responses of the orienting system remain present in the culturally determined gaze patterns that characterize social interaction and inspection of visual scenes. Our results suggest that mechanisms guiding the implicit learning of where to orient are quite similar in 4-month-olds and adults.

Orienting can also momentarily soothe the infant. During these occasions the caregiver trains the infant to develop control over the emotions. We believe that the caregiver's early involvement in the infant's learning where to move his or her eyes and moderation of the infant's emotions are critical steps on the road to the self-regulation of emotion and cognition. Later this system will be important for the development of the ability of the child to control their own cognitions and emotions. We turn to this topic in the next chapter.

4

A MIND OF ONE'S OWN

Children who at 4 months of age look at all the stimuli presented return to the lab a year and a half later with their own agenda. It is hard to get them to attend to our displays because their own plans take precedence. After making heroic efforts we can only shake our heads and mumble that they have a mind of their own. In this chapter we consider what it means to have a mind that can regulate one's own emotions and behavior.

ANATOMY OF VOLUNTARY CONTROL

In infancy, most behaviors are heavily under the control of the child's current state and of external events, mainly those presented by caregivers. Even the ability to regulate the infant's distress is heavily influenced by external stimuli introduced by caregivers (see Figure 3.5). It has long been believed that the development of the frontal cortex allows the child to move away from being bound to external stimuli. The development of frontal control mechanisms allows children to demonstrate voluntary control of actions and to delay gratification. The child's ability to resist control from current input gives rise to our feeling that toddlers, unlike infants, have a mind of their own.

The 2nd year of life ushers in a period of development that is critical for the child's ability to participate in the school experience. We think that executive control by frontal structures may begin to develop in the caregivers' early efforts in soothing the infant, which help to train the ability to regulate emotion. These activities may aid infants in control of distress and other emotions. Children develop structures that can then be applied to the selection, inhibition, and control necessary to acquire the complex skills taught in schools.

Neuroimaging studies show that frontal areas are crucial for the representation of information when it is absent from the senses, the aspect of attention that William James (1890) called "streams of thought." Frontal areas are also critically involved in working memory. These systems make it possible to relate pieces of information that have been stored in widely separated locations in memory. The toddler also produces words in attempting to express ideas to others; these words in turn influence the internal representation of thought. In this chapter, we describe how the ability to act independently of current input is related to the development of an attentional network that supports internal regulation of emotion and thought.

In *Attention in Early Development*, Ruff and Rothbart (1996) related attention to self-regulation, viewing attention as "part of the larger construct of self-regulation—the ability to modulate behavior according to the cognitive, emotional and social demands of specific situations" (p. 7). They further proposed that self-regulation places emphasis on inhibitory control, strategies of problem solving, memory, and self-monitoring. In addition to their argument that attention is a part of the mechanisms of self-regulation, Ruff and Rothbart discussed how individual differences in attentional efficiency play a part in successful self-regulation. We further develop this idea in chapters 5 and 6 (this volume).

CONTROL OF COGNITION AND EMOTION

We start by considering the functions of the executive attention network in adults. Adult studies allow the exploration of the anatomy and circuitry of the executive attention network by use of neuroimaging. A surprising aspect of the adult data is that attentional control of cognition appears to arise out of brain areas also noted for their involvement in emotion (Bush, Luu, & Posner, 2000). We use marker tasks (see chap. 2, this volume) to trace the development of this network in toddlers and young children. In later childhood the growth and development of this system can be examined by the use of pediatric neuroimaging.

Executive attention is important for a form of memory that is often called *explicit learning*. This is the kind of memory involved in school examinations in which performance is based on the ability of the child to bring to mind material previously encountered. Attention is needed to put the memory in a form that can be brought to mind and reinstated later.

This chapter emphasizes that executive attention is central to the regulation of both emotions and cognitions. Of course all children regulate their emotions to some degree. However, there are important temperamental differences in the timing and success of emotional reaction. The control of emotion is central for the adjustment of the child to the school situation. This theme is developed more fully in chapter 6 (this volume).

Executive attention is also of great importance in the learning of specific skills that are required in schools. The kinds of explicit learning necessary to acquire high-level skills of reading, calculation, and abstraction are all related to the efficiency of executive attention. Attention is crucial for acquiring new ideas and relating them to already learned concepts. This role of attention is the main topic of chapters 6, 7, 8, and 9 (this volume).

MEASURING EXECUTIVE ATTENTION

The idea of a high-level executive attention network arose first in cognitive psychology as a way of dealing with the inevitable conflicts that occur when separate processing systems (see Figure 4.1) are in competition for the control of behavior. Donald Norman and Tim Shallice (1986)

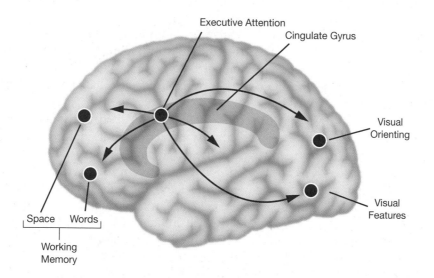

Figure 4.1. The interaction of the anterior cingulate with other brain areas that control various domains of cognition. From *Images of Mind* (p. 173), by M. I. Posner and M. E. Raichle, 1994, New York: Scientific American Books. Copyright 1994 by W. H. Freeman & Co. Adapted with permission.

thought that such a network would be needed to resolve conflict between competing responses, to correct errors, and to plan and develop novel responses.

Tasks

When neuroimaging began, it was shown that whenever we orient to a sensory event there is an increase in the activation of the brain areas involved in processing that stimulus (Posner & Raichle, 1994). The same principle seems to apply everywhere in the brain. When a person attends to the computation carried out by any area of the brain, the activity associated with that area increases, heightening the priority of the computation performed there.

Adult neuroimaging studies have been fairly consistent in showing activity in midline frontal areas during tasks that might be thought to involve conflict (Bush et al., 2000), detect error (Carter et al., 1998), or produce novel ideas (Posner & Raichle, 1994), the definitions proposed by Norman and Shallice (1986) to be important for executive attention.

Conflict Tasks

The most frequently studied conflict task shown to activate the frontal midline areas is the Stroop effect. In this task the subject is required to name the ink color in which a conflicting color word is written. Results from this task suggest that the frontal midline areas might serve as part of a network that is the source of changes in brain activity occurring as the result of executive attention. This is the basis for Figure 4.1, which shows in cartoon form that the anterior cingulate, a portion of the midline of the frontal lobes, interacts with a variety of other areas to regulate their activity (Posner & Raichle, 1994).

Figure 4.2 shows that the anterior cingulate is divided into a ventral area (the black area in the figure) that is active for emotional tasks and a dorsal area (the lighter area) that is activated in purely cognitive tasks. The cognitive tasks (such as the Stroop) have in common the need to provide a less dominant response when a more dominant one is present. They represent tasks involving cognitive conflict. Many tasks, such as the Stroop effect (e.g., saying "blue" to the word *yellow* in blue ink), are language tasks. Another language task involves giving the use of a noun (e.g., stimulus is *hammer*, response is *pound*) rather than naming the actually presented word.

Figure 4.2 distinguishes tasks that are purely cognitive from those that contain emotional elements. Although the anatomical separation is not absolute, there is a clear difference in the anatomy between the more dorsal cognitive area and the more ventral emotional area. The more ventral

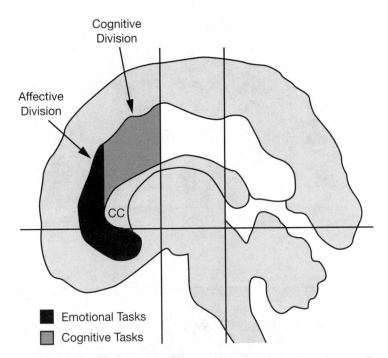

Cognitive
Division

Affective
Division

CC

■ Emotional Tasks
▨ Cognitive Tasks

Figure 4.2. Cognitive and affective division of the cingulate. This diagram illustrates the results of many studies that show increased activity in the anterior cingulate during control of cognitive (medium gray) or emotional (black) tasks. The idea is that the cingulate is part of an executive attention network that serves to modulate activity in many brain areas (see Figure 4.1) during attention. CC = corpus callosum. From "Cognitive and Emotional Influences in Anterior Cingulate Cortex," by G. Bush, P. Luu, and M. I. Posner, 2000, *Trends in Cognitive Sciences, 4,* p. 217. Copyright 2000 by Elsevier. Reprinted with permission.

area has close connections to the limbic system, including the amygdala, important in the processing of fear. The dorsal part has strong reciprocal connections to other attentional areas in the lateral frontal and parietal cortex.

Stroop tasks are not ideal for children. Children do not show the Stroop effect before they can read, because when they cannot read, there is no conflict between the word and the ink color. Children do show conflict when the dimensions of the identity of a stimulus and its location are made incongruent, as in the spatial conflict task illustrated in Figure 4.3. They also show conflict in a child version of the Attention Network Test (ANT; also see the bottom of Figure 4.3).

A neuroimaging study of adults used the color Stroop task and the two child-appropriate conflict tasks (Fan, Flombaum, McCandliss, Thomas, & Posner, 2003). A common network consisting of the dorsal anterior cingulate as well as an area of the left prefrontal cortex was activated in

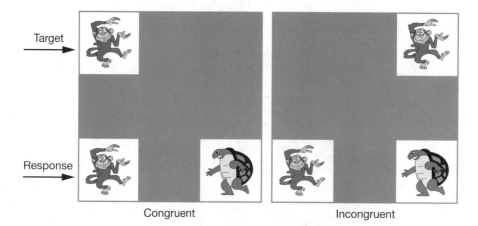

Target →

Response →

Congruent   Incongruent

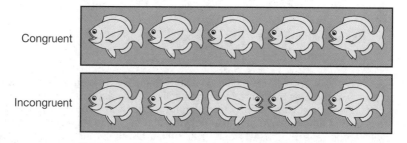

Congruent

Incongruent

Figure 4.3. Conflict-related tasks for young children. The upper panel shows a cognitive conflict task appropriate for children. The participant must respond by matching the top figure to the correct figure on the bottom (identity), but the matching figures may be on the same side or opposite side (location). The conflict between location and identity can be used to study the resolution of conflict in children 2 to 3 years of age (Gerardi-Caulton, 2000). The lower panel shows a child-friendly version of the Attention Network Test (see Figure 2.7). The arrows are replaced by fish and the child must press the left key when the center fish swims left and the right key when it swims right. Otherwise the task is the same as that in Figure 2.7. From "Development of the Time Course for Processing Conflict: An Event-Related Potentials Study With 4 Year Olds and Adults," by M. R. Rueda, M. I. Posner, M. K. Rothbart, and C. P. Davis-Stober, 2004, *BMC Neuroscience, 5,* p. 39. Copyright 2004 by M. R. Rueda, M. I. Posner, M. K. Rothbart, and C. P. Davis-Stober. Reprinted under license of BioMed Central.

common by all of these tasks. Although other areas were activated for individual tasks, these were the only common brain areas. These data identify tasks that will activate the network involved in executive attention and that can be used as marker tasks with young children.

Despite the common network involved in the three conflict tasks, there was little evidence that people who were good on one task were necessarily good on the other tasks. Each task achieves conflict by different methods. For example, the color Stroop depends so much on reading speed that young children do not show the Stroop effect at all, whereas the spatial conflict task uses a conflict between visual location and identity, two of the earliest developing visual dimensions in the infant brain. Thus the spatial conflict task can be used with young children.

Response to Error

The incongruent condition of conflict tasks in which the person must inhibit a dominant action to produce a subdominant one produces longer reaction times, more errors, and greater experience of effort than does the congruent condition. Immediately following an error, subjects are often conscious of having made a mistake. When aware of making an error in speeded tasks, they show a very specific change in scalp-recorded electrical potentials (see Figures 2.3 and 2.4 for illustrations of this method). Research has shown that this change comes from the anterior cingulate gyrus (De-haene, Posner, & Tucker, 1994). The error-related response generated by the cingulate occurs only when subjects know they have made an error. A similar negativity in response to an error was discussed in chapter 2 (this volume). Because people usually correct such errors or slow down on the following trial, this effect has been associated with a form of self-regulation of behavior.

Imaging studies have also shown that the conflict between responses is sufficient to generate activity in the cingulate (van Veen & Carter, 2002). The cingulate activity seems to occur under high-conflict conditions that occur on incongruent trials irrespective of whether an error actually occurs.

Emotional Control

The ventral part of the anterior cingulate (black part of Figure 4.2) is closely connected to the brain's emotional system (limbic area of the brain). Studies of negative emotion in adults have generally suggested that distress is related to activity in a limbic structure called the amygdala. When pictures depicting frightening or horrible scenes are shown to subjects, there is strong activation of the amygdala. This result also occurs with words associated with threatening events either in general (cancer) or specific to the person being tested.

There is some evidence that cingulate activity is related to our aware-ness of emotion rather than to the emotion itself. One method of measuring emotional awareness of individuals is to have them describe how they feel about situations and code their use of emotional terms and descriptors in the written responses. In a neuroimaging study, subjects were shown each of three highly emotional movies and three neutral movies during a positron emission tomography scan (Lane et al., 1998). Differences in anterior cingulate blood flow between the emotional and neutral movies were correlated with the person's emotional awareness score. These data suggest that something about the subjects' awareness of their emotions during sad or happy events is related to changes in the anterior cingulate. This result is similar to the finding of Rainville, Duncan, Price, Carrier, and Bushnell (1997) that cingulate activity is more related to the painful feelings than to the intensity of the stimulus inducing the pain.

Interaction of Cognitive and Emotional Regulation

Because the anterior cingulate is involved in both cognitive and emotional processing, it becomes important to ask how these functions might interact. This question is important for several reasons. First, the interaction between cognition and emotion is a central focus for psychological research. Second, there have been few opportunities to relate anatomical adjacency to behavioral or psychological interactions. Although the separation of these two systems within the cingulate might indicate functional independence, it is also possible that their close physical proximity within the cingulate supports important connections between the two. Next, we review what is known about the function of these two areas and discuss examples of psychological interactions between cognition and emotion.

Neuroimaging data provide an important perspective on possible interactions between cognitive and emotional portions of the anterior cingulate (Drevets & Raichle, 1998). Positron emission tomography studies of negative emotionality suggest that strong activation of the emotions suppresses or reduces blood flow in the cognitive area of the cingulate. This suppression can occur as a result of pathological disorders, such as depression, or when emotions are induced in otherwise healthy individuals, as when normal subjects anticipate an electric shock. Anterior cingulate activity has also been known to decline during vigilance tasks that do not involve emotion, when the subject is simply waiting for an event to occur. When attention-demanding cognitive tasks are performed, blood flow to the dorsal cingulate increases whereas blood flow to more anterior emotional areas tends to decrease (Drevets & Raichle, 1998).

A specific test of the idea that attention and self-regulation are closely related in the control of affect involved exposing male adults to erotic films, with the requirement that they regulate any resulting arousal. Cingulate activity shown by functional magnetic resonance imaging was found to be specifically related to the regulatory instruction (Beauregard, Levesque, & Bourgouin, 2001). In a different study, photographs known to produce negative affect were shown with the instruction to interpret them in a way that avoided any emotional response. There was a correlation between extent of cingulate activity and reduction in negative affect (Ochsner, Bunge, Gross, & Gabrieli, 2002). In a similar way, in a study using hypnotism to control the perception of pain, cingulate activity reflected the perception of pain but not the strength of the physical stimulus (Rainville et al., 1997). These results show a role for this anatomical structure in regulating limbic activity related to emotion, and provide evidence for a role of the cingulate as a part of the network controlling affect (Bush et al., 2000).

These data suggest a degree of mutual inhibition between emotional and cognitive control systems. However, there is also behavioral evidence that mild levels of positive affect such as those induced by rewards can improve subsequent cognitive processes, including creative problem solving (Ashby, Isen, & Turken, 1999). A study of the Stroop effect (J. Kuhl & Kazen, 1999) demonstrated that positive affect induced by priming with a happy face could reduce the size of the interference. Because the Stroop effect is consistently associated with cingulate activity, this reduction indicates an interaction between affect and attention, probably within the cingulate. Ashby et al. (1999) suggested that increased dopamine activity brought about by positive affective states enhances cognitive processing. This mechanism suggests a positive interaction between emotional states and cognition. Note that the main findings from PET studies relate to negative emotions and deal with blood flow at the time of the emotional induction, whereas the data described in this paragraph deal with cognitive processing following elicitation of positive emotion.

Further evidence for the interaction between affective and cognitive regulation comes from a study exploring the influence of personality traits on reactions to making an error. Relative to subjects low in negative emotionality, subjects high in negative emotionality slow down more after an error and show larger error-related negativity (Luu, Collins, & Tucker, 2000). The error-related negativity is an electroencephalogram component that occurs shortly after an error response that is thought to arise in the anterior cingulate. This result is consistent with the view that negative emotions interact with cognitive processes at the level of the anterior cingulate. However, this study relates to patterns of results across individuals rather than the interaction of cognition and emotion within a single brain.

It seems likely that strong negative emotions may inhibit the processing of cognitive information whereas strong positive emotions may have the opposite effect, at least if measured after a delay. Moderate levels of both positive and negative emotion may actually work in conjunction with attention to increase its effectiveness. Although these possibilities are tentative, they suggest methods to investigate further how cognitive and affective processing might interact within the frontal midline and how this interaction may be related to learning.

Imaging studies have begun to provide a basis for exploring frontal networks involved in effortful control (Dehaene, Kerszberg, & Changeux, 1998). These studies suggest that both anterior cingulate and areas of the lateral prefrontal cortex operate together during tasks involving high levels of mental effort. Dehaene et al. (1998) proposed a global work space, suggesting that both medial and lateral frontal areas exert a common influence during mental processing. However, neuroimaging studies of orienting of attention to visual stimuli show that within the large-scale distributed network found to orchestrate shifts of attention, each specific area plays a different role (Posner & Raichle, 1994). We expect that a similar story will eventually emerge with respect to the lateral and medial frontal structures involved in focal attention.

Some proposals have been made as to what this role might be for frontal activation, but none are clearly supported by the current data. One possibility is that the more lateral areas are involved as holding circuits in which domain-specific activity is represented while acted on by midline circuits. This situation would fit with the role of lateral frontal cortex in working memory. Consider obtaining the use of a noun (e.g., *pound* for *hammer*). The word name might have to be held in a system during the process of evaluating candidate uses. Focal attention would include both the representation of the input (lateral frontal) and the control operations (anterior cingulate) that would coactivate areas of semantic memory where associated concepts might be stored.

A different idea about how lateral and medial frontal areas might interact comes from the finding of both automated and attended routes to output (Raichle et al., 1994). According to this idea, the cingulate is part of a pathway used when effortful control is required, such as when a use is generated for the first time (see Figure 1.1). The anterior insula represents a more automated pathway to word output, which is active in reading aloud and when the association has been recently practiced.

Another view involves the distinction between the monitoring of conflict and the operation needed to implement control (Carter, Botvinick, & Cohen, 1999). According to this view, the cingulate is involved in the detection of potential cross-talk or confusions between separate processing modules. Lateral areas of the cortex are then activated to provide control operations, which might include increased activation or inhibition to eliminate confusion between modules.

These three views all propose breaking down executive attention into components and preserving the general approach to brain activity in which specific anatomical locations are related to mental operations (Posner & Raichle, 1994). Future research will have to determine whether high-level attention involves distributed components, each of which carries out a specific function, or whether the frontal lobe activity follows new principles of brain organization.

DEVELOPMENT OF EXECUTIVE ATTENTION

As discussed in chapter 3 (this volume), the control of distress or negative emotionality is a major task for the caregiver in the early months of life (see Figure 3.5). We believe that efforts by the caregiver (or by the infant him- or herself) to soothe the infant may train regulation of distress and be important to the development of the midfrontal area as a control system for negative emotion.

The importance of such control, even in adult life, is supported by a negative correlation between negative affect and ability to control attention (Derryberry & Rothbart, 1988). Adults who report themselves as able to concentrate and switch attention are also those who report less negative emotionality, and mothers' report of temperament in their children produces a similar finding. We believe this correlation is an adult version of infants' control of distress by orienting.

The 2nd year of life ushers in a period of development that is critical for the child's ability to participate in the school experience. Children develop executive attention processes that can then be applied to the selection and inhibitory control necessary to acquire the complex skills taught in school.

Test of Executive Attention for Children

During the period of later infancy there is evidence of the development of frontal structures that provide the person with the ability to free themselves from complete reliance on sensory input.

Reaching

For example, Diamond (1991) identified the period from 9 to 12 months as pivotal in infants' progress toward being able to resolve conflict between reaching for an object along the line of sight and retrieving an object from the open side of a three-sided transparent box. At 9 months, the line of sight dominates completely. Even if the child's hand touches the toy through the open side of the box, if it is not in his or her line of sight the infant will withdraw the hand and reach along the line of sight, striking the closed side. Three months later, infants are able to look through the closed side but reach through the open end of the box to retrieve the toy. However, being able to reach for a target away from the line of sight is only a very limited form of conflict resolution. This specific form of conflict appears to depend on the dorsolateral prefrontal cortex.

In chapter 3 (this volume) we discussed the ability of infants of 4 months to anticipate the location of an event by moving their eyes in anticipation of the target. Our studies showed that it was not until about 24 to 30 months that children could resolve conflicts about the correct spatial location in ambiguous sequences. We regard this form of anticipatory looking and conflict resolution as related to the development of the anterior cingulate and the executive attention system.

Verbal Conflict

Gerstadt, Hong, and Diamond (1994) adapted a verbal conflict task modeled on the Stroop paradigm for children as young as 3.5 years. Two cards were prepared to suggest day and night to the children. One depicted a line drawing of the sun, the other a picture of the moon surrounded by stars. Cards for the control condition were intended to suggest neither day nor night. Children in the conflict condition were instructed to reply "day" to the moon card and "night" to the sun card. Children in the control condition were divided into two groups and instructed to say "day" to either a checkerboard or ribbon card and "night" to the other. At every age, accuracy scores were significantly lower for conflict trials relative to control trials. Although all children also performed at 80% accuracy or better for the first 4 trials of the session, by the last 4 trials, performance of the youngest declined to chance. Older children were able to maintain above-chance performance throughout the 16-trial session. Latency scores for conflict relative to control trials were also significantly longer for 3.5- and 4-year-old children, suggesting that younger children needed more time to formulate their responses when faced with conflict. Other efforts have been made with Stroop-like tasks and with the Wisconsin card sort task to study children as young as 31 months, where little evidence of successful resolution of conflict below 3 years has been found.

Spatial Conflict

A more direct measure of the development of executive attention might be reflected in the ability to resolve conflict between simultaneous stimulus events, as in the Stroop task. Because children of this age do not read, we reasoned that the use of basic visual dimensions of location and identity might be the most appropriate way to study early resolution of conflict.

The spatial conflict task was designed to be appropriate for ages 2 to 3 years. As shown in Figure 4.3 (upper panel) it involves presenting a simple visual object on one side of a screen directly in front of the child and asking the child to respond with a key that matches the stimulus shown (Gerardi-Caulton, 2000). The appropriate key could be either on the side of the stimulus (congruent trial) or on the side opposite the stimulus (incongruent trial). The prepotent response was to press the key on the side of the target, irrespective of its identity. However, the task required the child to inhibit that response and to act instead on the basis of identity. The ability to resolve this conflict is measured by the accuracy and speed of the child's key-press responses.

Study results strongly suggested that executive attention undergoes dramatic change during the third year of life. Performance by toddlers at the very beginning of this period was dominated by a tendency to repeat the previous response. Perseveration is associated with frontal dysfunction and this finding is consistent with the idea that executive attention is still very immature at 24 months. Even at this young age, however, toddlers were already showing a significant accuracy difference between compatible and incompatible trials (63% vs. 53%). By the end of the 3rd and beginning of the 4th year, children showed a strikingly different pattern of responses. Three-year-olds at 38 months performed with high accuracy for both congruent and incongruent conditions (92% and 85%, respectively) and also demonstrated the expected slowing for incongruent relative to congruent trials (30% longer reaction times).

The sequential eye movement task discussed in chapter 3 (this volume) and earlier in this chapter also provided evidence that children 24 to 30 months old can resolve conflicts between spatial locations, a form of learning that in adults appears to require access to the kind of higher level attention needed to resolve conflict. As expected, performance of children at 3.5 years in resolving conflict in the spatial conflict task was positively correlated with their ability to respond to ambiguous locations in the eye movement task described in chapter 3 (this volume; Rothbart, Ellis, Rueda, & Posner, 2003). Thus we now have eye movement methods to examine the resolution of conflict from early infancy to adulthood. We have also found that individual performance of children in conflict tasks was related to important aspects of their ability to delay gratification and parental reports of their effortful control. These findings are discussed in detail in chapter 6.

Simon Says

In the Stroop task, conflict is introduced between two elements of a single stimulus. We reasoned that an even more difficult conflict might be introduced when the child is asked to execute instructions from one source while inhibiting instructions from another (L. Jones, Rothbart, & Posner, 2003). This conflict task is the basis of the Simon Says game, and previous studies suggested that the ability to perform this task emerges at about

4 years of age (Reed, Pien, & Rothbart, 1984). Children 40 to 48 months old were instructed to execute a response when it was given to them by a toy bear but to inhibit the response when given by a toy elephant (or the reverse). Children up to 40 months were unable to carry out the inhibition instruction at better than a chance level, and they performed just as rapidly in making incorrect responses to the elephant as they did in making correct responses to the bear. Although children could repeat the instruction, they did not seem to be able to use it to control their own behavior. The difficulty of young children in inhibiting their behavior is well known. However, in our study, just a few months later, they performed virtually perfectly.

When the children begin to be able to perform this task, they tend to use physical control to inhibit themselves from executing the commands given by the elephant. They will sit on their hands when the elephant gives the instruction, or squeeze their hand between their knees. It is quite amazing to observe the lengths to which they go to physically control their own behavior. After they gain some skill, the use of this kind of physical control disappears, but they are still quite slow in dealing with responses to the bear. They appear to control themselves with the elephant by delaying their responses to the bear, as though they are carefully considering the source of the instruction.

Attention Network Test

We have used the Attention Network Test (ANT; Figure 4.3, lower panel) with children 4 years of age and older as well as adults. Recall that in this task children must respond to the central fish but ignore the flankers.

We find that reaction time in the child ANT steadily improves from age 4 to adult performance (see Table 4.1). However, the components of attention show rather different developmental time courses (Rueda, Fan, et al., 2004). Orienting is already well developed by age 4 and shows little change thereafter. Warning signals rather surprisingly have a much larger effect in childhood than in adulthood. As discussed in chapter 3, much of this occurs during the 1st year of life. Adults seem to maintain a highly prepared state even when there is no specific warning, whereas children seem to be caught unaware on trials in which the target occurs without warning.

Most interesting is the conflict effect. We found dramatic improvement from age 4 through age 7 (see Table 4.1). However, after age 7 we found no additional improvement in the ability to resolve conflict. When we compared 10-year-olds with adults on both the child and adult version of the ANT, we found that their ability to resolve conflict was the same. Of course many aspects of performance on complex tasks involving attention improve to adulthood; however, our data suggest that a crucial element of the circuitry underlying executive attention appears to be developed as early

TABLE 4.1
Reaction Time (RT) and Time to Resolve Conflict

Age (years)	Task	Congruent trials		Incongruent trials		Conflict effect		Study reference
		RT (ms)	% correct	RT (ms)	% correct	RT (ms)	% correct	
2	Spatial conflict	3,476	69.1	3,378	53.9	−98	−15.2	Rothbart, Ellis, Rueda, and Posner, 2003
2.5		2,489	80.8	3,045	57.8	556	−23.0	
3		2,465	90.1	3,072	80.3	607	−9.8	
4	Flanker (child ANT)	1,490	89.4	1,913	77.1	424	−13.0	Rueda, Posner, Rothbart, and Davis-Stober, 2004
6	Flanker (child ANT)	890	92.0	1,005	76.4	115	−15.6	Rueda, Fan, et al., 2004
7		828	94.6	891	93.9	63	−0.7	
8		791	95.0	862	95.3	71	+0.3	
9		724	98.1	791	96.5	67	−1.6	
10		624	98.7	693	96.6	69	−2.1	
Adults		473	99.5	534	97.9	61	−1.6	

Note. The top three rows are from studies using the spatial conflict task (see Figure 4.3). The remainder represent a study using the child Attention Network Test (ANT).

as age 7. Table 4.1 (Rothbart, Posner, & Kieras, 2006) puts together data on the spatial conflict and child ANT to give an indication of the development of executive attention from preschool to middle childhood.

Cells and Circuits

One advantage of understanding where in the brain something takes place is that one has a chance to examine the cellular structure of the area involved. Although the anterior cingulate is an ancient structure, there is evidence that it has evolved significantly in primates. Humans and great apes appear to have a unique cell type found mainly in Layer V of the anterior cingulate and insula, a cell type not present in other primates (Nimchinsky et al., 1999). Although the precise function of this cell is not known, high correlations between its volume and encephalization suggest a likely role in higher cortical functioning. The proximity of these cell clusters to vocalization areas in primates led Nimchinsky and her colleagues to speculate that these cells may link emotional and motor areas, ultimately resulting in vocalizations that convey emotional meaning.

There is evidence for development in the connectivity of this cell in the child's brain. It is also known that Layer V of the cingulate expresses all of the various forms of the dopamine receptors. Genetic studies of families with members with attention-deficit/hyperactivity disorder (ADHD) have shown that they possess a variant of the dopamine-4 receptor. We examine this and other genes in relation to the development of attentional networks in chapter 5 (this volume).

Although as yet no direct evidence links the cellular architecture of the anterior cingulate to cingulate activity detected during neuroimaging studies, the importance of this area for emotional and cognitive processing makes further exploration important. The existence of animal models for the Stroop task (Washburn, 1994) suggests avenues for the pursuit of these ideas at the cellular and genetic levels.

INDIVIDUAL DIFFERENCES IN EFFORTFUL CONTROL

Executive attention provides a neural substrate for differences in effortful control among individuals. *Effortful control* is a measure of individual differences in the ability to inhibit a dominant response to perform a subdominant response.

The original discovery of effortful control as a broad dimension of temperament came from factor analyses of the Children's Behavior Questionnaire (Rothbart, Ahadi, Hershey, & Fisher, 2001), a questionnaire which assesses temperament in children ages 3 to 7. This research identified three broad factors, including a general factor of Effortful Control. Effortful control includes dimensions of attentional focusing, attentional shifting, and inhibitory control, along with perceptual and affective sensitivity.

Parents notice their children's ability to regulate their own behavior and can systematically report it in questionnaires. Effortful control is correlated with the ability to resolve conflict in tasks such as spatial conflict and the ANT during childhood (Gerardi-Caulton, 2000; Rueda, Fan, et al., 2004). The correlation of effortful control with the ability to resolve conflict suggests that the remarkable developments in the children's development of self-regulation over this period reflect the maturation of the underlying mechanisms of conflict resolution as measured by the ANT and other conflict tasks.

BRAIN SIZE

How do individual differences in the ability to resolve conflict and effortful control relate to what is known about the developing brain? Our general intuition is that larger brain area indicates greater capacity to carry out mental operations. This conviction is likely related to the general excitement about the finding that Albert Einstein's brain had greater brain area in the inferior parietal lobe than did a set of control brains. It is known (see chap. 8, this volume) that this general area of the brain is related to numerical computations, so it stands to reason that one of the world's great thinkers in physics might have more brain area related to mathematics. Just think what the reaction to the report might have been if this area had been smaller than normal in Einstein's brain.

It is now possible to study this intuition directly by examination of the size of regions of the brain as children develop, using magnetic resonance imaging (MRI). Although some evidence supports the brain-size intuition, not much data have been found to relate changes in the size of brain regions with developmental gains in cognition. One National Institutes of Health study of 145 healthy children examined the brains of individual children at 2-year intervals from 4 to 22 years (Giedd et al., 1999). Linear increases were found in the parts of the brain that involved connections between areas (white matter) over this period. However, the brain areas involved in cortical computations tended to increase at first and then decrease. For example, the frontal lobes showed a maximum size at 11.7 years, followed by a decrease postadolescence, so that from 4 to 22 years there was actually a net decline. These findings fit with the general result for cellular studies that the number of brain synapses and the density of cell structure tend to decline at adolescence. Another study of brains of children from 5 to 17 years old (Reiss, Abrams, Singer, Ross, & Denckla, 1996) confirmed this finding by showing little change in overall brain volume after age 5, but found a correlation (.4 to .5) between the size of gray matter in frontal areas and measured intelligence from IQ tests.

Intelligence as measured by IQ tests is a gross measure of overall performance. Although cognitive studies have often identified IQ with frontal function, IQ undoubtedly reflects a number of general capacities. So far there has been relatively little evidence that MRI measures of regional brain areas can be strongly related to intelligence or personality. The theories of temperament and personality arising from psychometric and experimental studies of children and adults show quite consistent major dimensions of individual differences, and it would be expected that these differences could be related to the size of regional brain areas. However, to date, very few studies using morphometry have taken advantage of these theories in examining differences in the size of brain area.

One area in which evidence is available involves individual differences in the size of the anterior cingulate in childhood in relation to conflict reduction and error correction. In a study driven by theory relating the anterior cingulate to high-level attention, the size of the anterior cingulate was measured in children ages 5 to 16 (Casey, Trainor, Giedd, et al., 1997). A significant correlation was found between the volume of the area of the right anterior cingulate and the child's ability to perform a go–no go task. In this task, the child must respond as rapidly as possible to an X stimulus while withholding response to all non-X stimuli. The correlation was present even when data were corrected for age and other factors that might be related to size. A reaction time control task, in which subjects responded to all stimuli and did not have to inhibit responding, showed no relation to the size of the cingulate.

A further study used functional MRI with a go–no go reaction time task (respond to X, inhibit to non-X). This task has some similarity to the bear–elephant task we discussed previously as relying on focal attentional control. Children from 7 to 12 years of age were observed. The go–no go task was compared with control tasks in which subjects responded to all stimuli and never had to withhold a response. Both children and adults showed strong activity in prefrontal cortex and cingulate when required to withhold responses. These activations were stronger and somewhat larger in children than in adults (Casey, Trainor, Orendi, et al., 1997). Moreover, the number of responses to nontargets (false alarms) made in the task was significantly correlated with the extent of the activation in the anterior cingulate. This finding fits well with the role of the cingulate in error detection found in adults.

Another approach to individual differences in brain size is the study of developmental pathologies. Pathologies such as attention deficit disorder or obsessive–compulsive personality relate to and may even be a result of temperamental differences among children in activity level, perseveration, extraversion, risk taking, and other temperamental characteristics (Rothbart, Hershey, & Posner, 1995; Rothbart & Posner, 2006). Although it would be extreme to suppose that these pathologies are merely the result of extremes of normal personality, it seems likely that the symptoms of disorders such as ADHD overlap with the normal tendency of some children to perseverate in responding, seek out high levels of stimulation, and lack concentration.

Studies of the brains of children diagnosed with ADHD by means of brain morphometry have shown some common characteristics, generally involving the frontal cortex and areas of the underlying basal ganglia. In general, children with ADHD showed abnormalities in the right frontal cortex and in parts of the basal ganglia including the globus pallidus and caudate nucleus (Filipek et al., 1997). Children with early bleeding in the area of the caudate are at greater risk for later diagnosis of ADHD and show evidence of difficulties in cognitive control (Casey, Durston, & Fossella, 2001). These findings of basal ganglia and frontal deficits in the brains of children with ADHD fit with the special roles of these areas in attention.

SUMMARY

In adults we find that control structures for cognition and emotion are represented in the frontal midline of the brain (anterior cingulate). The portions related to cognition and emotion are anatomically separated, but there is evidence that they interact in actual behavior. These mechanisms are closely related to lateral frontal and basal ganglia areas, but we do not yet know how the midline and lateral structures share the functions of executive control.

Control structures undergo a remarkable development in middle childhood. Two-and-a-half-year-olds are unable to voluntarily regulate their cognitive processes. When confronted with simple challenges between competing responses, they fail. By age 7, although slower than adults overall, children resolve conflict with almost the same efficiency as do adults. Children differ greatly both in the strength of their responses to stimuli and in their ability of effortful control. The school environment needs to be adaptive to these differences if children are to be made ready to make optimal use of their learning. Chapter 6 (this volume) deals in more detail with temperamental differences in attention and affect among children in relation to their readiness for schooling.

5

GENES AND ENVIRONMENT

The common brain mechanisms of attention we have examined in this volume are, in part, specified by the genetic instructions stored in each human cell. The study of molecular genetics has produced a map of the human genome (Venter et al., 2001) and enhanced the potential for understanding genetic contributions to brain development and to individual differences in behavior. This work has already altered the basis of the traditional nature–nurture debate. Gene expression depends on the environment, and thus, the interaction between nature and nurture goes all the way to the molecular level.

This solution to the traditional debate between nature and nurture means that thought, emotion, and behavior are both genetic and also influenced by the environment. However, there still remains the problem of whether specific educational experiences of the type that occur in schools can alter the course of brain development. It is already known that brain imaging can reveal new activations not present prior to educational intervention (see chap. 7, this volume), but it is not clear whether these experiences are simply allowing us to see the brain areas specific to the trained task or whether they have a more general effect on brain networks.

GENETIC BASIS OF ATTENTION

A view of genetic expression as environmentally dependent allows for acceptance of genetic influences on the part of the behavioral sciences without the need to forfeit the important role played by the social environment. Research into the genetic basis of attention is at the very beginning stages. In this chapter we review this effort, relate it to specific educational experiences, and indicate the potential for understanding the interaction of genes and environment.

Selectionist and Constructivist Views

Although much of the nervous system develops prior to birth, for primates and particularly humans, a long period of postnatal development is needed to complete the basic formation of the brain. Two basic biological ideas have dominated our understanding of how nervous systems are put together. The first stresses genetic influences and the second, learning. The idea that embraces the strongest form of genetic influence argues that neuronal connections are specified with great precision during development. A view that proposes a weaker form builds on this analysis to argue that experiences shape or select from an innate repertoire of connections (Gazzaniga, 1994). This view stresses the overproduction of synapses in early life and their pruning in development. Findings of the surprising capabilities of very young infants in processing features of language, number, and objects provide some support for this selectionist viewpoint. A selectionist may place emphasis on innate individual differences in children, which can lead to views such as the one expressed by Gazzaniga (1994) when he argued that education is about finding out what a particular brain is good for.

The learning principle, presented by D. O. Hebb (1949), indicates how correlated firing of cells leads to stronger connections between them. This principle ensures that cells that fire together will be strongly represented in connections. Hebb's idea has led to more constructivist views (e.g., Quartz & Sejnowski, 2000), according to which development involves a progressive increase in the representational properties of the cortex. Here the environment shapes the specific organization of sensory systems tuned to visual, auditory, or other aspects of stimuli. In support of this view is evidence that children deprived of sensory input (e.g., deaf from birth) show specific alterations in the organization of other modalities (Neville, 1995). Areas of visual system related to peripheral information appear to expand in the deaf, whereas central foveal information remains similar to that in the sighted. These findings stress how experience can reorganize brain circuits, but also show the limits of such reorganization. These findings support the plasticity of brain networks, but do not support more extreme views such as those sometimes held by Herbert Simon and his followers, that expertise depends only on a rich semantic memory built from hours of intense practice.

This volume illustrates how these selectionist and constructivist views can be combined. Current research shows that neural networks underlying self-regulation develop under the influence of specific experiences from caregivers (see chaps. 3 and 4, this volume) and later formal education (see chaps. 7 and 8). In this chapter we further our goal of integrating selectionist and constructivist views by reporting how candidate genes influence a specific attentional network important for development of self-regulation, and then examine specific educational experiences that may modify this development.

Findings of Molecular Genetics Research

As we have seen in chapter 4 (this volume), neural systems related to executive attention make a crucial contribution to temperament and to learning. Individuals can voluntarily deploy their attention, which allows them to regulate their more reactive tendencies and to suppress a dominant response to perform a subdominant response. In chapters 7 through 9 we review how this attentional network aids in the acquisition of school subjects. However, to relate individual differences in attention to candidate genes, we must first understand the chemical system that influences the attentional system's operation.

The brain's attention system is influenced by different transmitter systems arising in subcortical areas. We have discussed how orienting toward sensory stimuli involves the posterior parietal lobe. Studies of alert monkeys carrying out the cued detection task described in chapter 3 (this volume) have examined the role of modulator systems in alerting and orienting of attention.

Alerting and Norepinephrine

A major aspect of orienting to sensory events is being able to maintain the alert state. Speed of responding to external events declines remarkably as one goes from the fully alert state to a relaxed and then to a drowsy state, and tends to disappear completely during sleep. Levels of alertness can be manipulated by presenting a warning signal prior to a target to which the person responds. The warning signal enhances the speed of responding to the target by altering the level of alertness of the organism. In adults this alteration is rather slight, but in children it can be much more dramatic (see chap. 4, this volume).

Studies with alert monkeys (Marrocco & Davidson, 1998) have shown that drugs such as clonidine and guanfacine that reduce the availability of the transmitter norepinephrine appear to eliminate the beneficial effect of a warning signal on reaction time. In the case of clonidine, the overall speed of responding is reduced, whereas in the case of guanfacine, reaction time is enhanced; yet both drugs have a similar influence on the warning signal effect (Marrocco & Davidson, 1998). Monkeys under the drugs' influence are no better when a cue indicates that a target is about to occur than when there is no such cue. When they are drug free, the same monkeys show a clear warning signal effect. Though the studies conducted to date have involved systemic administration of the drugs, it is thought that the drugs act on the locus coeruleus to reduce the availability of norepinephrine to cells in the posterior parietal lobe (Marrocco & Davidson, 1998). Many other studies have confirmed the influence of norepinephrine on arousal or alerting functions.

Orienting and the Cholinergic System

Drugs such as scopolamine that influence the cholinergic system affect the ability to switch attention to a cued location without having any influence on the effects of a warning signal. One study involved local injections of scopolamine into the area of the lateral intraparietal sulcus known to contain cells involved in shifts of attention (M. C. Davidson & Marrocco, 2000). These injections produced difficulties in switching attention toward the hemisphere opposite the injection, but did not influence the effect of a warning signal. Thus alerting and orienting of attention are separable not only in anatomy, but also in terms of the transmitters involved at the cellular and synaptic level. These studies show remarkably clear evidence for the dissociation of two transmitters within the same task, relating them to different functions, even though it is known that the transmitters frequently interact and influence each other at many levels.

Some patients in the initial phase of Alzheimer's disease show an abnormality in their ability to orient attention (Parasuraman & Greenwood, 1998). These patients also show a reduction in blood flow within critical areas of the parietal lobe. One of the important characteristics of Alzheimer's disease is a marked loss of cells in an area of the basal frontal lobe called the nucleus basalis of Meynert, an important source of the cholinergic system. Indeed, removing this structure in monkeys reduces their ability to shift attention toward cues (Voytko et al., 1994).

Thus patients with Alzheimer's disease may shed light on how the cholinergic system deficit influences attention. Some patients with early Alzheimer's disease have a particular version (allele) of the apolipoprotein (APOE) gene called the e4. The occurrence of this version of the gene is associated with an earlier decline in cognition in those persons with Alzheimer's disease, but normal individuals also possess this genetic variant. An experimental study compared the attention shifts of normal people who had the e4 genetic variant with the shifts of those who did not (Greenwood, Sunderland, Friz, & Parasuraman, 2000). Researchers observed specific deficits in the use of visual cues to direct attention in normal persons who had this genetic variant. Thus it appears that the e4 variant of the APOE gene is related to a specific function of attentional networks in both normal persons and persons with Alzheimer's.

The relation of orienting to the cholinergic system led Parasuraman and colleagues (Parasuraman, Greenwood, Kumar, & Fossella, 2005) to examine two candidate genes known to influence the cholinergic system. In each case, they compared a group of individuals with one form (allele) of the gene with another group who had a different form of the same gene. In both of these comparisons the genes influenced the efficiency of visual orienting. They also tested a gene known to influence the transmission of norepinephrine and found it had no effect on the efficiency of orienting. Although many genes must be involved in the control of attention, the specific attentional function of switching attention represents a component operation that may be determined by a much smaller set of genes. This work shows that knowledge of the specific brain areas and of transmitters involved in orienting may assist the search for genetic controls. As in many other cases of cognitive neuroscience, understanding of function at one level provides a basis for studying its control at other levels.

Dopamine and Executive Attention

Two other abnormalities also produce deficits in attention. Attention-deficit/hyperactivity disorder (ADHD) is often diagnosed in the second or third grade at age 7 or 8 when children are required to concentrate for long periods. A very different disorder, schizophrenia, usually appears in late adolescence or early adulthood and often involves difficulties in concentration, thought disorder, and hallucinations. Both disorders have commonly been thought to involve attention in some form, but their surface symptoms are quite different.

There are reasons to connect the two disorders at both the neurosystem and the neurochemical levels. Studies of schizophrenia have often pointed to abnormalities in the frontal midline as a prominent feature of the disorder (Benes, 1999; Early, Posner, Reiman, & Raichle, 1989). Benes (1999) reported that schizophrenic brains in autopsy showed a striking deficit of control systems within the anterior cingulate in comparison with normal brains (see Figure 5.1). In her recent anatomical studies, she related such deficits to a circuit that includes the hippocampus and amygdala as well as the anterior cingulate.

The anterior cingulate is only one synapse away from the ventral tegmental area, which is one source of dopamine neurons. In addition, all of the dopamine receptors are expressed within the cingulate, and dopamine has been frequently associated with schizophrenia. Drugs that reduce the symptoms of delusions and thought disorder influence dopamine

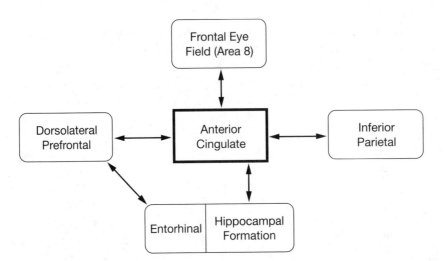

Figure 5.1. A network of areas centered on the anterior cingulate thought to be involved in schizophrenia (Benes, 1995).

transmission. A more direct test of the hypothesis that schizophrenia influences executive attention was conducted (Wang et al., 2005) using the Attention Network Test (ANT; see Figure 2.7). There was a dramatic abnormality among patients with schizophrenia in the executive attention network (see Figure 5.2), with a small deficit in orienting and no apparent deficit in alerting.

In a similar way, ADHD has often been associated with dopamine because methylphenidate, the main drug used to control the disorder, apparently does so in part by altering the availability of this transmitter. It has been shown that adults who had ADHD as children continue to display symptoms of the disorder and show a striking abnormality when required to perform a conflict task in which the person responds to the number of stimulus words presented (Bush et al., 1999). The words are numerals that might be incongruent with the response (e.g., four repeats of the word *two*) or congruent (e.g., two repeats of the word *two*). The adults with ADHD perform only slightly worse on this numerical task than controls, but unlike the controls they do not activate the anterior cingulate. Instead they activate a quite different pathway. Other studies (e.g., Swanson et al., 1991) have shown that children with ADHD may also have an alerting deficit.

These findings suggest that there might be a common executive attention abnormality in both ADHD and schizophrenia, even though the symptoms and ages of the disorder seem so different and they may also involve different additional attention network problems.

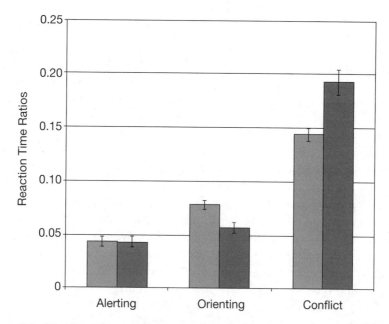

Figure 5.2. Attention Network Test results for patients with chronic schizophrenia (dark gray bars) compared with those of normal participants (light gray bars). Patients show a large deficit in the executive network and a very small deficit in orienting and none in alerting (Wang et al., 2005).

The common executive attention deficit in ADHD and schizophrenia, as revealed by the numerical Stroop and ANT, provided a new means of examining the genetic basis of the disorder. A number of correlational studies, using both population- and family-based methods, have suggested that the behavioral manifestation of ADHD appeared to be related to a particular form of a gene called the dopamine-4 receptor gene (Swanson et al., 2001). One version (allele) of the gene (+7 repeat) has seven repeats of a 48-base-pair sequence within a region of the gene that influences the proteins associated with the gene (coding region). Other alleles of this gene have only two or four repeats of this specific 48-base-pair sequence. Thus in the case of ADHD, there is a candidate gene that might be related to the symptoms of the disorder.

Children diagnosed with the behavioral symptoms of ADHD ($N = 32$) and normal children of the same age without the disorder ($N = 21$) were genotyped (Swanson et al., 2000). They were then compared in their performance on three reaction-time tasks related to attentional networks. The children with ADHD were slower than were the normal children and much more variable in their performance. However, when the children with ADHD were divided into those with and without the 7-repeat version, Swanson et al. (2000) were surprised to find that the slowness and variability in all three attention tasks came from the children with ADHD without the 7-repeat allele.

The 7-repeat allele has been found to be related to aspects of normal temperament that are sometimes called sensation or novelty seeking, but it also fits within the dimension of extraversion. Infants with the 7-repeat allele at 2 months showed a stronger tendency to look away from a toy and showed generally less sustained attention than did those without the allele (Auerbach et al., 1999). Infants with long alleles of the DRD4 gene showed less negative emotionality at 2 months and reduced distress to limitations.

Mice without the DRD4 gene show a deficit in their exploration of the environment (Grandy & Kruzich, 2004). These findings suggest that one pathway to ADHD might be through a temperamental variant related to a high need to explore the environment and low negative emotionality. These children might show reduced attention in environments that did not allow sufficient exploration. A second route to attentional deficit might be through some form of early brain injury. In children without the 7-repeat allele, 7 of 19 showed very long reaction times and high variability symptoms, which often accompany forms of brain injury (Swanson et al., 2000).

Heritability Studies of Executive Attention

To determine whether there was sufficient evidence of genetic influence in the development of the executive attention network in normal persons to support the hunt for candidate genes, it was important to determine its heritability. Heritability is a rough measure of the degree to which genes are important for the trait being considered. It is usually studied by comparing monozygotic twins who have identical genes with dizygotic twins who, like siblings, share about half of their genes. The heritability measure assumes that the mono- and dizygotic twins do not differ systematically in the environmental influences on their development. Because this assumption is somewhat doubtful, heritability remains only an estimate. However, in a small-scale study, the executive network showed high heritability sufficient to justify the search for specific genes (Fan, Wu, Fossella, & Posner, 2001).

DNA from cheek swabs of subjects who performed the ANT were then used to examine differences in candidate genes (different genetic alleles or polymorphisms) related to dopamine. To date, studies of genes related to dopamine have demonstrated four genes that influence performance of the executive network.

Behavioral Studies

One of these genes is the DRD4 gene that we discussed in association with ADHD and the personality trait of sensation seeking. The COMT gene has also been found to be associated with exeutive attention in a number of conflict-related tasks (Blasi et al., 2005; Diamond, Briand, Fossella, & Gehlbach, 2004).

Moreover, this gene has also been associated with schizophrenia (Egan et al., 2001). The deletion of the COMT gene in a severe childhood disorder (22 q11 deletion syndrome) also produced difficulties in executive attention as measured by the ANT and an increased risk of schizophrenia (Simon et al., 2005; Sobin et al, 2004). Other genes related to the executive network are the MAOA gene, which is involved in the synthesis of both dopamine and norepinephrine, and the Dopamine Transporter gene (DAT1; Fossella et al., 2002; Rueda, Rothbart, McCandliss, Saccamanno, & Posner, 2005).

We previously mentioned that children diagnosed with ADHD had a disproportionate representation of the 7-repeat version of the DRD4 gene. The findings with persons without ADHD provide a more complete perspective on this ADHD result. The 7-repeat allele associated with ADHD does not produce difficulties in the executive network. Instead, the presence of the more common 4-repeat allele appears to be associated with more difficulty in resolving conflict. The association of a different allele of the DRD4 gene with conflict among normal subjects provides additional impetus for considering the role of this gene in disorders such as ADHD. Evidence from detailed evolutionary studies suggests that the 7-repeat is under positive selective pressure (Ding et al., 2002), indicating that it might convey some advantages. This advantage may be related to the association of the 7-repeat with sensation seeking, a personality trait that might have conveyed an advantage during human evolution (Ding et al., 2002). These findings are all rather new and require further confirmation and extension. However, they do show possible usefulness in relating genetic differences to specific networks and temperaments.

Neuroimaging Studies

Neuroimaging can serve as a tool to examine the role of genetic variation in influencing brain networks. Two of the genes associated with differences in conflict reaction time (DRD4 and MAOA) also produced differences in brain activation within the anterior cingulate gyrus, although the finding involved different alleles of the gene (Fan, Fossella, Sommer, Wu, & Posner, 2003). This finding is illustrated in Figure 5.3.

The number of subjects required to find a significant difference in brain activity was far fewer than those needed to do so when looking at behavior. A similar result was reported for the BDNF gene (Egan et al., 2003), which was thought to be related to long-term memory storage. It required several hundred subjects with each allele to show a behavioral difference in a memory test, but fewer than 10 subjects per group were needed to establish a difference in degree of activation within the

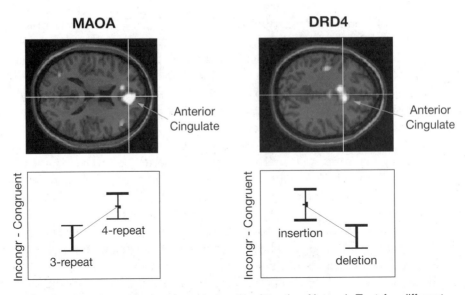

Figure 5.3. Imaging of brain areas during the Attention Network Test for different genetic alleles. Different versions of two genes (MAOA and DRD4) were shown to produce different levels of efficiency, as measured by error rate, in the executive attention network (bottom panels). In a neuroimaging study they also showed an altered activation pattern in the anterior cingulate gyrus (see arrow in top panels). Incongr = incongruent. From "Mapping the Genetic Variation of Executive Attention Onto Brain Activity," by J. Fan, J. Fossella, T. Sommer, Y. Wu, and M. I. Posner, 2003, *Proceedings of the National Academy of Sciences of the USA, 100,* p. 7409. Copyright 2003 by National Academy of Sciences, USA. Reprinted with permission.

hippocampus. These findings suggest that imaging may play an important role in examining the influence of genetics on neural networks.

The findings discussed thus far show how genetic differences can influence normal efficiency of the executive network. However, in chapters 3 and 4 (this volume), we have shown how common attentional networks are important in human development. It seems likely that the same genes that show differences among individuals will prove important in the common development of these networks and thus in the future will serve as clues both to normal development and to disorders.

TRAINING OF ATTENTION

One way in which specific experiences can alter brain function is through sudden injury to the brain. Brain injuries often produce a loss in the ability to concentrate as well as other difficulties in attention and short-term memory. Brain injury patients report problems with concentration, distractibility, forgetfulness, difficulty doing more than one thing at a time, and problems with aspects of memory strongly related to attention. Even relatively small decrements in an individual's attention ability may significantly reduce their capacity for new learning. Attention impairments are also found in executive attention. Patient complaints and laboratory research document problems with the allocation of attentional resources, switching between tasks, the ability to deal with two tasks at the same time, and overcoming automatic responses when faced with nonroutine situations. These are all aspects of executive attention.

Rehabilitation of Attention

Most efforts to rehabilitate patients with closed-head injury rely on some combination of education and social support, practice, and process training. Education and social support supply individuals with relevant information about their injuries and suggest strategies to help manage the consequences of the brain damage. They also give opportunities to share feelings about changes in circumstances in a supportive environment.

Practice refers to specific training on a task to improve performance on that task. Practice may be a deliberate part of the therapy or it may be accomplished through repeated administration of tests designed to determine amount of improvement. Practice alone may also be found to improve performance more generally if it results in transfer to tasks that have not been practiced.

Attention process therapy (APT) refers to a deliberate effort to use a therapeutic program to improve a wide range of tasks involving attention (Sohlberg & Mateer, 1989). Exercises include careful listening for targets, marking auditory targets on score sheets, and many other tasks requiring sustained careful attention to auditory information. Several studies have reported that APT improves memory, learning, and some aspects of executive control (Sohlberg & Mateer, 1989).

One study compared APT training with an educational and support method (Solhberg, McLaughlin, Pavese, Heidrich, & Posner, 2000). Ten neuropsychological tests were used to assess changes that accompanied the interventions. The attentional networks of orienting, alerting, and executive attention, together with working memory, were studied. To determine whether the therapy improved the prospects of patients in their everyday life, a battery of questionnaires and structured interviews was used with patients and their caregivers.

Results of this study provided support for differential effects of therapeutic strategies in the rehabilitation of patients with acquired brain injury. Practice, whether by repeating the tasks in the assessment or by training general processes with APT, improved performance. In contrast, teaching about the brain appeared to improve the attitude of patients by providing them with a systematic way of thinking about the nature of their deficit but did not improve attention. On the basis of these results we speculate that teaching children about the brain and how it changes with learning might itself be a good educational tool.

Patient reports from structured interviews suggested an even more robust effect of APT on improved executive control and working memory than was noted with the neuropsychological tests. Patients also reported more changes in cognitive function following APT and more changes in psychosocial functioning following brain injury education. Those who reported more cognitive changes also showed greater improvements on the executive attention tasks.

Developmental Interventions

The evidence that some executive attention might be restored following closed head injury, along with the findings discussed in chapter 4 (this volume) of important developments that occur at 2 to 7 years of age, raise the possibility that early training of executive attention might have a favorable influence on a wide variety of cognitive and emotional behavior.

Animal Studies

After extensive training, Rhesus monkeys and chimpanzees can carry out the numerical Stroop, a task known to produce activation of the anterior cingulate in human adults. The animals needed many months of training to perform the tasks. The training methods began with their learning how to use a joystick to track objects (Rumbaugh & Washburn, 1995). In one phase of the training, the animals learned to attend to objects even when they were not present in the field, anticipating the location at which they would appear. In another phase, animals were trained to choose one of two objects. They started with relatively simple problems, such as choosing the object that matched the one they saw previously. They learned to wait for varying periods before getting the object to match. The animals were also trained to understand the quantity of digits. The presentation of a digit yielded the number of rewards that corresponded to their quantity. This training led to trials on the numerical Stroop task in which they had to move the joystick to the larger of two arrays. After some training, digits were used so that the numerical value of the digit could be either congruent or incongruent with the array size.

In one study Washburn (1994) found that monkeys show similar reaction time performance on the numerical Stroop and other conflict tasks as do humans. The monkeys, however, made many more errors, particularly

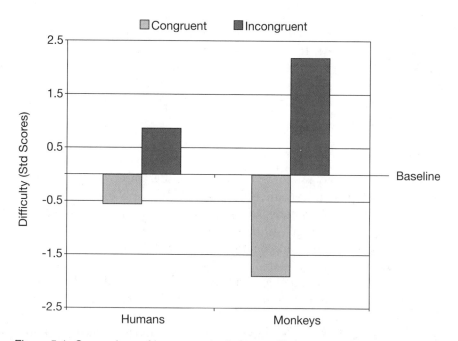

Figure 5.4. Comparison of human and primate conflict resolution scores. This figure includes data from humans and monkeys in the numerical Stroop task. The *y*-axis shows the relative difficulty of both kinds of trials: congruent, when the larger number of objects also has the larger digit, and incongruent, when the larger number of objects has the smaller digit. Monkeys showed larger interference effects than did adult humans. Std = standard. (Printed with permission from D. A. Washburn.)

on the incongruent condition. The scores achieved by the two species are compared in Figure 5.4.

Additional research showed that cues helping to direct the subject's attention to the target location are more effective with monkeys than with humans. However, rewards operating through executive attention are more effective in humans than in monkeys. In general, results of the tests with monkeys seemed more like those of young children whose executive attention is still immature than like those of human adults.

Informal observations made by Rumbaugh and Washburn (1995) indicated that the animals enjoyed performing these tasks. They particularly seemed to enjoy choosing which of the tasks they would perform at a particular time. It was also observed that the animals tended to become less aggressive and more sociable after training. These observations fit with the idea that training in executive attention might influence both cognitive and emotional tasks. This association would fit with the common influence of the anterior cingulate on both types of tasks as illustrated in Figure 4.2.

These observations of animals raise the question of whether it might be possible to influence both the cognitive and the emotional controls on behavior by systematic training of young children in tasks similar to those used with the monkeys. In laboratory studies with children, it would clearly not be possible to match the number of trials used with monkeys, but it might be possible to perform training designed to make subtle improvements in the children's executive attention during the period when it is undergoing development.

Child Studies

We have created a set of training exercises designed to help preschool children develop their executive attention skills, with exercises adapted from the work previously done with primates to train monkeys for work in outer space (Rumbaugh & Washburn, 1995). Each program was in the form of an exercise that the child could enjoy and was designed to teach a set of cumulative skills that would allow training on the elements of executive attention. We chose 4- and 6-year-old children for the test because we have shown that executive attention as measured by conflict develops between 2.5 and 7 years (Rueda et al., 2005). We felt that 4- and 6-year-olds would be in the process of developing this network and would have the best chance for improvement.

Figure 5.5 illustrates the training exercises. The upper portion shows a subject working with a joystick and an experimenter. The child's face provides some idea of the high degree of attention involved in carrying out the training. Some of the programs are illustrated in the lower slide. They began by teaching the child to use a joystick to control the movement of a cat. The cat had to be brought to the grass without getting in the mud. Over trials, the area of grass shrank and the area of mud increased. Another exercise required the child to put and keep the cat under the umbrella, which moved randomly. After joystick training the exercises required prediction. A duck jumped into a pond and swam in a straight line. The child had to position the cat to meet the duck. At first the duck was visible across its trajectory, but in later trials it disappeared under the water. Several exercises involved working-memory training. The child was trained on the value of digits (most children already were familiar with digits). After the training the child was told to move the joystick to the larger of two arrays. During conflict trials more copies of the smaller digit appeared on one side, with fewer copies of the larger digit on the other. Thus the child, like the monkeys, had to resolve the conflict between the value of a digit and the number of items in the array.

Effects of Training

Because this was the initial test of the exercises, children in the control group either participated in the pre- and postassays or viewed interactive

Figure 5.5. Examples of exercises for training attention in young children. Upper left: A 4-year-old participates in attention training under the watchful eye of a researcher. Bottom right: Several exercises from the attention training program are illustrated. The children learn to control a cat with the joystick to keep it out of the rain (a), to move the cat to grass (b), and to catch a duck when it leaves the pond (c).

videos. Two groups of 4-year-olds and one group of 6-year-olds underwent training. Each experimental and control group consisted of 12 children, selected from volunteers in the Eugene, Oregon, area. These studies involved only 5 days of actual training for about 30 to 40 minutes per day in addition to one pre- and one posttraining assessment day.

During the pre- and posttraining days, children performed the ANT while wearing a net with 128 scalp electrodes to measure activity level by means of an electroencephalogram (EEG). They also were given an IQ test, and their parents filled out the child temperament scale. We realized this amount of training was minimal, nothing like the hundreds of thousands of trials that were given to the monkeys. It also was not like what might happen if attention training were used over a full year in a school setting. However, because these were normal volunteers, we felt that seven visits

TABLE 5.1
The Effects of Training in Comparison With Age Effects

Task	Score	Training	Age differences
Child ANT	OV RT	−12.6	−43.8
	OV errors	−18.1	−86.3
	Conflict	−32.0	−63.8
K-BIT	VOC	+6.1	+28.0
	MAT	+9.6	+51.1
	IQ	+7.3	+36.4
CBQ	SUR	+0.5	−2.1
	EC	−1.5	+5.0
	NA	−0.8	−7.1

Note. Data are the percentage of change as a result of training—[(posttraining score − pretraining score)/pretraining score] × 100—or as a result of age—[(4-year score − 6-year score)/4-year score] × 100—for the Attention Network Test (ANT), IQ, and temperament. Note that all training changes for the Child ANT and IQ are in the same direction but smaller than the difference related to age from 4 to 6 years. OV = Overall; RT = reaction time; K-BIT = Kaufman Brief Intelligence Test; VOC = Vocabulary; MAT = matrix task; CBQ = Children's Behavior Questionnaire; SUR = Surgency (Postive Affect); EC = Effortful Control; NA = Negative Affect. From "Training, Maturation and Genetic Influences on the Development of Executive Attention," by M. R. Rueda, M. K. Rothbart, B. D. McCandliss, L. Saccamanno, and M. I. Posner, 2005, *Proceedings of the National Academy of Sciences of the USA, 102,* p. 14934. Copyright 2005 by National Academy of Sciences, USA. Reprinted with permission.

for child and parent were about the maximum we could require. We hoped to obtain some hint of whether the training was useful and, if so, how.

Results of the pre- and postassays for overall reaction time and the various network scores on the ANT are shown in Table 5.1. To compare the relative size of the training effects we included the improvement found from 2 years of normal development by showing the percentage change between age 4 and age 6. Two years of development showed a large improvement in the overall reaction time (a minus sign means the older children are faster) and in conflict reaction time and error rates. The trained group showed the same direction of improvement in reaction time and conflict scores when compared with the normal development of the control group, but the percentage of change was much smaller.

We also used an IQ measure to test for the possibility that the training might extend to measures remote from the trained activity (Table 5.1). We used the Kaufman Brief Intelligence Test (Kaufman & Kaufman, 1990), a child IQ test that includes separate subscales for vocabulary (VOC) and for analogical reasoning from visual information in matrix tasks (MATs). Before training, the experimental and control groups were closely matched in overall IQ, vocabulary, and the visual matrix scale. We found that the training produced increases in overall IQ and in the visual matrix scale (MAT). Again, the changes in IQ resulting from training were in the same direction but smaller than those found for 2 years of normal development. As expected, the temperament scores did not show a change with training in either group.

Electroencephalogram Data

During the day before and after training, we ran children in the ANT and monitored the EEG from 128 scalp electrodes. Previous results with adults (Rueda, Posner, Rothbart, & Davis-Stober, 2004; van Veen & Carter, 2002) showed that during conflict tasks the anterior cingulate gave rise to an electrical signal (N2), which could be recorded from the scalp. Incongruent trials in adults gave rise to a larger N2 than did congruent trials (see arrow for adults in Figure 5.6). No similar N2 effect was found in either the control children in pre- or posttest or the experimental children before training (see Figure 5.6). After training, however, the trained children showed an N2 effect strikingly similar to that found in adults. These results suggest that training might change the underlying network involved in self-regulation to make it more adult-like in response to the conflict-related task. We found that the 4-year-olds showed most of their improvement from training in far anterior electrodes that are related to the emotional part of the anterior cingulate, whereas the 6-year-olds showed training effects that appeared to come from the more dorsal part of the anterior cingulate involved in regulation of cognition (Rueda et al., 2005).

We genotyped the 6-year-olds run in the training study. Because the sample was very small, we found that only the DAT1 of the four-dopamine genes related to executive attention in adults had sufficient data for a test between two alleles of the genes. To carry out this test, we combined children in the experimental and control groups and then examined their performance on the two occasions on which they took the ANT. We found that one of the alleles proved to be related to significantly poorer performance on the conflict network than did the other. In addition, this allele also was related to lower levels of effortful control as reported by parents in their temperament questionnaire and to poorer regulation of conflict as measured by the EEG. These encouraging results indicate that different genes might show important differences in self-regulation in childhood. If so, it might be possible to choose children more in need of attention training to study in detail the relation of genotype to training effects.

We found that the training exercises were appropriate for preschool children, who enjoyed them and could carry them out. The training study also indicated that children will show a generalized improvement in executive attention following training. We also found a significant difference in IQ, particularly in the matrix measure, which is similar to the adult Ravens'

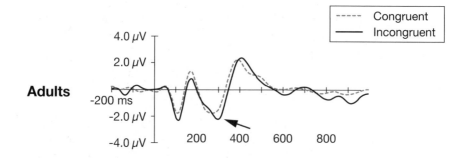

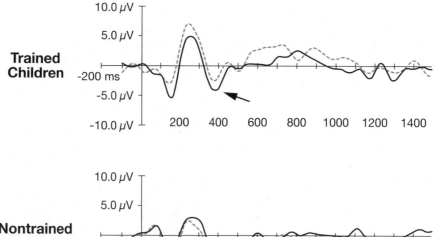

Figure 5.6. Scalp electrical activity in trained and nontrained children with and without attention training compared with adults. Note that after training, the scalp electrical activity in the trained children resembles that of adults but not that of nontrained children. The arrows indicate the N2, which has been shown to be related to conflict and to have a generator in the anterior cingulate. From "Training, Maturation, and Genetic Influences on the Development of Executive Attention," by M. R. Rueda, M. K. Rothbart, B. D. McCandliss, L. Saccamanno, and M. I. Posner, 2005, *Proceedings of the National Academy of Sciences of the USA, 102,* p. 14935. Copyright 2005 by National Academy of Sciences, USA. Reprinted with permission.

Matrices test. In light of the small sample sizes and short period of training, this finding was remarkable. A similar result was obtained in training the working memory of older children with ADHD (Klingberg, Forssberg, & Westerberg, 2002). This study found changes in brain areas related to working memory (Olesen, Westerberg, & Klingberg, 2004). Our study and the study of Klingberg et al. (2002) both showed that the training improved a general intelligence measure that was far removed from the specific training. Replication is needed with larger numbers of normal children and children with attentional deficits and with training for a longer period to determine whether the changes observed are genuine, whether they will be maintained over time, and whether they produce important changes in brain networks.

Evidence is accumulating that even adults can be trained in some aspects of attention by use of certain forms of fast paced video games (Green & Bavelier, 2003). It appears that this training may primarily involve the orienting network in situations where there are many distracting stimuli. Whether such training also changes the executive network could be an important focus of future research.

Currently, it is unknown whether there might be special sensitive periods for training related to the time of intense development of the network or whether attention is equally open to training at any age. However, even if training could occur at any time, it may still be of great practical importance to improve attention prior to or at the same time as entry into schooling. This could be true because of the importance of success in early schooling and the consequences of being unprepared for the critical areas such as literacy and numeracy to which the child is introduced in elementary school.

Attention Training in Schools

Even if computer-based remediation methods prove to be a successful way to train attention in early childhood, they are unlikely to be the only or even the best way. Children need to gain experience in social settings, and social settings can also be used to help in the training of executive attention. Some schools, particularly in central Europe, have adopted methods of preschool education designed to reduce the socioeconomic and genetic variation found in young children's attentional skills, to pass on to primary schools more homogeneous groups of children who can be taught together. The methods they have used to achieve this goal involve training of component skills such as attention, listening, and memory skills (Mills & Mills, 2000).

For the youngest age groups, several simple but effective attention-developing devices were used and observed by Mills and Mills (2000) in Hungarian kindergartens. The most common were eye-contact exercises (e.g., children sit in a circle around the teacher and each child needs to catch the teacher's eye before being allowed to leave the group). In a related exercise, teachers used various stop–go games in which children pursuing different activities must listen for a specific signal to stop, such as a drumbeat or even a specific number or rhythm of beats.

For older children, Mills and Mills (2000) observed much more sophisticated listening and auditory memory games. These exercises were used across the curriculum, although they were featured particularly in music sessions. Perhaps the most common was discriminating among and matching the sounds of musical instruments. For example, six instruments are displayed and played in turn; a child is blindfolded while one instrument is picked up, played, and then returned to its original place; and the child is then asked to identify that instrument.

As their attention and listening skills develop, children were introduced to games and activities intended to improve auditory memory. Such games build attention and listening skills and make increasing demands on children as they grow older. For instance, in a typical game observed in Hungary (Mills & Mills, 2000), a bean bag was passed around a group of 5-year-olds; when the teacher signaled stop, the child with the bag gave a number between 0 and 5; the bag then continued to circle the group until the teacher again signaled stop and a second child gave a number; the bag circled again, and when it stopped a third time, the child holding it was asked to add the two numbers.

The Hungarian Ministry of Education's kindergarten handbook (see Mills & Mills, 2000) puts particular stress on the value of music lessons in developing memory, saying that children ages 3 to 4 should be taught to recite six short nursery rhymes. At 4 to 5, they should be taught to sing, with help from the teacher, 3 to 4 songs. By 5 to 6, they should be taught to sing 10 songs on their own. Indeed, the arts appear to be a good way to enlist the interest of children and thus the high level of attention needed to train the network.

The Montessori tradition also stresses the training of children's concentration through the use of interesting materials (Lillard, 2005). Montessori and others noted that as the children's concentration changed, their behavior became normalized, and they showed greater calmness, joy, affection, and respect for others (Montessori, 1917/1965).

We believe that the studies described in this chapter and in chapter 4 (this volume) support the development of exercises for preschool children that would train them to have greater self-control of their behavior. Such exercises would be appropriate to prepare the way for learning specific subjects during the early school years. Even if psychological science has shown that most learning is domain specific, the unique nature of attention as a critical aspect in all domains of explicit learning supports its use as a preparation for schooling. We believe a strong national priority should be given to adopting the best and most appropriate methods to assist all children in the important goal of self-regulation. Some further suggestions along these lines are included in chapter 10 (this volume).

SUMMARY

This chapter has examined the role of genes and experience in shaping the neural networks underlying the brain's attention system. Specific genes related to individual differences in orienting and executive attention have been studied. These genes are likely to be important in the stages of development of these networks (discussed in chap. 4, this volume).

Despite the importance of genes in the development of the network, it is also clear that specific experiences can modify the efficiency of network performance. Training can improve executive attention following brain injury and training has also been shown to improve performance and underlying neural networks in children. Training exercises adapted from work with monkeys have given some evidence of the ability to modify performance and improve networks underlying executive attention and self-regulation. These results argue for a role of attention training in preschools. Chapters 7 through 9 further examine the role of attention in the development of specific school subjects.

6

TEMPERAMENT AND LEARNING

From the earliest days of life, children differ from one another in their levels of activity, distress proneness, orienting, and positive emotion. Individual differences in children's temperament have been intensively studied over the past 3 decades and have important implications for children's learning. We define *temperament* as constitutionally based individual differences in reactivity and self-regulation in the domains of emotion, activity, and attention (Rothbart & Bates, 2006; Rothbart & Derryberry, 1981). Temperament is biologically based and influenced over time by genes, environment, and experience. *Temperamental reactivity* refers to the time of onset, intensity, and duration of emotional, motor, and orienting reactions in response to external and internal stimuli. *Reactivity* describes broad behavioral dimensions, such as positive or negative emotionality, or more specific physiological reactions, such as heart rate reactivity. Temperament also includes individual differences in self-regulation (as discussed in chap. 4, this volume), which modulates reactivity.

The networks that underlie temperament systems are ones we all share; only the strength of a given temperamental disposition differs from one person to another. As researchers have over the past 3 decades attempted to identify the basic dimensions of temperament, they have often found differences in the primary emotions, including fear, anger–frustration, sadness, and positive affect. These emotions are also a part of motivations directed toward, away from, or against environmental stimuli and other people. Temperamental individual differences are also found in attention, including more reactive orienting, and in effortful control, including more voluntary focusing and shifting of attention.

Brain systems underlying the emotions and attention have been studied with imaging techniques, and the way in which attention and emotion influence each other has also been observed (see, e.g., Figure 4.2; Rothbart & Sheese, in press). In this chapter, we consider some of the basic emotions and attention systems underlying temperament, their contributions to the classroom, and their relations to children's motivation to learn and solve problems. First, we discuss temperament systems and their likely underlying brain mechanisms, and then we discuss temperament in connection with learning and education.

THE DEVELOPMENT OF TEMPERAMENT

A number of theorists originally believed that temperament is fixed early in development and changes little over time (e.g., Buss & Plomin, 1975), but we have since learned that temperament changes with development (Rothbart, 1989b; Rothbart & Bates, 2006). Children's tendencies to react with fear, frustration, and positive affect, and their orienting response to events in the environment, can be observed early in life, but as discussed in chapter 4 (this volume), self-regulatory executive attention develops relatively late and continues to develop during the early school years. Because the executive attention involved in the effortful control of behavior and the regulation of emotions is highly variable, some school-age children will be lacking in controls of emotion and action that other children can demonstrate with ease.

Until recently, almost all of the major theories of temperament have emphasized temperament's more reactive aspects, including positive and negative affect, sensitivity to reward and punishment, and arousal to stimulation. Individuals were seen to be at the mercy of their dispositions to approach or avoid an event or object, in accordance with cues signaling reward or punishment. More extraverted individuals were seen as sensitive to reward, showing tendencies to rapid approach of novel or potentially rewarding stimuli; more fearful or introverted individuals, sensitive to punishment, were seen to show inhibition or withdrawal from excitement (Gray, 1982). Recently identified systems of effortful control, however, allow the person to approach in the face of immediate cues for punishment, and to avoid in the face of immediate cues for reward. In addition, the programming of effortful control is critical to the internalization of socialization.

As early as infancy, there is evidence for broad dimensions of surgency–extraversion, negative affectivity, and orienting–regulation (Rothbart & Bates, 2006). Broad and narrow dimensions of the Children's Behavior Questionnaire for children 3 to 7 years of age (Ahadi, Rothbart, & Ye, 1993; Rothbart, Ahadi, Hershey, & Fisher, 2001) have also been identified. The first broad dimension is *surgency–extraversion*, composed of scales of Positive Anticipation, High Intensity Pleasure (Sensation Seeking), Impulsivity, Activity Level, and a negative loading from Shyness. A second broad dimension is called *negative affectivity*, with scales of Discomfort, Fear, Anger–Frustration, and Sadness, and negatively related Soothability–Falling Reactivity. The third dimension, *effortful control*, has scales of Inhibitory Control, Attentional Focusing, Low-Intensity Pleasure, and Perceptual Sensitivity.

The temperamental variable related to the development of executive attention is effortful control. Effortful control represents the ability to inhibit a dominant response to perform a subdominant response and to plan and to detect errors. Effortful control is important for linking the influence of temperament on behavior to the underlying attentional network involved.

Emotional Aspects of Temperament and Neural Processing

Emotions are broadly integrative systems that order feeling, thought, and action (LeDoux, 1989). Whereas object recognition systems and spatial processing systems of the brain address the questions "What is it?" and "Where is it?", neural emotion processing networks give answers to the questions "Is it good for me?" and "Is it bad for me?", in turn influencing the organism's behavioral answers to "What shall I do about it?" or simply "What shall I do?" These networks have been evolutionarily conserved to allow the organism to deal with environmental and internally generated threat, opportunity, and social affiliation.

In the neural processing of emotion, thalamic connections route information about the object qualities of a stimulus through sensory pathways, while simultaneously routing information for an emotional (evaluative) analysis to the limbic system and amygdala, where memories of the affective meaning of the stimulus further influence emotion processing (LeDoux, 1989). Later stages of object processing can update the emotional analysis based on further sensory information, but in the meantime, back projections from the amygdala influence the subsequent sensory processing of the stimulus. If one is afraid, for example, sensitivity to threat and escape routes will be heightened. Output of the amygdala to organized autonomic reactions via the hypothalamus and to motor activation via the corpus striatum underlies the motivational aspect of the emotions, supporting needed action.

In this brain-based view, the processing of emotions is a variety of information processing. Attentional neural networks can then act on emotional information similarly to how they act on other data processing systems, such as those involved in object recognition, language, and motor control, each of which in turn has its own underlying neural networks (Crottaz-Herbette & Mennon, 2006; Posner & Petersen, 1990). Neuroimaging studies demonstrate connections between emotional processing networks and the executive attention system, including the anterior cingulate, allowing attention to influence the selection of emotional information for conscious processing. One consequence of these connections is that people may or may not be aware of their emotional evaluations (Bush, Luu, & Posner, 2000; Posner & Rothbart, 1991). However, the attentional controls on emotion may be somewhat limited and difficult to establish. Panksepp (1998) laid out anatomical reasons why the regulation of emotion may pose a difficult problem for the child:

> One can ask whether the downward cognitive controls or the upward emotional controls are stronger. If one looks at the question anatomically and neurochemically the evidence seems overwhelming. The upward controls are more abundant and electrophysiologically more insistent: hence one might expect they would prevail if push came to shove. Of course, with the increasing influence of cortical functions as humans develop, along with the pressures for social conformity, the influences of the cognitive forces increase steadily during maturation. We can eventually experience emotions without sharing them with others. We can easily put on false faces, which can make the facial analysis of emotions in real-life situations a remarkably troublesome business. (p. 319)

Attentional systems can influence the conscious aspects of emotional control (see chaps. 3 and 4, this volume; Derryberry & Reed, 1994a, 1996; Gray, 1982; Lane et al., 1998; Rothbart & Sheese, in press). An important aspect of the child's adaptation to the school setting, for example, involves the appropriateness of the child's social interaction with the teacher and classmates, and the others' acceptance of the child (Parker & Asher, 1987). Information about the emotional state of others is an important contributor to appropriate social action, and any failure of access to this information can be a critical element in the development of disordered functioning (R. J. R. Blair, Jones, Clark, & Smith, 1997). When the child's attention is focused on stimuli that threaten the self, access to information about others may become less available, and later in this chapter we discuss some of the ways in which schooling can threaten a child's self-worth.

Neural Models for Temperament

We now briefly consider neural models developed to describe neurophysiological substrates for temperament, beginning with approach–positive affect and fear–inhibition.

Dopamine, Positive Affect, and Approach

Panksepp (1982, 1986, 1998) has reviewed the literature on dopamine (DA) effects, concluding that "the general function of DA activity in appetitive behavior is to promote the expression of motivational excitement and anticipatory eagerness—the heightened energization of animals searching for and expecting rewards" (Panksepp, 1998, p. 91). Cloninger (1986) specified a novelty-seeking dimension related to DA functioning, as did Zuckerman (1984) in his dimension of sensation seeking (see review by Rothbart, 1989a).

Approach behavior is controlled by basolateral amygdala projections to nucleus accumbens and the pedunculopontine nucleus, two of the primary centers controlling locomotion. Approach is also facilitated by midbrain dopamine systems projecting from the substantia nigra and the ventral tegmental area.

In functional magnetic resonance imaging research, Canli et al. (2001) found that the brain's activation to positive and negative pictures varied, depending on the subject's temperament. Persons higher in extraversion showed greater brain response to positive than to negative stimuli in widespread frontal, temporal, and limbic activation of both hemispheres. Subjects higher in neuroticism (negative affect) reacted more to negative than to positive stimuli, and showed more circumscribed activation (frontotemporal on the left side) and deactivation in a right frontal area. This research also demonstrated a positive emotional bias for extraverts and a negative bias for those high in neuroticism.

A quite different set of brain areas has proved to be active in studies of persistence, a dimension of personality related to effortful control in temperament (Gusnard et al., 2003). The effects of persistence acted strongly on midline and lateral prefrontal areas rather than those areas found to be related to positive and negative affect, which suggests a regulatory role for persistence. An increasingly popular view (Posner & Rothbart, 2000; Rothbart & Rueda, 2005) is that effortful control (persistence) is represented in midline frontal areas and regulates brain areas such as the amygdala that are more clearly related to reactive negative affect.

Fear and Behavioral Inhibition

The amygdala has been identified as a critical structure in the processing of emotional information (LeDoux, 1987, 1989), and there is evidence that emotional networks involving the amygdala respond more strongly to novel than to familiar stimuli (Nishijo, Ono, & Nishino, 1988). The amygdala's lateral nucleus receives conditioned fear signals and projects to the central nucleus. In turn, the central nucleus projects to brain-stem areas where components of fearful activity, including facial and vocal expression, heart rate changes, behavioral inhibition, and startle potentiation, are regulated.

Amygdala lesions in rodents disrupt autonomic and cortisol reactions and activate behavioral freezing and fear vocalizations, and similar findings have been reported in primates (Lawrence & Calder, 2004). In humans, functional neuroimaging studies by Calder, Lawrence, and Young (2001) and others support involvement of the amygdala in both acquiring and expressing fear, although not in the voluntary production of facial expressions of fear (Anderson & Phelps, 2001). The amygdala also is involved in the recognition of fear in the human face (Calder et al., 2001), and there is evidence in humans that amygdala damage is related to reduced fear experience (Adolphs et al., 1999; Sprengelmeyer et al., 1999).

Projections from the amygdala implement autonomic and behavioral components of fear, including startle, motor inhibition, facial expression, and cardiovascular and respiratory changes supporting defensive actions (Davis, Hitchcock, & Rosen, 1987). Individual variability in the structure and functioning of any of these subsystems may be related to variations in behavioral expressions of fear, and we would expect multiple components of other affective motivational systems such as approach–positive affect and anger–irritability to be found as well.

The amygdala also appears to affect information processing within the cortex. For example, the basolateral nucleus of the amygdala projects to frontal and cingulate regions involved in the executive attention system (Posner & Petersen, 1990), as well as to ventral occipital and temporal pathways involved in processing object information. These connections are consistent with findings that anxious individuals show enhanced attention to threatening sources of information (e.g., Derryberry & Reed, 1994a).

Frustration and Aggressive Behavior

In Gray's (1991) model, the fight-or-flight system is constituted by circuits connecting the amygdala, ventromedial nucleus of the hypothalamus, central gray region of the midbrain, and somatic and motor effector nuclei of the lower brain stem. These circuits process information involving unconditioned punishment and nonreward. When painful or frustrating input is detected, brain-stem effectors produce aggressive or defensive behavior. Individual differences in reactivity of this system are also thought to underlie aggressive aspects of Eysenck's general psychoticism dimension, and Panksepp (1982) described similar neural circuitry in a rage system (see review by Rothbart, Derryberry, & Posner, 1994).

More recently, important distinctions among varieties of aggression and anger and their underlying neural networks have been made. On the one hand, aggression as a self-defense reaction seems to be based on the functioning of the same amygdala circuits involved in the production of fear (Blanchard & Takahashi, 1988). Aggression linked to protection of resources, competition, and offensive aggression, on the other hand, involves a different system based on DA (Lawrence & Calder, 2004). The DA system has been linked to both the production of offensive aggression (Smeets & González, 2000) and the recognition of anger in the human face (Lawrence, Calder, McGowan, & Grasby, 2002). In the Lawrence et al. (2002) study, DA blockade impaired the recognition of anger while sparing recognition of other emotions and of facial identity.

Negative Emotionality

The need for identification of neural systems related to negative emotionality is also evident in recent psychological models (Rothbart & Derryberry, 2002). Factor analyses of infant temperament questionnaires have reliably yielded two distress factors: one involving distress to novelty, and the other, irritability, including distress to limitations or frustration (Rothbart & Mauro, 1990). In the recent revision of the Infant Behavior Questionnaire, a higher order negative emotionality factor that includes fear and frustration is also found (Gartstein & Rothbart, 2003). Distress to novelty is linked to an extended latency to approach new objects (Rothbart, 1988), and a combination of behavioral inhibition (Kagan, 1994) and distress proneness to novelty is similar to the introverted pole of a broader extraversion–introversion dimension. Negative emotionality is a general dimension that subsumes emotions such as fear, anticipatory anxiety, sadness, frustration–anger, guilt, and discomfort.

As previously noted, separable neural systems have been found to be related to fear and frustration. There are nevertheless several possibilities for identifying higher order negative emotional reactions. One is the link between systems supporting fear and defensive aggression (Blanchard & Takahashi, 1988). Defensive aggression in animal models seems to be based on the same amygdalar circuits as fear, and in humans, anger in response to threat to self structures may also be linked to fear.

Negative affect systems are also regulated by more general neurochemical systems including dopaminergic and serotonergic projections arising from the midbrain, and by circulating gonadal and corticosteroid hormones (Rothbart, Derryberry, & Posner, 1994; Zuckerman, 1995). Neurochemical influences may thus provide coherence of emotional states within the organism and support more general factors of temperament such as negative emotionality. For example, serotonergic projections from the midbrain raphe nuclei appear to moderate limbic circuits related to both anxiety and aggression (Spoont, 1992). Low serotonergic activity may thus increase an individual's vulnerability to both fear and frustration, contributing to a general factor of negative affectivity, including depression. Gonadal hormones are related to both positive affect and aggressiveness (Zuckerman, 1991) and may influence individual differences in positive and angry states. Neural structures can thus support variability at broad as well as specific levels. In any case, more research in the area is needed.

Affiliativeness

In considering neural bases for affiliativeness, humans share with other animals, including mammals, birds, and fish, systems of affiliation that support pair bonds and the care of the young (Insel, 2003). Panksepp (1986) indicated that affiliative and prosocial behaviors may depend in part on opiate projections from higher limbic regions (e.g., amygdala, cingulate cortex) to the ventromedial hypothalamus, with brain opiates promoting social comfort and bonding, and opiate withdrawal promoting irritability and aggressiveness. Because ventromedial hypothalamic lesions dramatically increase aggression, Panksepp (1986) also suggested that this brain region normally inhibits aggressive behaviors controlled by the midbrain's central gray area. Hypothalamic projections can also allow for friendly, trusting, and helpful behaviors between members of a species by suppressing aggressive tendencies. Mechanisms underlying prosocial and aggressive behaviors would in this way be reciprocally related, in keeping with the bipolar agreeableness–hostility dimension found in five-factor models of personality. Panksepp (1993) has also reviewed research suggesting links between social bonding and the hypothalamic neuropeptide oxytocin, involved in maternal behavior, feelings of social acceptance and social bonding, and reduction of separation distress. Oxytocin is also released by both females and males during sexual activity.

Regulatory Functions of Attention

Chapters 3 and 4 (this volume) have reviewed evidence for attentional networks common among people and discussed how the efficiency of these networks varies among individuals. The anterior cingulate gyrus, one of the main nodes of the executive attention network, has been linked to a variety of specific functions in attention. In emotion studies, the cingulate is often seen as part of a network involving orbital frontal and limbic (amygdala) structures. The frontal areas seem to have an ability to interact with the limbic system (R. J. Davidson, Putnam, & Larson, 2000) that fits well with the idea of its subserving self-regulation.

As discussed in chapter 4 (this volume), the neural networks related to effortful control show important development between 2 and 7 years, but effortful control continues to develop during childhood and into adolescence, allowing more sophisticated forms of self-regulation based on verbal information, representations of the self, and projections concerning the future. We now discuss some of the links between reactive emotions, self-regulatory attention, and children's learning.

In developmental studies, an early appearing inhibitory influence on temperamental approach is behavioral inhibition or fear. Fearful inhibition is well developed by the end of the 1st year of life, and if a disposition to fear is strong, both positive and negative expressiveness and approach–avoidance may be moderated under novel or challenging situations. Children who were high in fearfulness during the 1st year as measured in the laboratory tended to be low in parent-reported impulsivity, activity, and aggression at age 7 as well as more susceptible to guilt and shame, two powerful socializing emotions (Rothbart, Ahadi, & Hershey, 1994; Rothbart, Derryberry, & Hershey, 2000).

These relationships suggest that fear plays an important role in moral development, and this hypothesis is supported in the work of Kochanska on the early development of conscience (Kochanska, 1991, 1995). Kochanska found that temperamental fearfulness is a source of early internalization of rules of conduct. More fearful children showed more internalized conscience, although this effect was chiefly present during the younger ages of toddlerhood and the preschool period. As children grew older, by 4 to 5 years, this direct link was gradually replaced by a more complex interaction with maternal socialization. Fearful children whose mothers used gentle discipline, likely capitalizing on the child's temperamental tendency to experience anxious states, developed highly internalized consciences. These findings suggest that there are developmental pathways that change with age through which temperament and socialization influence the development of high-level social–cognitive processes.

Fear takes on an important inhibitory role in early development, constraining approach and aggression, acting as a protective factor for the development of externalizing disorders, and contributing to the development of conscience (see review by Rothbart & Bates, 2006). In addition to Kochanska's (1991, 1995) findings, children with symptoms of both attention-deficit/hyperactivity disorder and anxiety show reduced impulsivity in comparison with children with attention-deficit/hyperactivity disorder alone (Pliszka, 1989), and aggressiveness decreases between kindergarten and first grade in children who show tendencies to fear (Bates, Pettit, & Dodge, 1995).

These findings may seem surprising, given that fear is frequently seen as a maladaptive emotion, at least in North American culture. From an evolutionary point of view, however, fearful inhibition protects the individual from potentially harmful objects or situations. It can also support children's following of the rules in educational settings. Nevertheless, the fearful form of inhibitory control remains a reactive process elicited by situational or internal cues. In the course of development, this system can lead to rigid and overcontrolled behavior that limits the child's positive experiences with the world (Block & Block, 1980; Kremen & Block, 1998).

Temperament fortunately also involves effortful control, supported by the development of executive attention as described in chapter 4 (this volume), which provides greater efficiency and flexibility than that afforded by fear. Both fearful behavioral inhibition and effortful control inhibit approach behavior. At the same time, a greater disposition to approach is likely to require greater inhibitory mechanisms for control (Rothbart & Derryberry, 2002).

Reward and Punishment

We have touched on possible neural substrates for approach–positive affect systems related to reward seeking and for fear, linked to the inhibition of behavior that might lead to punishment (*harm avoidance*). An important aspect of these constructs suggests that some children will be more activated by reward, and some children will find stopping an activity easier when there is a high likelihood of punishment (Rothbart, Ahadi, & Hershey, 1994). When a situation involves both potential rewards and punishments, such as interactions with a stranger, the balance between approach and fear tendencies on the basis of temperament and previous experience will be critical to behavioral outcomes.

This model of individual differences in susceptibility to reward and punishment has direct applications to child socialization and education. If we consider a toddler performing an enjoyable act, such as shredding the pages of a book, the child's activities will be influenced by the approach or extraversion system. If the parent now gives a sharp, punishing command for the child to stop, will the child's activity be inhibited? Patterson (1980) found that parents of nonproblem children were effective in stopping their children's aversive behavior on three out of four occasions when they punished. When parents of problem children used punishment, however, children were likely to actually continue the punished behavior (Patterson, 1980; J. A. Snyder, 1977). Although parenting skills are also involved, children's temperament is likely to make a basic contribution to effects of punishment and reward.

APPROACH, INHIBITION, AND MASTERY MOTIVATION

In Piaget's (1936/1952) view, the infant's understanding of early concepts of the object, of causality, and indeed all of his or her sensorimotor gence, is rooted in exploratory and playful interactions with the environment. Related work by Hunt (1961) described intrinsic motivation and its contributions to the development of intelligence. Though these authors stressed the cognitive aspects of exploratory play, important roles are also played by emotion and attention in generating, sustaining, and terminating exploration. Observations of infants and young children exploring objects reveal a broad array of emotions, including pleasure, fear, boredom, frustration, and even anger. The study of mastery motivation in child development has therefore attempted to explore emotional contributions to interactions with objects and attentional interactions.

Morgan, Harmon, and Maslin-Cole (1990) defined *mastery motivation* as a "psychological force that stimulates an individual to attempt independently, in a focused and persistent manner, to solve a problem or master a skill or task that is moderately challenging to him or her" (p. 319). A common measure of mastery motivation is the child's persistence at challenging tasks, such as examining and manipulating interesting objects, working on puzzles, and appropriately using cause-and-effect materials. Challenging toys or situations are presented to infants and young children, and the persistence of their action toward making the objects "work" is taken as a sign of motivated action.

Shiner (1998) defined *mastery motivation* as a disposition to curiosity and interest, taking pleasure in mastering problems set by their environments and preferring more challenging tasks to easy ones. Shiner noted that mastery motivation may be seen as a motivational aspect of Tellegen's (1985) positive emotionality system,

> tapping a person's tendency to approach situations and tasks with enthusiasm and zest. From this perspective, achievement is distinguished from behavioral control and discipline (Watson & Clark, 1992). . . . Persistence and mastery motivation may represent two distinctive but related personality dimensions, with persistence primarily tapping behavioral control and mastery motivation primarily tapping positive emotionality. (Shiner, 1998, p. 324)

Shiner identified both surgency–extraversion and effortful control as aspects of temperament related to achievement. However, we have found that surgency–extraversion also contributes to sustained attention. Indeed, before the development of effortful control in the preschool period, surgency–extraversion may be the chief contributor to interest sustained involvement. These findings have clear application to schooling. To the degree that positive involvement with tasks can be fostered as opposed to fear or coercion, genuine interest may help to support children's learning.

Positive Affect and Sustained Engagement

The power of interest or positive emotion in influencing competence and achievement is suggested by a meta-analysis of the studies involving children in Grades 5 through 12 (Schiefele, Krapp, & Winteler, 1992). In a review of 121 studies conducted in 18 different countries, Schiefele et al. (1992) found that interest accounted for 10% of the variability in children's achievement. In our research with college students, we have also found that self-reported surgency–extraversion is positively related to the personality dimension of openness to experience, which in turn is an indicator of interest in a broad array of topics (Evans & Rothbart, 2004).

Positive affect is related to sustained engagement. Spangler (1989) related observations of 24-month-old toddlers' play to their mental and emotional dispositions. When children showed expressions of positive emotion, either when alone or with their mother, they remained engaged in an activity for longer periods. In our laboratory, Chu (as cited in Rothbart & Hwang, 2005) and later Hwang (1999) found that 13-month-olds who smiled more in the laboratory also sustained interest in a toy for a longer period; Chu found that infants who showed more distress maintained interest in a toy for a shorter period. We gauged interest through the amount of time the child remained engaged with a small toy before pushing or throwing it away twice in a row. Hwang (1999) found that smiling was related to the duration of time spent manipulating the toy while looking at it but not to length of gaze toward the toy without manipulation.

Is positive emotion related to mastery motivation in adults? Erez and Isen (2002) induced positive and neutral moods in subjects. Subjects in the positive mood condition performed better, showed more persistence, and reported higher levels of motivation. In a second study, subjects in the positive affect condition were more likely to have high levels of expectancy of success and higher evaluations of reward. Erez and Isen concluded that positive affect enhances expectations about goals and the feeling that one can reach them. Surgent–extraverted individuals, who are more prone to experience positive moods (Tellegen, 1985), may then be more likely to experience enhanced evaluations, and in general, positive mood can be used to facilitate performance.

Developmental Changes in Mastery Motivation

Intrinsic pleasure is seen in the performance of young children, even in challenging tasks. With age, however, children move from taking direct pleasure in mastering tasks to being concerned about how their efforts will turn out and whether others will approve of their performance (Harter,

1981). Affect is still critically important to mastery motivation, but it is now at least partially mediated by children's views of how others view their performance (Harter, 1981).

The relation between extraversion and performance appears to change with development. Shiner (2000) studied a sample of third- through sixth-grade children (8 to 12 years old) who were later seen at 15 to 19 years and 17 to 23 years. Parent-reported extraversion predicted social competence both concurrently in the younger children and late in adolescence. Academic achievement was predicted positively from children's extraversion in childhood, but the correlation did not hold up when IQ was controlled for. High school and college academic achievement, however, were negatively related to earlier extraversion. Shiner suggested that extraverted individuals may have more impulses that require restraint during later schooling. Her results suggest developmental changes in the link between surgency–extraversion and school competence as well as the importance of IQ as a mediator.

Fear and Mastery Motivation

The fear system is related to avoidance or inhibition of action in settings that are novel, threaten punishment, or are evolutionarily prepared, as with fear of snakes or the dark (Gray, 1971). Because individual differences in temperament include fear or behavioral inhibition as well as approach or incentive motivation, they are likely to influence the development of effectance and mastery motivation. Models such as Susan Harter's (1978) stress the influence of reward and punishment in accounting for approach, whereas dispositions to approach (surgency–extraversion) and avoidance (fear) can also be related to individual differences in temperament.

When temperamental high approach is linked with low fear, approach may not be inhibited under circumstances that might lead to punishment. Children with strong approach tendencies who are also fearful, however, can inhibit approach tendencies when they might lead to negative outcomes. Dispositions to positive affect–approach and fear tend to be independent unless they are measured in the same setting. Children can be thus both approaching under safe conditions and relatively inhibited under threat. Because fear or anxiety is linked to enhanced attention to threats (Derryberry & Reed, 1994a, 1996; Vasey, Daleiden, Williams, & Brown, 1995), fear may enhance sensitivity to possible negative events and allow the child to avoid problems. However, extreme fear may lead to problems with rigid overcontrol of behavior, as reflected in the Blocks's description of overcontrolled patterns that can limit positive experiences (Block & Block, 1980; Kremen & Block, 1998).

Fear and Competence

Blair (2003) developed a parent-report version of the Behavioral Activation System measure (related to surgency–extraversion) and the Behavioral Inhibition System (related to fear) measure to assess the temperament of 4-year-olds in Head Start programs. He found that fear-related scores were positively related to teacher reports of social competence in the children; both fear- and activation-related scores were also related to lower persistence. In this instance, the fear-related measure was related to both a competence variable and lower persistence.

In their research on temperament and personality, Victor, Rothbart, and Baker (2005) have linked mother-reported achievement of children at ages 2 to 12 to aspects of temperament. Children who were more fearful, angry, and sad were described as showing less achievement, and children who were more sociable and positive showed more. More highly achieving children were also described as more active and assertive, higher in perceptual sensitivity and openness, and higher in effortful control.

Elliot and Harackiewicz (1996) distinguished between an orientation toward attaining competence (approach) versus avoiding incompetence (avoidance) in adults. Subjects were asked to solve a puzzle, and instructions stressed the possibility of either success or failure. Those in the avoidance-of-failure condition performed less well and were less cognitively involved in the task. It was concluded that performance goals aimed at avoiding incompetence can undermine intrinsic motivation.

Frustration and Aggression

Depue and Iacono (1989) suggested that when there is blockage of a goal, irritable aggression is elicited, which can serve to remove the obstacle. Their view suggests links between approach and frustration–anger, and we have found that activity level and anger are consistently positively related in parent-reported temperament. Seven-year-old children who had been active in infancy were both more positive in affect and higher in anger–frustration (Rothbart et al., 2001). Together with our earlier reported finding relating 7-year surgency–extraversion to concurrent aggression (Rothbart, Ahadi, & Hershey, 1994), this finding suggests that strong approach tendencies may contribute to negative as well as positive emotionality (Derryberry & Reed, 1994b; Rothbart, Ahadi, & Hershey, 1994). Children who showed strong approach by quickly grasping novel objects at 6.5, 10, and 13.5 months showed high levels of positive anticipation and impulsivity and high anger–frustration and aggression at 7 years, which again suggests that strong approach tendencies contribute to later negative as well as positive emotionality.

Children who showed higher frustration at 6 and 10 months were higher in anger–frustration but not fear at age 7 (Rothbart et al., 2000). Greater infant frustration was also related to higher 7-year activity level, positive anticipation, impulsivity, aggression, and high-intensity pleasure. Whereas infant fear is thus related to relatively weak approach behavior in childhood, infant frustration is related to stronger approach and to later lack of emotional control. This finding is consistent with Panksepp's (1998) suggestion that unsuccessful reward-related activities may activate the anger–frustration functions of a rage system. Strong approach tendencies often result from positive expectations, and frustration results when those expectations are not met.

Children who showed rapid approach as infants also tended to be low in attentional control and inhibitory control at age 7. These findings suggest that strong approach tendencies may constrain the development of voluntary self-control. If approach tendencies are viewed as an "accelerator" toward action and inhibitory tendencies as the "brakes," stronger accelerative tendencies may weaken the braking influence of inhibitory control (Rothbart & Derryberry, 2002).

Another interpretation of this finding is that early self-regulation of motor behavior reflects a developing executive attention system. We are currently carrying out longitudinal research to investigate the early signs of developing executive attention and effortful control.

Affiliativeness and Agreeableness

Agreeableness, including, at the high end, the prosocial emotions and behaviors and affiliative tendencies, and at the low end, aggression and manipulativeness, has been increasingly studied in childhood (Graziano, 1994; Graziano & Eisenberg, 1997; Graziano & Tobin, 2002). Like other originally bipolar dimensions of temperament, prosocial and antagonistic dispositions have also been studied separately (Bohart & Stipek, 2001), and Graziano and Eisenberg (1997) suggested that the two dispositions may be separable, even though they are negatively related. Shiner and Caspi (2003), for example, pointed out that antisocial and prosocial behavior have different etiologies (Krueger, Hicks, & McGue, 2001). Any temperamental predisposition to prosocial behavior needs to be seen as an open system, interacting with social experience for its outcomes.

In research linking temperament to personality in early and middle childhood, two forms of surgency–extraversion have been identified; one involves prosocial behavior and the other, impulsivity, antisocial behavior and aggression (Victor, Rothbart, & Baker, 2005), again suggesting that socialization can steer approach tendencies toward pro- or antisocial behavior. The education setting is one in which prosocial behavior can be strengthened and supported for all children.

Effortful Control

We have discussed the way fear inhibits impulsivity and approach. A second inhibitory influence on impulsivity is the attentionally supported capacity to withhold prohibited responses, an aspect of effortful control. This function may be divided into monitoring for conflict and executing inhibitory control (Botvinick, Braver, Barch, Carter, & Cohen, 2001). Monitoring for conflict has been related to anterior cingulate function, whereas lateral prefrontal areas may be more related to executing the inhibitory operation. In our 7-year-old sample, inhibitory control was predicted by infants' longer latency to approach toys at 11 and 13 months, and by their lower activity level in the laboratory at 13 months (Rothbart et al., 2000). At 7 years, inhibitory control was positively related to attentional control and empathy and negatively related to aggression. Inhibitory control was also positively related to guilt or shame, but uncorrelated with fear.

Development of Effortful Control

As discussed in chapter 4 (this volume), the neural system related to effortful control shows rapid development between 2 and 4 years, and other research suggests some stability of executive attention during childhood. There is also some stability in effortful control after 2 years. Kochanska and her associates (Kochanska, Murray, & Harlan, 2000) developed a battery of laboratory-based effortful control tasks for children between 22 months and 5 years. Beginning after age 2, children's performance showed considerable consistency across tasks, indicating that the tasks were measuring a common underlying capacity. Children showed improvement in their performance on the battery, but were also remarkably stable in their individual performance over time, with correlations ranging from .44 for the youngest children (22 to 33 months) to .59 for 32 to 46 months, to .65 for 46 to 66 months (Kochanska et al., 2000).

Olson, Bates, Sandy, and Schilling (2002) found that parent–child interaction, child temperament, and child cognitive competence in toddlerhood all predicted variations in children's later self-regulatory capabilities. Olson et al. tested for individual differences in children's self-regulatory competence using laboratory tests and observations. The toddler temperament predictor of later low competence was a measure of the child's unoccupied "wandering" during a 2-hour home visit. The authors speculated that the children who walked about without apparent goals may be showing early difficulties with organization and deployment of attention, a construct underlying effortful control (Olson et al., 2002).

Additional evidence for stability in constructs similar to effortful control has been found in research by Mischel and his colleagues (Mischel, Shoda, & Peake, 1988; Shoda, Mischel, & Peake, 1990). Preschoolers were measured on their ability to wait for a delayed treat that was preferable to a readily accessible treat. Delay of gratification in seconds predicted later parent-reported attentiveness, concentration, competence, playfulness, and intelligence when the children were adolescents. Preschoolers better able to delay gratification were also seen as having better self-control and an increased ability to deal with stress, frustration, and temptation. Seconds of preschool delay predicted later academic competence in SAT scores, even when intelligence was controlled for. In follow-up studies, preschool delay behavior predicted goal-setting and self-regulatory abilities when the subjects reached their early 30s (Ayduk et al., 2000), suggesting remarkable continuity in self-regulatory tendencies age 4 and later.

Questionnaire studies of 6- to 7-year-olds have found an Effortful Control factor to be defined in terms of scales measuring attentional focusing, inhibitory control, low-intensity pleasure, and perceptual sensitivity (Rothbart et al., 2001). Effortful Control is negatively related to both Surgency and Negative Affectivity temperament factors. These negative relations are in keeping with the idea that attentional skill may help to regulate negative affect while also constraining impulsive approach tendencies. An interesting example involves the negative relation between effortful control and aggression. Aggression also relates positively to children's reactive surgency and negative affectivity (especially anger; Rothbart, Ahadi, & Hershey, 1994).

Effortful control may regulate aggression indirectly by controlling reactive tendencies underlying surgency and negative affectivity. For example, children high in effortful control may be able to direct attention away from the rewarding aspects of aggression, or shift attention away from the negative cues related to anger. Eisenberg and her colleagues found that 4- to 6-year-old boys with good attentional control tended to deal with anger by using nonhostile verbal methods rather than overt aggressive methods (Eisenberg, Fabes, Nyman, Bernzweig, & Pinulas, 1994).

It was also possible to examine the relationship of our laboratory measures of conflict resolution (see Figure 4.3) with a battery of tasks requiring young children to exercise inhibitory control over their behavior (Gerardi-Caulton, 2000). These measures included standard tasks involving delay of gratification, such as waiting to receive a reward. We found substantial correlations between these standard measures and our laboratory task. Even more impressive, elements of the laboratory task were significantly correlated with aspects of effortful control (positively) and negative affect (negatively) in the parent reports of the children's usual behavior. The cognitive measure of conflict resolution appears to have a substantial relation to the naturalistic aspects of the infants' self-control that parents can report.

Establishing Theories of Mind

Another study (Carlson & Moses, 2001) replicated these relationships between the spatial conflict task (see Figure 4.3), delay tasks, and parent reports of effortful control. They also found that control was related to the children's performance on theory-of-mind tasks. Considerable evidence suggests that children between the ages of 3 and 4 are developing the ability to understand the beliefs, intentions, and actions of others, that is, a theory of how the human mind works. In this study, children of 3 and 4 years of age were told a story involving two puppets who were enjoying playing ball together. One of the puppets then placed a ball inside one of two containers and left the room. After he left, the other puppet removed the ball from the first container and placed it in another container that appeared very different. When 3-year-old children are asked where the absent puppet will think the ball is, they often report that the absent puppet knows it is where the second puppet had placed it in his absence. That is taken as evidence that young children have little awareness of the actual beliefs of others. By 4 years old, many fewer children make this and similar errors.

The ability of children to recognize the fact that the absent puppet cannot know where the ball really is located was positively related to their effortful control capacities as measured by their performance on conflict trials of the spatial Stroop conflict task. We believe that both the spatial Stroop conflict and theory-of-mind tasks require control over a dominant response (i.e., to respond with where the ball really is) to be able to respond with a less dominant one (to recognize the deception). We know that when adults are given conflict tasks or are given stories similar to those used in the theory-of-mind tasks, there is strong activation in the frontal midline areas related to executive attention (Frith & Frith, 2001).

Learning Empathy, Morals, and Social Competence

Children high in effortful control also exhibit strong empathy with others. In a study of elderly hospital volunteers, Eisenberg and Okun (1996) found that attentional control was positively related to sympathy and per-spective taking, and negatively related to personal distress, whereas negative emotional intensity was positively related to both sympathy and personal distress. Effortful control may support empathy by allowing the individual to attend to the thoughts and feelings of another without becoming over-whelmed by their own distress. In a similar way, guilt or shame in 6- and 7-year-olds is positively related to effortful control and negative affectivity (Rothbart, Ahadi, & Hershey, 1994). Negative affect may contribute to guilt by providing the individual with strong internal cues of discomfort, thereby increasing the probability that the cause of these feelings will be attributed to an internal rather than an external cause (Dienstbier, 1984).

Effortful control may contribute further by allowing the flexibility needed to relate these negative feelings of responsibility to one's own specific actions and to negative consequences for another person (Derryberry & Reed, 1994b, 1996).

The work of Kochanska, Murray, Jacques, Koenig, and Vandegeest (1996) indicates that the development of conscience is related to temperamental individual differences in effortful control. The internalization of moral principles appears to be facilitated in fearful preschool-age children, especially when their mothers use gentle discipline (Kochanska, 1995), but, in addition, internalized control is facilitated in children high in effortful control (Kochanska et al., 1996). Two separable control systems, one reactive (fear) and one self-regulative (effortful control), thus appear to regulate the development of conscience. Whereas fear may provide reactive inhibition and negative affect for association with moral principles, effortful control provides the attentional flexibility needed to link negative affect, action outcomes, and moral principles.

These findings suggest the importance of temperament in general, and effortful control in particular, to the child's emotional, cognitive, and social development. Without underestimating environmental influences, the underlying temperament systems may serve a central role in the self-organization of personality. This role is particularly evident in the functions of attention, which select and coordinate the most important information, contribute to the storage of this information in memory, and provide an important regulatory function. In addition to influences of the immediate environment on children's behavior, children are also highly thoughtful and can use attention to replay their positive and negative experiences. Across development, one would expect these emotional and attentional processes to progressively stabilize certain forms of self- and other-related information and thus to shape the child's representation of the self and world instantiated in the brain and provide a means of further regulating their behavior (Derryberry & Reed, 1994b, 1996; Rothbart, Ahadi, & Hershey, 1994).

Effortful Control and Education

Because it goes beyond models that find human beings are moved chiefly by affect or arousal, effortful control allows people to resist the immediate influence of affect. Bramlett, Scott, and Rowell (2000) looked at relationships between temperament, social skills, academic competence, and reading and math achievement in first-grade children. The children's temperament, particularly their persistence, predicted academic competence, and teacher ratings of behavior were better predictors of classroom behavior and academic status than were parent ratings.

Internalization occurs through self-regulation that redirects or suppresses behavioral urges, and Ryan, Connell, and Grolnick (1992) developed a theory relating internalization of social norms to self-regulation. Internalization is important in school adjustment and societal achievement, because these areas involve situations that may not be intrinsically motivating. Teachers and parents play critical roles in the development of internalized self-regulation, through supporting autonomy, providing structure, and promoting positive involvement.

Eisenberg et al. (1996) examined kindergarten through third-grade children, measuring both negative emotionality and a composite measure of attentional or effortful regulation. Eisenberg et al. (1997) also examined socially competent (socially appropriate and prosocial) behaviors in the same sample. At all levels of emotional intensity, children high in effortful self-regulation exhibited higher levels of social competence than did children lower in effortful self-regulation. However, this relationship was strongest for children higher in general emotional intensity. In addition, attentional control was related to resiliency, and was particularly important for children prone to negative affect.

Although the effortful control system can support both the internalization of competence-related goals and their achievement, more research tracing the developmental balance between approach, fear, and effortful control as well as anger, sadness, and overstimulation will be helpful in coming to understand children's adaptation (Rothbart & Sheese, in press). This research will require the use of temperament measures. We also realize that some adaptations helpful to children in the short term may not be adaptive in later development. Longitudinal research will make essential contributions to knowledge in this area, and using temperament measures for assignment of subjects to control conditions will also be important additions to intervention studies.

TEMPERAMENT AND THE SCHOOL ENVIRONMENT

We now introduce and reprise some of the findings on temperament with special application to the school environment. Teachers in the United States have clear ideas about the qualities a model student possesses (Keogh, 1989), including temperament characteristics such as high attention span, approach, low activity, and low negative reactivity. These attributes as perceived by the teacher contribute more than does high IQ or lack of academic deficiencies in predicting teachers' beliefs about their students' potential (Keogh, 1982). Child temperament is also related to the behavior of teachers. In one study, Martin (1989) found that children who were distractible and low in attention (low in effortful control) received more criticism from their teachers. Pullis (1985) found that when teachers thought children were capable of but not practicing self-control, they were more likely to discipline the children with punitive and coercive techniques.

Motivation for School Subjects

How do temperament systems relate to children's motivation for school subjects? The intrinsic interest and positive approach to challenge we discussed earlier are important in the school setting, and intrinsic interest may later be supplemented or supplanted by extrinsic interest through social and material rewards. We noted in chapter 1 (this volume) B. F. Skinner's (1968) stress on the importance of reward in instrumental learning. Skinner argued on the basis of animal data that punishment was not effective, although researchers later noted that he based his conclusions on the effects of intense shocks on laboratory animals, which probably disturbed any learning that might take place. In fact, milder social punishments do inhibit children's behavior. In the school setting, grades and praise or criticism from the teacher can serve as either extrinsic rewards or punishments.

Although fear may inhibit children's response to novel tasks, fear is also helpful in the school in inhibiting overactivity or aggression, encouraging following the rules, and promoting early conscience (Rothbart & Bates, 2006). Negative affect is also linked to the ability to detect errors so as to be able to correct them (Luu, Collins, & Tucker, 2000). However, fear or anxiety may increase the likelihood of perceiving threat and create attentional biases that make disengagement from negative information difficult (Reed & Derryberry, 1995).

Ego Development and Personality

To understand how approach and fear systems serve or fail to serve children's responses to school, one must include aspects of ego development and personality as well as temperament. Personality includes how children and adults see themselves and the world, and as a sense of self develops, children come to assess the content of the self and make evaluations of self-worth. Figure 6.1 depicts mechanisms whereby children's temperament can come to shape their experience in school (Teglasi & Epstein, 1998, p. 536), but it is important to remember that these processes apply to all children. It is also important to remember that coping strategies that are useful and rewarded in one situation may prove to be ineffective or harmful in other settings or later in development.

As children develop a strong sense of self, their feelings of positive or negative self-worth also become more affected by rewards and punishments (Harter, 1999). As early as the preschool years, children develop ideas about

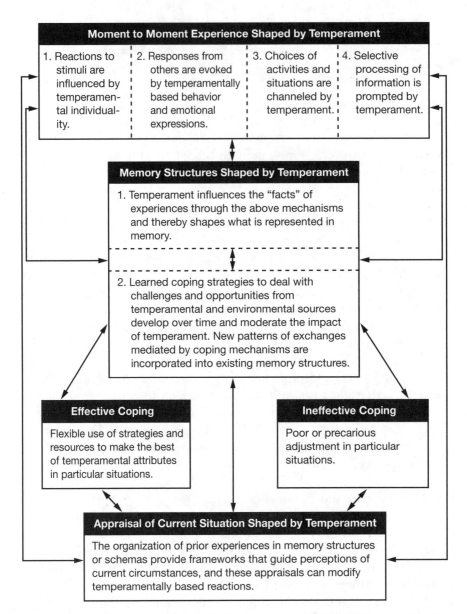

Moment to Moment Experience Shaped by Temperament

1. Reactions to stimuli are influenced by temperamental individuality.	2. Responses from others are evoked by temperamentally based behavior and emotional expressions.	3. Choices of activities and situations are channeled by temperament.	4. Selective processing of information is prompted by temperament.

Memory Structures Shaped by Temperament

1. Temperament influences the "facts" of experiences through the above mechanisms and thereby shapes what is represented in memory.

2. Learned coping strategies to deal with challenges and opportunities from temperamental and environmental sources develop over time and moderate the impact of temperament. New patterns of exchanges mediated by coping mechanisms are incorporated into existing memory structures.

Effective Coping

Flexible use of strategies and resources to make the best of temperamental attributes in particular situations.

Ineffective Coping

Poor or precarious adjustment in particular situations.

Appraisal of Current Situation Shaped by Temperament

The organization of prior experiences in memory structures or schemas provide frameworks that guide perceptions of current circumstances, and these appraisals can modify temperamentally based reactions.

Figure 6.1. A model of mechanisms for the influence of temperament on subjective experience in school situations. From "Temperament and Personality Theory: The Perspective of Cognitive–Experiential Self-Theory," by H. Teglasi and S. Epstein, 1998, *School Psychology Review, 27,* p. 536. Copyright 1998 by the National Association of School Psychologists. Reprinted with permission.

goodness and badness, and feelings of shame, embarrassment, and pride have been observed in children younger than 2 years of age. With development, views of the self become more differentiated, and children come to distinguish among their social, athletic, and academic selves (Harter, 1978). Feelings of generalized shame may also become more specific, yielding guilt reactions (Dweck, 2000). In recent years, researchers have uncovered many negative effects of rewards as well as punishments, and although temperamental differences may lead some children to be more sensitive to reward or punishment than others, these systems are present in all children. Thus, motivational research becomes of basic importance to understanding children's development and functioning in learning situations. Carol Dweck (2000) commented on the power of self-related information:

> In all of our work, one thing that has struck me time and again is how attuned people (both children and adults) are to messages about the self. It never ceases to amaze me how our experiments, in one session, can teach people a "new" view of the self, influencing their motivation and behavior (see Jones, 1990). Although the influence of a short experience may be quite limited and temporary, these studies show the great sensitivity that people have to this kind of information. (p. 143)

Fear of Failure and Feelings of Inferiority

We also know that schooling may give children repeated information over long periods that can be applied to their perceptions of self-worth. Competitive schooling, for example, may give evidence to children who have failed that the self is flawed. Even children who regularly succeed often fear failure and the likely loss of a positive view of the self when their weaknesses are exposed. Thus, succeeding is frequently not enough for a secure self, and fear of failure can be found in some of the most achieving students (Dweck, 2000). Even students who have had a long run of achievement may fear that their imperfection will be "found out" on an upcoming test or other evaluation. When the dominant motivation of schooling is fear, it also becomes difficult to elicit intrinsic interest or involvement in the subject. In experimental studies, the introduction of competition decreases rather than increases student performance when the tasks are complex and meaningful (see review by Covington, 1998).

Excuses for failure, including feigning working, setting goals so high they can never be reached, choosing easy tasks to ensure success, setting low standards for success, cheating, blaming the teacher or the test, discounting school success (as is sometimes seen in minority students), or even blaming their own anxiety, are thus encouraged in children (Covington, 1992). The extensive application of excuses for self-protection is reviewed by C. R. Snyder and Higgins (1988). In addition, fear can extend to children's devaluing of cooperation, with children afraid they will contribute more to a group outcome than others or will not get the grade they feel they deserve.

Evaluative anxiety may also be potentiated by temperamental fearfulness. Harter (1980), for example, reported signs of fearful children's decreased interest in challenging tasks and behavioral withdrawal when they were scrutinized and evaluated by others. Longitudinal studies of the development of avoidant styles that take temperament into account will be important to an understanding of the emotions and education.

In the United States, people tend to have positive evaluations of autonomous achievement, forthrightness, and consistency between public and private selves (Harter, 1998). These ego values were traditionally related to gender, with individual success more important for boys and social approval and physical attractiveness more important for girls, although these values are likely changing. As children's representations of self develop, their vulnerability and anxiety about failure in the valued areas increase (Harter, 1998).

In personality theory, anxiety has been related to early experiences in the family. Children whose feelings of self-worth depend chiefly on their individual performance will be more anxious about the possibility of failure than will children who have more unconditional parental acceptance (Assor, Roth, & Deci, 2004; Ausubel, 1996). Feelings of inferiority can also lead to taking defensive positions of arrogance, dislike, and seclusiveness (Adler, 1946). Temperamental tendencies to fearfulness will contribute to anxiety reactions, but when there are strong pressures to succeed, even a temperamentally positive and approaching child can become vulnerable to anxiety about the possibility of failure. Feelings of inferiority engendered by performance threat may then be displayed in behavior that seems to be the opposite of inferiority, such as arrogance. In addition, children are subject to the frustration, avoidance, and depression related to decreased self-evaluation (Harter, 1998). In the development of these processes, temperament is likely to make only partial contributions, and longitudinal study of these self-related personality processes is much needed.

Learning Goals That Foster Motivation

In a competitive and judgmental atmosphere, the helpful informational value of mistakes is lost, and children spend much of their time trying to avoid any sign of failure. Children study and prepare for evaluations, but even so, some children are bound to perform relatively poorly. How are they then to deal with information that might lead them to think poorly of themselves? One possibility for older children is to use self-differentiation, preserving a positive self-view in at least one area and writing off the self in others, as in, "I'm not good in school, but I'm a great baseball player." It is discouraging, however, that a child may thereby write off a whole area of experience.

In older children, two kinds of academic achievement goals have been identified, one including intrinsic mastery motivation and task involvement, the other extrinsic motivation, performance evaluation, and ego involvement. In a review of the relations between these two orientations and children's cognitive engagement, Pintrich, Marx, and Boyle (1993) reported that a focus on mastery goals results in deeper cognitive processing on academic tasks than does a focus on the self (ego-involved) or a focus on performance (getting a good grade, besting others). Performance and ego goals are related to more surface processing and less overall cognitive engagement. Mastery motivation is also affected by school structure: Children are more oriented toward mastery when the goals they are directed toward are meaningful and challenging ones; when the children themselves have some control of the direction of their effort; and when evaluations are not highly focused on external rewards, competition, or social comparison.

One way of making learning more intrinsically rewarding and less punishing in the school has been to change children's ways of thinking about intelligence (Dweck, 2000). Some children view intelligence as a trait that is unlikely to change: A person is smart or dumb and there isn't much that can be done about it. In addition, when you have to work hard to succeed, this is a sign that you are not very smart. Another approach is more like the view of skill learning we present in chapter 9 (this volume): Intelligence is subject to incremental change; one can become smarter. Taking this view, children are able to learn that through effort and practice they can gain intelligence (Dweck, 2000). We illustrate this possibility in chapter 9. It is interesting that the way intelligence tests are constructed, as noted in chapter 1, children really do get smarter with age. It is just that when compared with other children of the same age, some receive higher and some receive lower IQ scores.

Other problems with the use of rewards in schooling have been identified. One is that when once rewarded for the performance of a task, a child may come to require a reward to do it and may discount any previous intrinsic interest in the task (Lepper, Greene, & Nisbett, 1973). Children may also choose easy tasks if they are linked to rewards (Harter, 1974) and follow the general approach of seeking the greatest award for the least effort (Kruglanski, 1978). Covington (1998) proposed that these problems can be dealt with by viewing academic gains as by-products on the way toward attaining more fundamental goals such as mastery, helping others, or the satisfaction of curiosity, rather than as signs of individual achievement linked to reward:

Ultimately, it is the value and meaning of what is learned—more particularly, the sense of satisfaction arising from enhanced understanding—rather than accumulating knowledge for the sake of power or prestige that will ultimately determine whether the will to learn is maintained. (Covington, 1998, pp. 136–137)

By stressing knowledge that can be used to pose and resolve questions, a different view will be taken of success and failure as information helpful for problem solution rather than as an index of self-worth.

SUMMARY

Temperament offers a level of analysis and understanding that provides new perspectives on children's education. Built on brain systems that have been increasingly studied in recent years, these individual differences provide the building blocks for motivation and learning experiences. Surgency–extraversion has been positively linked to mastery motivation; fear and sadness have been negatively linked to mastery motivation. Children who are more perceptually sensitive and open to experience are also reported to be more competent. One of the most important dimensions of individual differences in temperament is effortful control, based on the development of executive attention but also related to the motivational systems that temperament supports and shapes. As motivations change with development, children often become subject to ego anxiety, and some of the early positive zest for learning and challenges may be lost. Working with children's appropriate motivations and taking into account their temperamental characteristics creates an exciting challenge for parents and teachers as skill development is encouraged.

7

LITERACY

Perhaps the best example of how imaging the brain can contribute to the learning of school subjects is the process of learning to read. Reading is a complex task, but the crucial level of analysis is the acquisition of the skill of decoding the word unit. What is crucial are the operations involved in decoding words. The brain develops particular areas involved in chunking letters into a visual unit, obtaining the word name, and analyzing its meaning. Most of the imaging studies to date have examined adults reading individual words. The neuroimaging methods discussed in chapter 2 (this volume) have revealed areas of the brain active while one is reading. When these studies are conducted with fluent readers, they provide a picture of the end state of reading.

The goal of literacy education is to move the child toward this end state of fluent reading, but what is needed to acquire fluent reading cannot necessarily be inferred directly from adult studies. When reading was examined in children who either were proceeding normally in learning the skills or were having much greater than normal trouble (S. E. Shaywitz, 2003), frontal areas in the poor readers were found to be more active than in normal readers; however, areas in the back of the brain specifically related to decoding of words into their sounds were found less active or inactive in the poor readers. This finding suggests that the poor readers were exercising even more effortful control than were the normal reading controls to compensate for the brain areas that function automatically in fluent-reading adults. Whether children do this because they cannot yet read sufficiently well or because some prior problem with these brain areas makes reading acquisition difficult, we do not yet know. To understand what is known about how the child's brain becomes adapted for reading, we must first examine the process of reading in adults. In this chapter we examine how visual, phonological, and semantic operations are involved in adult reading of individual words and how they map onto specific brain areas that carry out mental operations on these three forms of representation. These results allow us to examine the process of the acquisition of literacy. It is surprising that the acquisition of phonological operations in reading can be traced back to early infancy when the phonemic structure of the native language becomes differentiated, yet the automatic chunking of letters into units that allow fluent reading comes relatively late in the development of reading.

METHODS FOR STUDYING READING

Most of the neuroimaging data that we discuss in this chapter involves the processing of individual visual words. To a rather surprising degree, the ability to read words shapes both the acquisition and the success of the overall task of skilled reading. During reading, the eyes are fixed for brief periods, separated by sudden jumps (*saccades*) that move the eyes from one location to another. The study of eye fixations during normal reading provides a natural connection between reading individual words and reading continuous text. During a single fixation, a skilled reader is able to see effectively only a small amount of the text, mainly the current fixated word, with some preview of one or two words to the right (Rayner & Pollatsek, 1989). During the approximately 40 milliseconds of the saccade, there is no detailed vision and the reader is effectively blind.

Neuroimaging studies suggest possible brain areas associated with components of word recognition in studies of the processing of single words. These components include analysis of visual features (orthography), word sounds (phonology), and word meaning (semantics). We discuss these studies and then we turn to the organization of these areas during the brief time we are fixated on a word (approximately 275 milliseconds in the fluent reader). Studies using scalp recording of electrical activity yield estimates of the time of activation of component processes, giving insights into the circuitry of visual word processing. Active connections between remote brain areas when information flows from one area to another can be determined by measuring correlations in the electrical activity recorded from different brain areas. In some cases, diffusion tensor imaging (see chap. 2, this volume) allows researchers to actually image the fiber tracts that send information from one brain area to another. Once one knows something about when

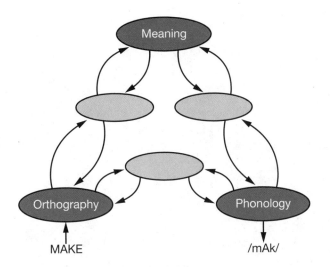

Figure 7.1. Model of operations involved in reading. According to this model of word reading, three computations related to orthography, phonology, and semantics cooperate to allow fluent reading. From "A Distributed, Developmental Model of Word Recognition and Naming," by M. S. Seidenberg and J. L. McClelland, 1989, *Psychological Review, 96,* p. 526. Copyright 1989 by the American Psychological Association.

brain areas are active, one can see if the time course of their activation fits with the fixation time found in studies observing eye movements during skilled reading. If fluent readers spend a given time fixated, and if the meaning of the word on which they are fixated influences the eye movement that ends the fixation, it follows that semantic brain areas are activated before the fixation ends. This analysis provides a test of whether the speed of brain events is fast enough to fit with the behavioral observations from actual reading. At the end of this chapter, we return to studies of word reading, this time as it accompanies acquisition of the reading skill first by adults and then by children.

Cognitive Operations

What are the cognitive operations that constitute reading a word (Everatt, 1999; Klein & McMullen, 1999)? According to most analyses, these include the visual operations of putting the individual letters into an orthographic unit (*visual word form*). The visual units can be translated into an internal sound (*input phonology*) or articulations (*output phonology*). It is also possible that people translate the visual unit directly into its semantic meaning just the way they recognize a chair as something to sit in even without first knowing its name. These operations are outlined in the form of an interconnected neural network in Figure 7.1. In addition to these

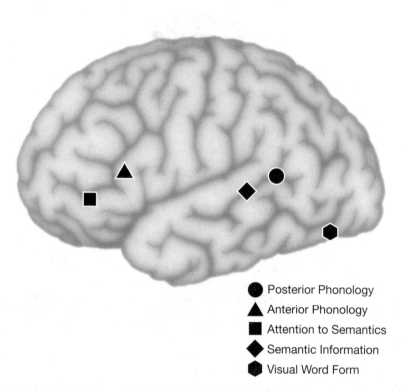

● Posterior Phonology
▲ Anterior Phonology
■ Attention to Semantics
◆ Semantic Information
⬡ Visual Word Form

Figure 7.2. Areas of the cortex critical to fluent reading acquisition. Imaging studies of word reading show the importance of two left lateralized posterior areas (visual word form [hexagon] and phonology [circle]) and an anterior area (square) related to mental effort (S. E. Shaywitz, 2003).

operations specific to reading, the attentional networks discussed in chapters 3 and 4 (this volume) provide the basis for modulating these operations in accord with instructions or intentions of the person.

Visual Processing

The first cortical processing of a visual word must occur in the primary visual cortex. However, neuroimaging studies in which subjects are instructed to look at words compared with nonword stimuli of the same visual complexity have shown that most of the differences occur in left lateral visual areas that follow processing by the primary visual cortex.

Figure 7.2 summarizes areas of the left hemisphere involved in the processing of words. An extrastriate visual area in the left fusiform gyrus (shown as a hexagon) is more strongly activated by strings of letters that could be words in English (e.g., *WERD*) than by nonsense material, even when the nonsense material consists of consonant strings composed of actual letters (e.g., *WRDN*). The specificity of this activation suggests that areas within this region are sensitive to the visual organization of those letters permitted within the English language. Hence, it has been dubbed the *visual word form area*. It appears to be active both when the string is an actual English word and when the string is meaningless but obeys English orthography.

The idea of a visual word form area has been controversial (McCandliss, Cohen, & Dehaene, 2003; Price, Winterburn, Giraud, Moore, & Noppeney, 2003). In our view there are many reasons for this controversy. One reason is that it is probably not a single area but a constellation of adjacent areas that are sensitive to different aspects of the letter string. These could be general features such as the length of the string and more specific features such as the proper organization of the strings into orthographic units. Another reason for controversy is that this area is not necessarily unique to words. The area can be activated by other stimuli when a similar operation of combining elements into a unit (chunking) is involved. For example, this might be the case in which the picture of an object is not grasped as a whole. In this case, chunking would require integration of the parts similar to the fusiform face area that is active when faces are shown, but also becomes active in response to other visual objects for which expertise has been acquired, such as a dog for dog experts or a car for those expert in identifying cars (Posner, 2004). These findings fit with the idea that brain areas often represent actions or operations that may be preferentially performed on a particular kind of stimulus but may also be activated by other stimuli when the same operation is performed. A third reason for controversy is that these two brain areas may differ when people learn to read in different languages or use different strategies. Reading English shows more evidence favoring a visual word form area in the left ventral occipital lobe, whereas reading Italian shows more activity in left lateral temporal areas closer to where auditory words are processed (Paulesu et al., 2001). Italian is a more regular language, and there is less need to process detailed information about the visual form of the words. In English, words such as *have* and *pint* cannot be spoken correctly by the same rule as can their neighbors *wave* and *lint*.

These three points have important implications for learning to read. They suggest the importance of the direction of attention of the novice reader who is acquiring the skill. Skilled readers have developed a network of brain areas within the visual system that organize the input string in accord with prior learning. So powerful is this device that skilled readers with injury to the right parietal lobe neglect the letters on the left side of nonsense strings but can still read words normally (Sieroff & Posner, 1988). Patients whose lesions are in areas of the left occipital and temporal lobe where the word form areas are located can lose the ability to read words as a whole, although they may retain the ability to sound them out letter by letter (Cohen et al., 2003).

Very strong evidence on this point comes from a study of a patient who was able to read words normally when they were presented in the right hemifield that goes directly to the left hemisphere (Cohen et al., 2003). When words were presented in the left hemifield, however, they could be read only letter by letter. Evidence showed that his stroke had severed connections between the visual areas of the right hemisphere and the left fusiform gyrus visual word form area. Without the ability to automatically chunk letters into a unit, the patient was unable to chunk the letters into a unitary word. Later we consider how the relatively late development of the visual word form area may contribute to the skill of fluent reading.

Phonological Processing

Many studies have shown that the best predictor of learning to read is the ability of children to deal with phonemes, the basic constituents of spoken language (Stanovich, Cunningham, & Cramer, 1984). Studies have shown that the ability of children to discriminate phonemes is present at birth. In fact newborns have the capability of discriminating phonemes in unfamiliar languages (P. K. Kuhl, 2000). Between 6 and 10 months, however, these children develop much improved sensitivity to and sharpened skills of discriminating phonemes in the native language to which they are routinely exposed than to other languages (P. K. Kuhl, 2000; P. K. Kuhl, Tsao, & Liu, 2003; Werker & Yeung, 2005). In fact, the ability to discriminate among sounds that represent the same phoneme in the native language begins to disappear. We are learning more about how phonemes come to underlie the development of word forms (Werker & Yeung, 2005). This remarkable achievement of learning starts early in infancy, even before the infant begins to show evidence of babbling. Although the spoken environment is important, there are also clear genetic influences on the development of phonology (Newbury, Bishop, & Monaco, 2005).

Moreover, it is possible to measure differences in scalp-recorded event-related potentials (ERPs) following a change from a frequent phoneme to another less frequently presented phoneme (Cheour et al., 1997; Guttorm et al., 2005; Molfese, 2000). The brain shows its discrimination of the two by responding differently when the novel phoneme occurs. Brain activity can be used to reveal whether or not the infant is making the discrimination between phonemes. This electrical difference serves as a measure of the efficiency of the brain in making the discrimination. Thus the effectiveness of caregivers in establishing the phonemic structure of their native language and also of additional languages that they might desire to teach can be examined. It is also possible to predict later difficulties in spoken language and in reading from these recordings (Guttorm et al., 2005; Molfese, 2000). Recent methods for combining data from six electrode sites suggest high accuracy in predicting difficulties in acquisition of literacy can be obtained from infant recordings (Kook, Gupta, Molfese, & Fadem, 2005). These methods make it possible to check for the development of a strong phonemic structure by use of electrical recording in early life just as brain-stem ERPs are now widely used to allow early detection of hearing deficits in infants.

A distinction can be made between two types of phonological coding in reading (Figure 7.2). One type, input or acoustic phonology, is related to recoding the visual word into a form similar to auditory input. This is like looking up the word sound. These operations take place in the posterior area represented by the circle in Figure 7.2. Another type of word sound is more closely related to articulation of the word and takes place in frontal areas of the left hemisphere (triangle in Figure 7.2).

Neuroimaging studies have provided evidence of both types of coding. When subjects were asked to determine if a pair of visual words rhymed, an area of the left superior temporal lobe (see circle in Figure 7.2) located anterior to the angular gyrus was found to be active (Petersen, Fox, Posner, Mintun, & Raichle, 1989). A nearby area was active when auditory words were presented. This area was not activated during visual word naming or during semantic analysis tasks. These findings have been used to support the view that phonological encoding of visual words is an optional part of fluent word reading, at least for well-known words in the English language, and that an alternative, direct, visual-to-semantic route is used for recognizing familiar words.

Many studies have reported that left frontal areas are also activated in tasks that involve rhyming, particularly when nonsense material is involved. Rhyming nonsense material often involves articulating the string to oneself, and it is not too surprising that the area of the frontal cortex closely associated with motor output becomes involved.

The need to design special tasks such as rhyming to activate phonological areas suggests that phonology is optional in skilled reading of simple words, with many words being read by a direct route from the orthography to semantics (see Figure 7.1). In recent years, however, this view has been questioned, and a more compulsory role for phonological processing has been advanced, even for skilled readers. This role is seen in Figure 7.1 in which phonology and orthography interact in processing a visual word. Languages with very consistent rules that map orthography to sound, such as Italian, may be particularly prone to rapid phonological distinctions. English requires learning to read many words whose correct articulation requires recognition of the specific word (e.g., *pint*). The idea expressed in Figure 7.1, in which orthography and phonology are in close coordination, suggests that there is no absolute answer to the question of which is most important in reading any particular word, and leads to disputes in this area between those who place more emphasis on orthographic analysis and those who stress phonology. Whatever may prove to be the case for skilled readers, as we discuss later in this chapter, it seems clear that phonology is important for the acquisition of reading skill (S. E. Shaywitz, 2003).

Semantic Analysis

When subjects are asked to provide the use for a visually presented noun (e.g., *pound* for *hammer*) versus just reading the noun aloud, several brain areas have been found to be active. Figure 7.2 (see square and diamond in figure) summarizes two cortical activations related to the semantic processing of words. These areas have been almost universally found in many studies that use different tasks that have in common the need to deal with meaning.

These two areas are both left lateralized in most readers. The first is a left inferior frontal activation that is anterior to Broca's area (square in Figure 7.2). This area has been implicated in nearly every auditory or visual study requiring a more elaborate analysis of word meaning. Thus, its activation does not appear to be uniquely associated with any particular task, but it is often accompanied by activation of the anterior cingulate and thus is associated with the need to exercise effortful control by attention during semantic processing.

A second left lateralized area is a posterior region of the temporal and parietal lobe related to Wernicke's area (diamond in Figure 7.2). Damage to Wernicke's area results in a fluent aphasia with impairment in understanding and ability to produce meaningful sentences. Cognitive studies have provided some constraints about the nature of such lesions for the processing of individual words. If a related word is presented prior to a target, patients categorized as having Wernicke's aphasia do show semantic priming even though their speech shows a deficit in semantic coherence. At least under some conditions, patients exhibiting Wernicke's aphasia are processing the meaning of words rather automatically (Milberg, Blumstein, Katz, Gershberg, & Brown, 1995), but they do not carry out the normal strategic processing needed to deal with sentences involving higher level semantics. If semantic information primarily involves Wernicke's area, what role does the left frontal area have? There is clear evidence that the left ventral lateral frontal cortex becomes active when people need to analyze the meaning of a word (Petersen et al., 1989), but its role is not completely clear.

One possibility is that the role of the frontal area is to be more involved in guiding the subject's attention to the correct response rather than as a storage system for semantic information. According to this view, the storage of semantic information is in the posterior temporal regions, but the frontal areas help in locating the correct answer, perhaps by temporarily storing information about the specific word being processed. In support of this idea is the finding that the frontal area is also active in a large number of problem-solving tasks involving thought (Duncan et al., 2000). What mental operation might be involved in all of these tasks? A likely possibility is that the input word is temporarily stored in the frontal region while the posterior area is involved in finding the correct association.

Another frontal area active in semantic tasks is the anterior cingulate gyrus (left and right) on the frontal midline. As discussed in chapter 4 (this volume; see Figure 4.2), activity in the anterior cingulate is generally related to executive attention in cognitive tasks, particularly when conflict is involved. When one has to give the use of a word, for example, it is necessary to avoid saying the word itself, the most frequent response, and instead give the associated use. The idea is that the conflict induced by the need to avoid the automatic tendency to say the word name activates this attention area. As previously discussed, the cingulate acts in conjunction with lateral prefrontal areas (square in Figure 7.2) during processing of individual words.

Despite many disputes and areas of uncertainty, anatomical studies suggest that the components of reading models such as the one shown in Figure 7.1 are localized in separate regions of the human brain. It is truly remarkable that portions of the visual system should come to reflect specific reading experiences in a particular language. To understand how brain areas relate to actual word processing, we must determine when they are activated during reading. We next ask how these brain areas become active during the 275 milliseconds of a fixation by the skilled reader.

Timing of Brain Activation in Reading

Understanding how reading is achieved in the brain requires a method of linking the time course of mental activity to brain activation. As discussed in chapter 2 (this volume), electrical studies (ERPs) can be used to make links between brain areas and their time course of activation (Posner & McCandliss, 1999).

Visual Activations

Anatomical studies summarized in Figure 7.2 suggest that left posterior brain areas are active during the processing of words. A band of scalp electrodes over the left occipital lobe showed a difference between words and consonant strings starting about 150 milliseconds following input (Posner & McCandliss, 1999). Depth electrodes in the visual systems of the left hemisphere of epileptic patients show differential responding to word and nonword stimuli at almost the same time course (Nobre, Allison, & McCarthy, 1994). Finally, magnetic recordings from outside the skull also showed that words activate a midline area of the left hemisphere (Tarkiainen, Helenius, Hansen, Cornelissen, & Salmelin, 1999).

Like the imaging data, these ERP data suggest that the left-hemisphere areas involved in chunking letter strings into unitary wordlike stimuli are rather complex and involve several subareas. However, the time course appears to argue that these activations begin within the first 200 milliseconds, even in tasks that might require 700 to 1,000 milliseconds to produce an actual response.

Semantic Activations

In an effort to investigate the time course of the brain activations associated with higher level semantic processing, studies were run in which subjects were required either to give the name of the word they saw or to generate its use (Abdullaev & Posner, 1998). In both cases the same visual activity was present, but the subjects were assigned either a decoding or a semantic analysis task.

ERPs in these two conditions were subtracted from each other. For the task of generating a use of a word there was an increase in frontal ERP positivity starting around 170 milliseconds. It is possible to use a mathematical algorithm to determine the location of the brain areas most likely to produce the recorded distribution of electrical activity on the scalp (Scherg & Berg, 1993). The results showed that these data were best fit by a single active brain area on the frontal midline, a location that matched the activation of executive attention in the anterior cingulate. By 220 milliseconds, a second generator was required to account for differences in ERP waves. This source was in the left lateral frontal cortex, matching the left frontal regions shown by the square in Figure 7.2. Around 600 to 700 milliseconds, ERP differences were found over left temporal parietal regions (diamond in Figure 7.2), close to Wernicke's area. These results suggest that activation of the left prefrontal cortex occurs at about 220 milliseconds, and Wernicke's area much later, at about 600 milliseconds after onset of the stimulus. Because time course in Wernicke's area is later than the reaction times produced in a number of rapid semantic tasks, and because patients with lesions in this area show semantic priming but have impaired semantic speech, the activation in Wernicke's area is likely involved in the integration of word meanings to obtain the overall meaning of phrases, sentences, and other units more complex than single nouns.

This assumption has received some support from further studies showing that a single-word semantic task elicits higher activation in the left prefrontal region than in Wernicke's area, whereas a sentence comprehension task elicits stronger activation in Wernicke's area than in the left frontal cortex (Posner & Pavese, 1998). It is also possible that Wernicke's area plays an important role earlier in processing that is similar or identical in both the semantic and decoding tasks so that it would be subtracted out when seman-

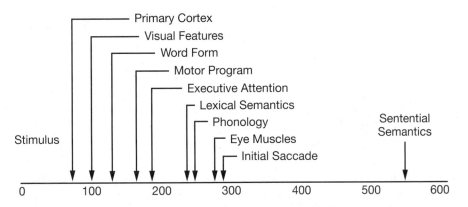

Figure 7.3. A time line for the activation of different forms of information and process during word reading. The *x*-axis shows milliseconds after onset.

tic tasks were compared with reading aloud. This situation might occur if the word's meaning was automatically activated in Wernicke's area regardless of whether the task was reading aloud or doing a specific semantic analysis.

Order of Operations

The time line of Figure 7.3 suggests a serial organization of processes during reading. However, it is misleading to think purely of a serial set of internal processes because attention can be used to reprogram the priority of operations.

The attention system, which is active quite early, can be used to reactivate any of these anatomical areas and thus reorder the priority of the cognitive operations involved. These processes reflect top-down attention-driven rather than bottom-up sensory activation of a given brain area. By now, a great deal of evidence shows that posterior brain areas, even sensory areas, can be activated either by input or by attention. For example, studies of visual imagery, in which people are asked verbally to generate a visual image of a letter or object, suggest that people activate the visual cortex (even primary visual cortex) in the absence of sensory input (Kosslyn & Thompson, 2000).

How does attention influence processes involved in the reading of single printed words (see Posner & Raichle, 1994)? In one study, subjects were asked to view the same stimuli under two different instructions. Half of the words had a thickened letter (e.g., **A**) and half appeared in normal font (e.g., A). In addition, half the words represented manufactured items (e.g., *piano*) and half represented natural ones (e.g., *tree*). In one task, subjects were asked to make a yes–no decision on the basis of a semantic category (manufactured). In another task the decision was defined on the basis of a sensory feature (thick letter, e.g., *APPLE*).

On one day, subjects performed the thick-letter task and were later asked to perform a new task that required pressing a target key only for items that had a thick letter and were also from the manufactured category. These instructions, together with the subjects' experience with the previous task, should have led subjects to first look for the visual feature and then make the semantic analysis. On another day, subjects performed the semantic task and were later asked to perform a new task of pressing the target key only for items that were manufactured and had a thick letter. This time, the instructions, together with their previous experience in the semantic task, should have led the subjects to first do the semantic analysis and then the physical feature. However, both tasks had the same input and identical correct responses. Only the priorities given to the underlying computations were reversed.

The expectation was that subjects who were trained on the thick-letter task and then asked to respond to targets that had a thick letter and were manufactured items would give priority to the visual search for a thick letter. The reaction times did suggest that the instructions were successful in getting the subjects to assign different priorities. The ERPs recorded over frontal semantic areas showed an earlier amplification of electrical activity when the semantic task was given priority than when the visual task had been given priority. The posterior visual area showed an earlier amplification of electrical activity when the thick-letter task was given priority than when the semantic task was given priority. These results show that subjects are able to reorder the priority of the underlying brain computations, and this observation may provide a basis for understanding how the brain can carry out so many different tasks. By reordering the component computations, we can produce novel thoughts.

Some of the underlying computations do not seem to be affected by the instructions at all. The visual attribute area of the right posterior brain, for example, seems to carry out the computation on the input string at 100 milliseconds irrespective of whether the visual features are identified as part of the task or not. However, when the task is identified as looking for a thick letter, these same brain areas are reactivated as seen in the scalp electrical activity, and presumably carry out the additional computations necessary to make sure that one of the letters has just enough thickening to constitute a target. Attention can increase neuronal activity (as measured by ERPs) within particular areas but often appears to do so by reactivating the same area that initially performed the computation, not by activating new higher level association areas.

The method of using attention to give priority to specific computations provides a very general tool for exploring the circuitry involved in brain activity. It is often tempting to think of brain circuitry as a set of fixed anatomical connections between brain areas or between neurons within an area. However, it is well known that any brain area can be anatomically connected to any other area by either direct or indirect routes, providing multiple possibilities for recombining component operations in novel ways. The act of attending to a particular type of information can be thought of as setting up a temporary circuitry from higher level to lower level areas. In this sense attention can control the order of the computations, such as those involved in the thick-letter and semantic category tasks.

If this hypothesis concerning the brain is correct, by temporarily combining information within a target, we can explore the relation between remote areas of the brain during specific cognitive tasks. This method uses the person's own attention to illuminate the order of the computations, with higher level circuits being used to execute the task instruction. For this very general hypothesis to be tested, new experiments will be required, taking as their elements anatomical areas shown to be active during simple computations. Subjects can then be asked to assemble the elements in different ways while researchers measure the impact of this cognitive reorganization on the neural circuitry recruited.

We can also observe some of these changes by examining the correlations that develop between brain areas during the processing of a task. Considerable work has been done in both neuroimaging and electrical studies to investigate the idea that when two brain areas are in communication, their activation will come into synchrony and they will exhibit a form of correlation.

For example, in the use generation task when compared with reading aloud, three general waves of correlated activity were discovered (Nikolaev, Ivanitsky, Ivanitsky, Abdullaev, & Posner, 2001). The first related frontal midline to temporal and frontal sites at about 100 milliseconds, suggesting that the attention system assisted the processing, perhaps by priming phonological systems. The second wave seemed to involve transfer of information from the left frontal area involved in lexical processing, with the more posterior areas chiefly involved in relating lexical meanings (see Figure 7.4). A much later set of correlations seemed to be involved in transmitting the motor output. These correlations fit quite well with the time course information and suggest that the two methods might be used together to specify the circuitry used in solving a particular task.

Words to Sentences

During normal skilled reading, the eyes typically remain fixed on a given word for about 275 milliseconds (Rayner & Pollatsek, 1989). This time constraint on word recognition can assist in interpreting research

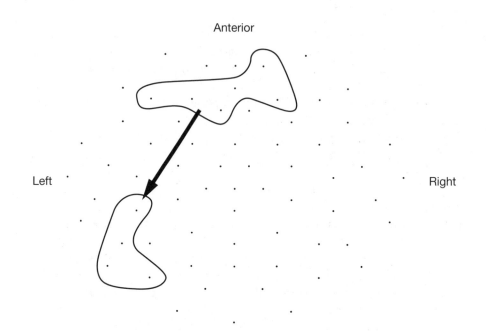

Anterior

Left   Right

Posterior

Figure 7.4. Transfer of information between brain areas during semantic analysis. Correlations between distant scalp electrodes reveal communication between frontal and posterior areas at about 450 milliseconds in the task of obtaining the use of a word. From "Short-Term Correlation Between Frontal and Wernicke's Areas in Word Association," by A. R. Nikolaev, G. A. Ivanitsky, A. M. Ivanitsky, Y. G. Abdullaev, and M. I. Posner, 2001, *Neuroscience Letters, 298,* p. 108. Copyright 2001 by Elsevier. Adapted with permission.

that uses a real-time measure, such as recording ERPs during single-word presentations. Readers typically follow each fixation with a rightward eye movement of seven to eight letters. Leftward regressions (looking back in the text) occur about 10% to 15% of the time. Although there is considerable variability within each of these measures, it is closely related to the characteristics of the text (easy or difficult) and the reader's skill level. For example, if a text is difficult, fixations are longer, saccades are shorter, and there are more regressions. The eye movement monitoring technique is remarkably sensitive to processing difficulties. Effects not only are reflected in the total number of fixations or the overall reading rate but also typically appear within the confines of a single fixation on a word.

The fixation time on a word during reading reflects its processing difficulty. Perhaps the best way to demonstrate how eye movements temporally constrain lexical processing is found in Figure 7.3, which shows the time course of generating the eye movement. Figure 7.3 summarizes the timing of activations within the anatomical areas that we have discussed. Although they are all rather tentative, they serve as a first approximation to coordinating the behavior of the eyes in reading with concurrent activity in the brain. Recall that eye movement studies summarized earlier showed that fixations during reading last about 270 milliseconds. The length of a fixation is influenced by the meaning of the fixated word, indicating that at least some semantic processing has taken place by that time. The fixation time is sufficient to allow left posterior areas to influence programming of the saccade and left frontal areas to influence the eye movement itself. These findings, though incomplete, suggest that the time course of brain areas provides a reasonable fit to the eye movement behavior of the skilled reader during comprehension of actual passages. In this sense, the analysis of individual words does provide a good start in understanding the brain mechanisms of natural reading.

EFFECTS OF EXPERIENCE ON READING

So far, most of the research strategies we have discussed for investigating the neural circuitry of reading skill have manipulated either the task instructions or the stimuli and observed the resulting changes in cortical activation. Another important strategy involves holding both task and stimuli constant but changing the experiences that the subject brings to the experiment. Responses to visual words can be altered by a person's experience within the last few seconds, as in the case of priming by a prior word; within the last few minutes as in the case of generating the same list of associations; over the last several weeks as in the case of learning the meaning of words in a new language; or even over several years as with the case of gaining the ability to read a new language or gaining literacy skill for the first time. Thus, experience-related changes in the brain's response to visual words can be investigated at many time scales. We examine each of these in turn and consider how such changes in experience might lead to different forms of changes in the neural circuitry of word reading.

Practice

Raichle et al. (1994) reported that they used a single list of nouns several times in a task in which the subject was required to generate a use for each word. After subjects went through the list a few times, reaction times to practiced words were fast, responses were always the same, and subjects found the task easier than for novel words. Changes in brain activations were traced through imaging before and after practice.

Automatic Route to Output

Activations in the left lateral frontal and posterior semantic areas (see square and diamond in Figure 7.2) and in the anterior cingulate were reduced with practice. However, the activation in the insular cortex actually increased (see Figure 1.1), becoming as strong as had been found during the reading aloud task. The anterior insula appears to be critical in automatically generating words (Dronkers, 1996). Raichle et al. (1994) suggested that the insula was part of an automatic route to output. When people have to search for the proper output, this route is suppressed and a more effortful route including cortical semantic areas and the anterior cingulate is engaged.

Retrieving Words

Abdullaev and Posner (1998) studied the role of practice in word generation while recording from scalp electrodes. In the Raichle et al. (1994) study, subjects generated uses for the same list of 40 items 10 times in a row, which produced a high level of automatic performance. The ERP study (Abdullaev & Posner, 1998) used a list of 100 items, and as subjects repeated the list, they were instructed to try to produce the same words each time they went through the list. In general, the strength of the scalp activity found over frontal regions and Wernicke's area was reduced by practice. However, a right frontal area of positivity was also produced by the practiced condition. This finding of right prefrontal positivity relates to findings of right frontal activation in tasks requiring the explicit retrieval of information from memory (Habib, Nyberg, & Tulving, 2003). The electrical activity suggests that the act of contacting a previous memory to obtain explicit information on the stored word starts by about 250 milliseconds after input over right frontal structures.

Generating New Thoughts

After subjects generated words to the same list for four successive trials, they were asked to generate a new and unusual use for the same items. Now the early frontal positivity found in the original generation task returned. Later, posterior temporoparietal positivity was as strong and significant as in the first naive-use generation task but was clearly bilateral with two peaks in symmetrical regions of the left and right hemisphere. Generating the new thought thus appears to recruit a right-hemisphere area symmetric to Wernicke's area. These results illustrate the temporal relations among brain areas involved in processing semantic associations and confirm the idea arising from cognitive and brain injury studies that unusual associations require additional processing resources from the right hemisphere.

Learning Vocabulary

Vocabulary learning represents another level at which experience can modify cortical activations to visual words. The activations associated with recognizing a well-known word are presumably quite different than the processes we apply when we encounter an unfamiliar word. Through weeks or months of learning, the same visual words that once struck us as meaningless can be transformed into rapidly accessible entries in our mental lexicon.

Improving Reaction Time

One study (McCandliss, Posner, & Givon, 1997) investigated changes that took place in neural circuitry as subjects spent several weeks learning novel words. The new words being learned were formed by an artificial orthographic rule system that combined letters into word forms according to a limited set of rules. These "words" are fully pronounceable but contain many elements that are unusual in English, and the word forms appear more like Italian or Spanish than English.

Half of the words produced by this orthographic system were used to form a miniature artificial language called Keki. The other half were reserved for testing purposes (Keki control strings). These stimuli provided an opportunity to examine the process of item-specific learning against a group of very well-matched control strings. Each Keki word was assigned a distinct meaning corresponding to a high-frequency English word (i.e., *GILKI* = bird, *PENKA* = black). Together, the set of 68 Keki words formed a small functional language that could be used to convey meaningful sentences.

A group of undergraduates learned Keki via a series of visual and auditory computer tutorials in a laboratory setting for 2 hours per day, 5 days per week, over a period of 5 weeks. During these 2-hour tutorials, subjects worked through interactive exercises that stressed reading Keki words in meaningful contexts. Thus, subjects received extensive visual and semantic experience (50 hours over 5 weeks) with a small word set created by a somewhat novel orthographic system.

A behavioral task was administered at several points across the training program to trace learning. Two successive visual strings were presented in rapid succession, followed by a same–different judgment. Stimuli were familiar English words, Keki words, and Keki control strings. Subjects demonstrated a consistent reaction time advantage for English words over Keki control strings at all three testing intervals (a form of word superiority effect). A similar benefit for Keki words was not present before training but developed over the course of the 5 weeks of training. This result supports the notion that after 5 weeks of training, Keki words were taking on some of the same processing qualities that were present for well-known English words.

Developing Word Forms

An ERP study (Posner & McCandliss, 1999) investigated how 50 hours spent learning Keki words might influence early posterior ERP effects related to processing visual word forms, and later, more broadly distributed ERP effects related to accessing word meanings. Investigators examined the impact of the processing goal of the subjects on the brain electrical response by presenting all stimuli under three different instructional conditions. A semantic condition required that subjects decide whether each string represented something tangible, a visual feature condition required only a judgment about the presence of a small thickened-letter segment embedded somewhere within the stimuli, and a passive condition required only that the stimuli be viewed (no task was performed).

ERP measures were collected in response to Keki strings, Keki control strings, and English strings before, during, and after training. In addition, consonant strings were included in the ERP experiments to provide a baseline stimulus. To examine how Keki training influenced visual word form processes, the same electrode sites and time course as had been used in previous studies of the visual word form area were examined. Real English words, consonant strings, Keki words, and Keki controls were studied.

Regardless of training, both Keki and Keki control items lay between consonant strings and English words. Thus the word form demonstrated sensitivity to the internal structure of letter strings by showing the largest response to strings that are highly consistent with English strings, a smaller but significant response to strings based on a similar orthography (Keki and Keki control), and only a weak response to consonant strings. This pattern remained stable across all three testing sessions (before, during, and after training) and all three task conditions (passive viewing, semantic judgments, visual feature judgments).

Investigators also examined the impact of word familiarity by comparing early posterior ERP response to fully trained Keki words with untrained Keki control items. Results demonstrated the training had no impact. ERP responses were virtually unchanged by 50 hours of familiarization and training. During the first 200 milliseconds of processing, the visual word form system in adult readers is apparently uninfluenced by the familiarity of particular word items yet is highly sensitive to the abstract orthographic structure of both novel and familiar letter strings. Taken together, effects revealed by the early posterior ERPs appear to reflect a visual word form system, which is very sensitive to orthographic regularities, insensitive to familiarity for specific visual words, and slow to change.

Word Meaning

Another goal of the study was to trace word-learning effects in other systems related to word meaning. Approximately 300 milliseconds after presentation, English words (compared with consonant strings) demonstrated a negative shift in the recorded electrical activity event under passive viewing conditions. This effect virtually doubled in magnitude under semantic task demands, and was greatly attenuated under the task requiring a nonsemantic decision for each stimuli (letter feature judgment). Unlike the earlier orthographic effect, which was isolated to posterior areas, this effect was widely distributed over the left hemisphere, including posterior and frontal regions. Examining the ERP responses for Keki versus Keki control words in the semantic task during this same time window (280 to 360 milliseconds) revealed a set of systematic changes occurring over the 5 weeks of training.

In the first session, Keki words and Keki control strings did not differ from each other, but both were more positive than were English words. Over the course of training, a difference emerged between the Keki and Keki control items, such that response to Keki words came to resemble the response to English words, whereas responses to Keki controls and consonant strings remained more positive than did responses to English words. After 50 hours of training, the ERP response to Keki words was equivalent to English words, and was significantly different from both Keki control and consonant strings. Like the effect for English words, the difference that emerged between Keki words and Keki control strings was broadly distributed over posterior and frontal sites.

Overall, these results demonstrate that the processes of learning lexical items can be traced in detail. Different aspects of learning can be related to changes in specific parts of the neural circuitry. Within the first 200 milliseconds of processing, the orthography of letter strings can influence processing by posterior brain mechanisms associated with visual word form information. However, the operation of these mechanisms is not influenced by task demands and did not change noticeably with 50 hours of practice. The effects of learning were also evident over left frontal and posterior sites, and this learning effect appeared strongest when subjects attended to the meanings of the words. These findings illustrate potential differences in the way the brain circuitry changes with experience, suggesting that some aspects of the neural circuitry of reading might be more easily modified by experience than others. We believe that the approach used in this study will allow examination of many questions about how different forms of learning can be understood in terms of changes in the neural circuitry that supports a task.

Even in adults, some of the circuitry underlying reading can be changed with practice and new learning. Although the basic brain areas involved in reading remain fixed, attention, practice, and learning alter the time course of their activation and give temporary priority to some computations based on instruction.

ACQUIRING LITERACY

A consensus has developed about what kind of reading instruction is of most aid to children. The National Reading Panel (Institute of Child Health and Human Development, 2000) has stressed the importance of awareness of the small units of speech called *phonemes* in learning to read. Phonemic awareness is often demonstrated by the child's ability to move sounds in spoken words around to produce rhymes or to use special auditory languages such as Pig Latin.

Phonemic Awareness

As discussed previously, infants enter the world with the ability to discriminate phonemes even in languages they have never heard. Studies have shown that infants' attention to a repeated phoneme wanes with repetition but is reinstated when the sound is shifted to a new phoneme. During the 1st year of life, even before babbling begins, infants begin to show evidence that representation of phonemes are adapting to the languages they hear. This adaptation involves sharpening of the boundaries around their native language phonemes, but also the loss of the ability to discriminate phonemes in other languages (P. K. Kuhl et al., 2003). There is some evidence that interaction with a human speaker of a foreign language can prevent the loss of these phonemes.

Phonemes in spoken language can be related to the alphabet of that language by specific instruction in phonics. Instruction in how to sound out words and nonwords has been shown to improve the child's ability to learn to read. Poor readers seem to lack the awareness of the constituent sounds of words and the automatic ability to connect letters with sounds.

Can we use this knowledge about how children learn to read to improve instruction? Many efforts have taken advantage of the importance of relating the nature of the sound structure of English to the reading skill (McCandliss, Beck, Sandak, & Perfetti, 2000). Early in reading, many children have a bias toward treating printed words as unanalyzed whole units without fully grasping the alphabetic principle that each grapheme can map to a phoneme, thereby allowing systematic learning to transfer from one set of trained words to a novel set of words.

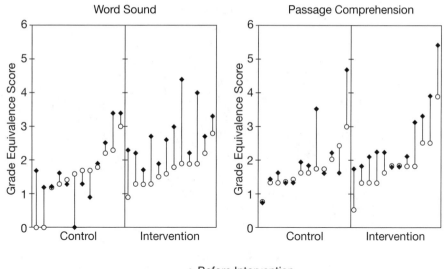

Word Sound

Passage Comprehension

○ Before Intervention
◆ After Intervention

Figure 7.5. Improvement in reading resulting from training. This figure shows improvement in individual word reading (left) and comprehension (right) scores of children reading below grade level after 20 sessions of a computerized phonics-based instruction compared with controls who underwent normal school experiences in reading. From "Focusing Attention on Decoding for Children With Poor Reading Skill," by B. McCandliss, I. L. Beck, R. Sandak, and C. Perfetti, 2000, *Scientific Studies of Reading, 7,* p. 95. Copyright 2000 by Lawrence Erlbaum Associates. Adapted with permission.

The use of specific instruction to train decoding skill has recently been combined with an imaging strategy to observe changes in the circuitry induced by the training (B. A. Shaywitz et al., 2004; S. E. Shaywitz, 2003). Instructional programs that incorporate various activities to help children focus on an analytic stance toward word decoding were used. Children's attention skills, which help them focus on particular constituent visual and phonological units, build automaticity in decoding words.

The results for children who had large difficulties in learning to read were very impressive. In 20 hour-long sessions, the ability to decode words jumped 1.4 grade levels. Even more important, nearly all of the children improved (see Figure 7.5). There was virtually no improvement in the children not given this specific phonics instruction. Although these studies were targeted mainly at the word decoding level, a very substantial gain in decoding skill as well as improved comprehension of sentences resulted. Another imaging study involved a year's training in phonological analysis (B. A. Shaywitz et al., 2004). Control groups received the usual reading instruction but no special work on phonics. Imaging prior to instruction showed that children who were having difficulty with reading failed to

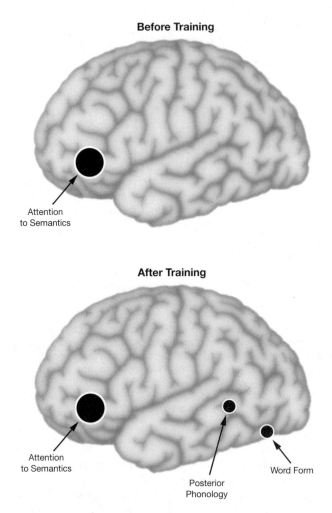

Before Training

After Training

Attention
to Semantics

Attention
to Semantics

Posterior
Phonology

Word Form

Figure 7.6. Brain activity during reading before and after training. Brain imaging of children with poor reading skills was conducted prior to and after phonics training. The left superior temporal gyrus (posterior phonological brain area) and the visual word form were areas showing improvement with training (S. E. Shaywitz, 2003).

activate the posterior visual word form and phonological areas found active during adult reading. Instead they showed much stronger than normal activation of the frontal area, probably reflecting their great effort. After the year of phonics training, children with low reading skills showed improvement in reading, and imaging showed better activation of both posterior phonological and visual word form areas (see Figure 7.6).

Reading skills were also improved in a study (Temple et al., 2003) of a group of children with poor reading skills. In this case, the intervention involved improved auditory phonemic analysis and language training with a commercial program called Fast Forward designed to teach children to understand and isolate phonemes, among other skills. In this study, children, after learning, also showed clearly increased brain activity in a frontal area that in adults was also related to phonological analysis (see triangle, Figure 7.2).

These studies suggest that in at least some children, improvements in reading and better automatic analysis of phonology can occur as the result of interventions. At the present time, there has been little effort to determine what sort of intervention relates to which kind of deficit. However, there is an important paradox in the results of phonics training for children with dyslexia. Although training in phonemic awareness and phonics improves performance and tends to correct the brain systems, it often does not by itself produce fluent reading. For fluent reading, apparently more than decoding skills is needed. An exception is the yearlong intervention described earlier (B. A. Shaywitz et al., 2004), which did seem to improve the visual word form and produce more fluent reading. The resolution of this paradox may depend on understanding the rather late development of the visual word form system.

Development of the Word Form Systems

One experiment with children was designed specifically to examine the development of the visual word form system (Posner & McCandliss, 1999). ERPs were collected as 4-, 7-, and 10-year-old children watched letter strings appear on a computer screen. The initial goal was to start the studies well before the children could read, so ERPs were collected when children were either passively watching strings of letters or actively processing them to decide whether a thickened-letter segment was present.

Although the overall waveforms were quite different from those of adults, the specific differences that emerged between active and passive conditions across ages were remarkably similar to the adults, with posterior channels showing increased positivity during the thickened-letter search task. As with many other developmental ERP findings, the latency of this effect generally decreased with age.

Half of the letter strings in these tasks formed high-frequency words that are common in first-grade curricula, and the other half were consonant strings. Recall that in adults, the earliest indication that the brain processes words and consonant strings differently occurs in posterior channels within the first 200 milliseconds of processing (McCandliss et al., 1997). In the Keki study this effect was present during both passive viewing conditions and the feature search task.

Our studies with 4- and 7-year-olds showed little difference between words and consonant strings, even though the 7-year-olds could read the words we showed them. However, for 10-year-olds, the story was quite different. The influence of word-specific knowledge appeared at about a 200-millisecond window and diminished by about 300 milliseconds, and it occurred almost exclusively in posterior inferior channels similar to those found for adults. Unlike the adult ERP results, however, the 10-year-olds showed no evidence of effects related to orthographic encoding. Instead, it appeared that early response in 10-year-olds occurred only with words that they already knew.

The results of this study suggest that 10-year-old children integrate visual letters into word forms differently than do adults. The 10-year-olds showed two distinct phases. The first phase appears to be related in location to the word form system but occurs 30 to 40 milliseconds later. In this phase, known words differ from unknown words and consonant strings, which suggests a visual word form system that is sensitive to familiarity but not orthography. It contrasts with the adult systems that respond to orthography whether or not the string is familiar.

In a second phase following 300 milliseconds and somewhat more anterior, the responses of the 10-year-old children seemed to be more fully based on orthography because they discriminated between consonant strings and words, whether familiar or not. This distinction could well be based on efforts to sound out the stimulus that would be much easier for the known words than for unknown words or consonant strings.

These findings suggest that the word form system may evolve out of differences in familiarity. In our work with 7-year-old children who had learned to read some words, evidence was found that familiar words began to be discriminated from unfamiliar words by about 300 milliseconds, but this result occurred only for items for which we had specially trained the children in the laboratory by a phonics method. By age 10, these familiarity-based effects occurred earlier and appeared for untrained items, which had been learned by the child outside the laboratory.

Some connectionist models of the processing of words, such as the one shown in Figure 7.1 or by Harm and Seidenberg (2004), suggest that what appears to be selection by orthography actually arises from a comparison of the input string with stored exemplars, which are close to its neighbors. The 10-year-old results are mainly consistent with this notion. If at age 10 the neighborhoods are rather sparse, there will be substantial differences between known and unknown words.

As learning continues into adulthood, however, the neighborhoods become very dense. In adults, rather than reflecting specific familiarity with individual items, output appears to reflect the degree to which the input strings activate their neighbors. So for adults a regularly appearing but unfamiliar string will be handled just as though it were a word. However, this would not be the case for young children.

According to this view, familiarity through storage of exemplars is the basic mechanism of word form development. Nonetheless, because of the dense neighborhoods present in adults, orthographically regular nonwords do not appear different from real words. This result could be made to fit with the data that show no difference between words and orthographically regular nonwords. However, if the basic mechanism of the word form is storage of exemplars, it is surprising that more than 50 hours of training did not establish a difference between trained and untrained Keki strings (McCandliss et al., 1997). Perhaps the Keki orthography is similar enough to English that it is subject to similar neighborhood effects, or perhaps the plasticity that allows new exemplars to alter the system easily at age 10 is no longer present for adults.

Whatever the specific mechanisms, these results provide evidence of automatic letter integration responses that are different in children than in adults. Children can integrate letters into visual word forms for known items but may have to rely later on more effortful mechanisms for unknown words. This result and the method that allows us to study the details of the processing systems present in learning to read should be of great benefit in future studies of the skill.

IMPLICATIONS FOR RESEARCH ON LITERACY

The new results provide a strong basis for the design and evaluation of specific interventions. Phonics training is common in many schools and has usually been successful in improving reading of children with low reading skills. The difficulty is that by itself phonics training may not produce fluent reading. Research is clearly needed to determine the optimal means of developing both decoding and fluent reading skills. Though phonics training seems to be a very good method for developing posterior phonological areas, the development of the visual word form area might be fostered by improving the motivation to practice reading by whole-word training or by other methods. Normal readers may acquire this ability through the act of reading, but poor readers may not expose themselves to sufficient reading to develop the word form area properly.

Imaging studies would be useful in helping to determine which curriculum influences which parts of the reading network. It may also be possible to use simple behavioral tests, such as nonword reading, to determine easily which form of instruction a particular child needs. The ability to image the circuitry may allow the fine-tuning of educational intervention that would target the specific difficulties that various children have in learning to read.

The studies reviewed previously suggest that learning to read is a process that begins well before school ever starts. In the 1st year of life, social interaction with caregivers provides a strong basis for sharpening and strengthening the boundaries of the phonemes of the native language. This process may be sufficient for speech but if weak may not provide the strong basis for phonemic awareness needed for reading. In chapter 4 (this volume) we examined the development of self-regulation. This development too begins well before the child begins formal reading instruction but may be critical for the success of that instruction. When more formal reading instruction begins in school, it seems crucial that the child learn to sound out words so that the connection between visual letters and the auditory language be secured. However, the process of fluent reading requires also that letters be automatically chunked into units. That development appears to occur at later ages than might have been expected. In many children the act of reading itself seems sufficient to develop this system. For children with special difficulties, exercises that lead to successful automatic chunking may need to be developed.

SUMMARY

Neuroimaging methods have proved to be a convenient way to image the circuitry of high-level skills in adults. In this chapter, we have attempted to illustrate the use of this strategy. It is possible to study the details of both the anatomy and time course of the operations of many components involved in reading. The time course of these component operations fits reasonably well with the demands needed to produce the structure of fixations and eye movements involved in skilled reading.

Although changes in specific brain circuitry can take place quite rapidly, they may also take many years of learning, as with the changes that have been found in the brains of children with poor reading skills after intervention. These studies have found evidence that specific interventions can improve processing in the posterior brain areas related to phonological processing and the visual word form system. Further research is needed to examine the changes in brain circuitry that will both lead to a better understanding of the difficulties some children have in learning to read and help in the development of methods for making instructing reading more effective.

8

NUMERACY

In chapter 7 (this volume), we presented some important principles that can be applied to the learning of new skills. We should not assume that the learning of all skills will be the same; indeed, the acquisition of number tells quite a different story about the skills of early childhood than does the development of reading. What is common to the study of both is the method of approaching the subject through an examination of its elementary operations.

The first task in understanding number is to isolate the appropriate level of analysis for comprehending the concept of quantity. We can then see how the brain deals with this computation and relates it to others involved in working with number. Recent studies have examined the understanding of number through the ability of humans and other organisms to know something about quantity, even without any verbalized counting. The idea is that just as objects are automatically evaluated for location, identity, and emotional valence, sets of objects at separate locations give rise to an impression of quantity.

UNDERSTANDING QUANTITY

This primitive understanding of quantity is present in nonhuman animals and in human infants. When rewarded, rats can learn to discriminate, for example, a two-tone from an eight-tone sequence, even if the two sequences are matched in duration (Meck & Church, 1983). Rats can also base their judgment on total duration if these differ, or if durations do not differ, on the number of events.

Monkeys can be trained to appreciate number as represented by Arabic digits (Boysen & Berntson, 1996). With extensive training they are able to relate the digits 0 to 9 to the quantity of a reward. In the research discussed in chapter 5, monkeys who were trained to associate digits with an equivalent size of reward were taught to manipulate a joystick toward the side of the greater number of objects (Washburn, 1994). If the objects were digits, monkeys demonstrated a numerical Stroop effect. That is, it took them longer when the digit was presented in a way that was incongruent with the larger number (e.g., the digit 6 was presented twice whereas the digit 3 was presented four times). The numerical Stroop effect in humans is known to produce a strong activation in the anterior cingulate.

The presence of the numerical Stroop effect in rhesus monkeys shows that digit training established a sufficiently rapid and automatic appreciation of digit quantity to have it interfere and produce a Stroop effect. The same sort of high-level attention system as the executive attention systems in humans described in chapter 4 (this volume) is presumably needed for monkeys to respond on incongruent Stroop trials. Because they make a very large number of errors, it also appears that the monkeys are not applying this form of control as consistently as adult humans do. Adult humans, like the monkeys, can base their analysis of number on implicit knowledge of quantity rather than counting, if the counting strategy is unavailable. For example, if presented with a series of light flashes too fast to allow explicit counting, adults can still provide accurate information on the basis of implicit enumeration, provided the rate is not too fast (Whalen, Gallistel, & Gelman, 1999). If the events occur at very fast rates, so that duration is a reliable guide to number, what is reported is how many 0.1-second intervals have accumulated (Cheatham & White, 1954). This latter finding suggests the possibility of a basic unit of duration. When electrical activity recorded from the scalp is broken down into its component rhythms, one of the strongest is at 10 cycles per second (the alpha rhythm). Cheatham and White (1954) speculated that this rhythm might be related to the reported number for very fast sequences. In any case, the data show clearly that both duration and quantity can be accumulated, even without any verbalization.

THE NUMBER LINE

When adult humans are required to determine which of two digits is larger, the speed of doing so depends on how far apart the two digits would

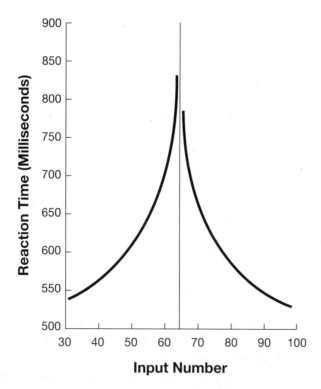

Figure 8.1. The distance effect in number processing: Reaction time as a function of distance from the comparison number 65. The figure illustrates the distance effect, the time to determine that two numbers differ, and a function of their distance. From "Is Numerical Comparison Digital? Analogical and Symbolic Effects in Two-Digit Number Comparison," by S. Dehaene, E. Dupoux, and J. Mehler, 1990, *Journal of Experimental Psychology: Human Perception and Performance, 16,* p. 627. Copyright 1990 by the American Psychological Association.

be if placed on a number line (see Figure 8.1). This effect can occur quite automatically. For example, when subjects are asked to determine whether two objects are the same physical size and if the objects are digits (e.g., 4 vs. 6), the subjects show a Stroop effect (Tzelgov, Meyer, & Henik, 1992). When the magnitude of the digits is compatible with the physical size, subjects respond more quickly than when it is incompatible. As in the monkeys and in the numerical Stroop task (chap. 4, this volume), there is automatic activation of quantity.

Brain imaging also demonstrates the automatic effect of quantity. In one study, adults were asked to determine if a target digit was above or below 5. However, prior to the target they were presented with a digit that they were not able to see consciously or report (the digit was presented for a very brief interval followed by superimposed visual noise called a *mask*). Nonetheless, the prime influenced both their speed of response (they were faster when it was on the same side of 5 as was the subsequent target) and the degree of activation of the motor system involved in the response, as determined from functional magnetic resonance imaging (fMRI; Koechlin, Naccache, Block, & Dehaene, 1999; Pinel, Dehaene, Riviere, & LeBihan, 2001).

The closer a digit is to 5, the longer it takes to determine if it is above or below 5. This finding implies there must be some underlying representation that is like a one-dimensional map of quantity. This form of analog representation of number is called the *number line*. It is thought to serve as a cognitive representation in which the distance along the line is related to quantity of the input. The number line relates to understanding number in somewhat the same way as the visual word form relates to understanding how letters form words. The input to the word form is separate letters, but its output is a unified chunk. In a similar way, the input to the number line can be in the form of spelled words, digits, or dots, but its output is quantity. A quantity means that the brain has related the stimulus to other potential stimuli in a way that reflects the different amounts to which they refer. The digit 7 is more similar in looks to 1 than it is to 6. Yet the number line places 7 in between 6 and 8, and thus provides a quantity. This property underlies the distance effect, as illustrated in Figure 8.1. Because almost all numerical tasks depend on understanding quantity, it is important to know how the number line works and how it develops.

Brain Anatomy and Circuitry for Determining Quantity

The basic anatomy and circuitry for determining quantity of Arabic (e.g., 2) and spelled digits (e.g., two) in normal adults have been worked out (Dehaene, 1996). The task used is to compare an input item (e.g., 4, four) to determine if it is above or below 5. Reaction times (RTs) for this task vary as a function of the type of input (Arabic or spelled), distance from 5 (close or far), and type of output; see Figure 8.2.

Results shown in Figure 8.2 indicate that the amount of increase in RT resulting from the type of input is the same irrespective of its distance from 5. Moreover, the decrease in RT as the distance from 5 increases is the same for both forms of input (spelled vs. Arabic digit) and for both left- and right-hand responses. This form of additivity between independent variables agrees with the serial processing stages as discussed in the additive factor method described in chapter 2 (this volume).

Areas of the Brain at Work

According to the additive factor logic as discussed in chapter 2 (this volume), the additive RTs shown in Figure 8.2 imply a set of serial stages.

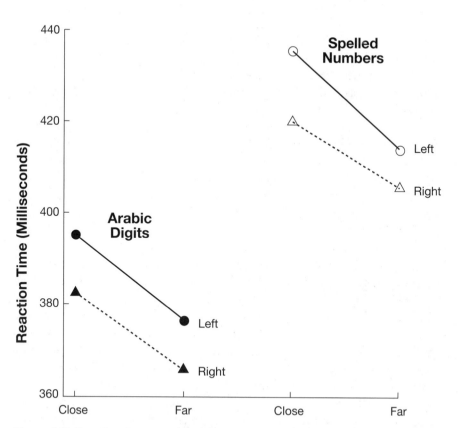

Figure 8.2. Reaction time as a function of notation, distance, and responding hand. The three effects are additive, indicating the likelihood of serial stages as discussed in chapter 2. From "The Organization of Brain Activations in Number Comparison: Event-Related Potentials and the Additive-Factors Method," by S. Dehaene, 1996, *Journal of Cognitive Neuroscience, 8,* p. 52. Copyright 1996 by the Massachusetts Institute of Technology. Reprinted with permission.

When the same task was used with high-density electrical recording from the scalp, it was possible to work out the location and time course of activation for each of the stages (Dehaene, 1996).

Order of Operations

Event-related potentials (ERPs) recorded during the performance of this task suggested that each of the stages produced activation in a different brain area that corresponded closely with what would be expected on the basis of functional anatomy. The occipital electrodes related to the encoding stage were affected 150 milliseconds after input by stimulus type. The spelled digits showed a stronger activation over the left occipital lobe, which would fit with a generator in the visual word form area. This effect contrasted sharply with the bilateral activation found for the use of Arabic numerals.

The distance effect (distance of input digit from 5) was found after about 200 milliseconds and was strongest over the right parietal lobe and, to a lesser degree, the left parietal lobe. This area had been related in lesion studies to the storage of numerical quantity, and supporting results have now been reported from studies using functional imaging with more precise localization (Pinel et al., 2001).

The use of the left or right hand in response produced very clear modulations in electrodes above the motor cortex on the side opposite the responding hand. On a small minority of trials, subjects made errors. When they did, about 70 milliseconds after the response there was an intense area of negativity over the frontal electrodes. As we have noted earlier, this activation comes from the anterior cingulate, showing how higher level attention relates to error detection. The location and times of each stage are shown in Figure 8.3.

These findings illustrate the use of additive factors as a way to examine high-level activation that might have a serial character, as in relating an input digit to a single stored quantity. We are not suggesting that all tasks, not even the task of mental arithmetic, are performed in serial stages. It is clear that the task of comparing the physical size of the digits 4 and 6 produces parallel activation of their magnitude, which can interfere with saying that 6 is physically smaller. The brain tends to look up many familiar codes in parallel. However, if one can design a task in which the stages are largely serial, as in Dehaene's task, one can use a factorial design to discover many interesting aspects of the brain's activity during the task.

Results obtained in this study suggest that the general finding we observed in chapter 7 (this volume) in studies of reading also applies to this simple numerical calculation. Performance of a task activates a small number of widely separate regions corresponding to the operations involved in the task. The additive factors method has been widely used to study many simple tasks that have a structure in which the operations occur one after the other. It appears that what are identified as cognitive stages in an additive factor design may correspond to separated anatomical operations related to these different operations or computations. It is important to note that a numerical task can recruit a brain area related to word reading when the input items are spelled digits.

Separate anatomical areas provide distinct functions during skilled performance. An implication of this statement is that whenever skilled performance requires a particular cognitive task component, the neural area that calculates that computation should be active. This localization of cognitive operations appears to be a general property of skilled performance. For example, similar semantic areas appear to be activated in

1. Vision (150 ms)

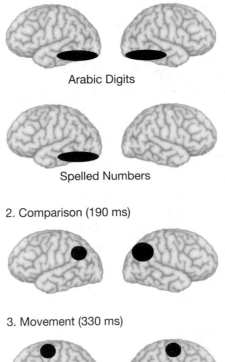

Arabic Digits

Spelled Numbers

2. Comparison (190 ms)

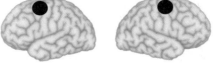

3. Movement (330 ms)

4. Error correction (470 ms)

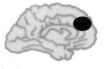

Figure 8.3. The anatomical locations involved in number comparison from electroencephalogram and functional magnetic resonance imaging studies. The panels show the location of the visual notation effect (1), the comparison of distance (2), the side of movement (3), and error correction (4). From *The Number Sense* (p. 224), by S. Dehaene, 1997, New York: Oxford University Press. Copyright 1997 by S. Dehaene. Reprinted by permission of Oxford University Press, Inc.

reading, listening, and naming pictures. Likewise, verbal working memory areas appear to be involved when the task is storing written words, verbally encoding a location, or otherwise using strategies that incorporate verbal description. In a working memory task, the same areas are activated for temporarily storing words (e.g., Broca's and posterior parietal areas), whether the words are presented aurally or visually (Schumacher et al., 1996). These results strongly suggest that component operations in skilled learning rely on the same neural areas whenever those component computations are called on.

DEVELOPMENT OF THE NUMBER LINE

The development of number has been examined in children by means of the same task as that reported earlier for adults: to determine if the input is above or below 5 (Temple & Posner, 1998). The basic brain areas involved in comparing the quantity of numbers do not change from 5-year-olds to adults, although the RT to respond to the task drops threefold over this period (see Figure 8.4).

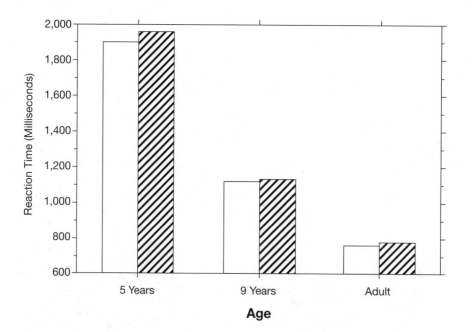

Figure 8.4. Development of number comparison. This figure shows reaction time for children when making comparisons with dots (striped bar) or digits (white bar) as a function of age (Temple & Posner, 1998).

Localization in Children

Do 5-year-olds show the same localization of function as adults? A 128-channel geodesic sensor net was used to record scalp electrical activity from 5-year-olds and adults as they performed number comparisons, and differences in the ERPs associated with the distance effect were examined. Both dot patterns and Arabic digits were used to determine if perceptual and symbolic representations of magnitude affected the localization or timing of the distance effect. RTs of both groups were significantly longer for stimuli close to 5 (average RT = 519 for adults and 1,665 for children) than for those far from 5 (average RT = 480 for adults and 1,495 for children; see Figure 8.4; Temple & Posner, 1998).

Significant effects for distance were found in each of the six chosen electrode pairs, and the waveforms at the selected sites had components similar to those reported previously by Dehaene (1996) for adults. The brain areas associated with the behavioral distance effect were the same for each age group.

Dehaene (1996), recording scalp voltage with a 64-channel recording net, reported voltage differences associated with the distance effect for both Arabic digits and written number words at electrodes at the parieto-occipito-temporal junction (slightly right lateralized) from 174 to 230 milliseconds after stimulus onset. Results led Dehaene to suggest that the distance effect represents a separate magnitude comparison step in number processing. This comparison is carried out in localized brain areas involved in the abstract representation of magnitude, or number comparison areas. The results with children replicated Dehaene's results with respect to comparison of digits in terms of both localization of the voltage difference and the approximate time after stimulus presentation those differences were observed.

The overall organization of brain activations seen in 5-year-olds was thus remarkably similar to those seen in adults, in terms of both brain localization and components of the waveform related to the distance effect. Despite RTs three times as long (about 1,600 milliseconds in children vs. 500 milliseconds in adults), the major components of the waveform at which a distance effect was observed were only slightly delayed in 5-year-olds compared with adults. The first positive wave of the ERP (P1) peaked at 124 milliseconds after stimulus onset, only 26 milliseconds later than in adults; the first negative peak (N1) was at 212 milliseconds after stimulus, 42 milliseconds after adult N1. Waveforms from more anterior areas were more delayed. The distance effect was similar for both forms of representation (dots and digits), and the localization and timing in 5-year-old subjects were remarkably similar to those seen in adults. These findings suggest that the system involved in rapid estimation of quantity develops prior to formal schooling in the same brain areas as found in adults.

The processing of arrays of dots showed a voltage difference associated with distance in the same electrodes and in the same time windows, as seen with the processing of digits both in Dehaene's adult study and in this study. This voltage difference was large, significant, and slightly earlier than that seen for digits. However, considering that only four easily discriminable dot patterns were used in our study, adults and children both seem to refer these patterns to the same comparison process as found with digits. This finding suggests that the analysis of quantity is highly similar irrespective of the input mode, and lends further support to the identity of a localized inferior parietal brain area involved in abstract magnitude comparison. Contrary to previous electroencephalogram results by Dehaene (1996), our results (Temple & Posner, 1998) suggest the area is bilateral rather than right lateralized.

Studies using fMRI with adults as well as cellular recording in monkeys (Piazza, Izard, Pinel, LeBihan, & Dehaene, 2004) have supported the bilateral parietal localization for the number line and its close association with attentional and spatial processing networks. Recent fMRI studies have produced some discrepancies. One study (Ansari, Garcia, Lucas, Hamon, & Dhital, 2005) found that children activated frontal rather than parietal areas during a simple numerical task, whereas another study (Cantlon, Brannon, Carter, & Pelphrey, 2006) found that both 4-year-olds and adults activated the same parietal areas. Although it is possible that the number line shifts between childhood and adults, it seems likely that children show more frontal activation because of the overall difficulty of the task for them. However, more research targeted on the development of the number line and particularly its connection to other areas is needed.

What might account for the long RTs of the 5-year-olds? One reason was clear in the behavior of the 5-year-olds who systematically looked down at about 1 second to verify the correct key to press. The association of the quantity computation with an arbitrary key press seemed to be much more difficult for the children than for the adults. We suspect that the difficulty in associating a behavior with the internal computation of quantity may reflect a more profound difficulty that children of this age have in organizing appropriate voluntary actions to reflect internal thoughts, particularly those computed by posterior structures. This idea is consistent with the slow maturation of frontal areas, but also requires further study.

Although there remains some doubt about whether the brain area for comparison of number in children is the same as in adults, the ERP data suggest that the comparison has a similar brain effect whether the input notation is in the form of dots, digits, or spelled numbers. The results suggest that the number line is developed before 5 years of age and without any formal mathematical training. Although Piaget concluded in the 1950s that preschoolers lack a basic concept of number, as discussed in this chapter there is evidence that children possess an elementary concept of quantity, and the concept of quantity is also present in many animal species.

Training

There have also been empirical efforts to train number comparison in low socioeconomic status children at risk for failure in elementary school arithmetic (Griffin, Case, & Siegler, 1995). One such program, called Rightstart, involves exercises such as board games that require the child to determine the number of spaces to move. The idea was to train the concept of quantity as part of learning to play the various games. Evaluative studies suggested that this learning allowed children at risk to succeed in elementary school arithmetic to perform about as well as children of high socioeconomic status who likely had more parental tuition.

The success of these training methods may lie in their ability to develop connections between input and a preexisting number comparison area. In more general terms, these studies identify tools that may be used to further understand how the brain is reorganized through learning and to examine educational strategies in school instruction.

The importance of detailed analysis of brain circuitry during the performance of these tasks is reinforced by striking differences between the acquisition of the visual word form in reading and the number comparison area. Studies of reading suggest that the visual word form undergoes a very lengthy developmental process and is still quite different from that found in adults even at age 10, when many children read quite well. However, the Temple and Posner (1998) study suggests that the number comparison area is close to adult form even by 5 years of age. The ability to study brain circuitry during reading and arithmetic offers the possibility of observing changes in circuitry during the acquisition of many forms of learning and could help to indicate which teaching strategies are most effective, not only in mathematics but also in listening, reading, and other skills.

Doing Arithmetic

Just as our goal in chapter 7 (this volume) was to go beyond the processing of individual words in model tasks to an understanding of reading in more natural contexts, in this chapter we seek to go beyond the appreciation of quantity to the learning of arithmetic. To do arithmetic, one needs to perform calculations on the data. Although infants have primitive abilities to deal with small additions and subtractions, the formal use of arithmetic operations apparently waits on two crucial things: The first is the

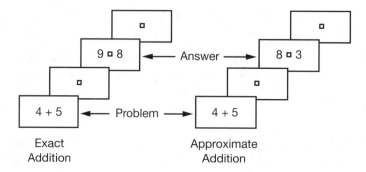

Figure 8.5. Paradigm for exact calculation (left) and for approximation (right) for simple arithmetic problems. Small squares are locations of fixation. From "Sources of Mathematical Thinking: Behavioral and Brain-Imaging Evidence," by S. Dehaene, E. Spelke, P. Pinel, R. Stanescu, and S. Tsivkin, 1999, *Science, 284,* p. 970. Copyright 1999 by the American Association for the Advancement of Science. Reprinted with permission.

development of language, or at least the language-appropriate areas of the brain, and the second is the acquisition, usually by tuition, of certain formal skills.

Involvement of Language Areas

An important study combining neuroimaging and ERPs has shown the involvement of language areas in more complex arithmetic skills (Dehaene, Spelke, Pinel, Stanescu, & Tsivkin, 1999). This study required subjects to verify which of two sums was either true or approximately true.

Examples of these two types of problems are shown in Figure 8.5. In the exact addition condition, one answer was exactly correct and the other was close but an error. In the approximate condition, one answer was close and the other distant. Dehaene et al. (1999) reasoned that the use of a number line system would be sufficient for the approximate question but that exact calculation would require careful enumeration, which might involve other systems. In support of this idea, the approximate solution produced activation mainly of the bilateral parietal areas known to be activated by the number line, with a few other areas related to spatial visualization also showing some activity. When the exact sum had to be calculated, the language areas of the left hemisphere described in chapter 7 (this volume) were active. These data clearly show that for adults, as arithmetic operations are added, language areas are drawn in. Further evidence in this regard comes from an fMRI study in which the task of comparing the quantity was contrasted with the task of multiplying numbers. A network of brain areas, including the parietal area associated with the number line and the anterior cingulate involved in attention, was activated. The comparison task involved mainly right hemisphere activity, whereas multiplication involved mainly left hemisphere activity related to language areas (Chochon, Cohen, van de Moortele, & Dehaene, 1999).

Counting

Generally speaking, children begin to learn to count in a primitive way about the same time as their language explosion, at about 2 years of age. Usually this ability develops well before formal schooling. It is interesting to note that languages that base their number systems on logical organization (such as the decimal system) foster faster development of counting skills in children, and the use of short number names provides a somewhat larger working memory for numbers.

The earliest abilities for addition and subtraction can be found even in infants of a few months, who have long and surprised looks when the number of objects does not fit the changes they see. For example, they are shown a single small toy behind a screen and then see a second toy added. When the screen goes down, they look longer and are more surprised with an incorrect result (one or three toys are shown) than when the correct result of two toys is shown (Wynn, 1992). This result had been interpreted as meaning that the infants expected two items and detected the error, but this idea has been disputed by others. As reported in chapter 3, Berger, Tzur, and Posner (in press) conducted the same study but recorded 128 channels of electroencephalogram. They found the infant brains, like those of adults, showed strongly increased negativity over frontal electrodes when the answer was wrong. Because the infant response is similar to that of adults and because this brain area in adults is known to involve self-regulation, it appears to support the idea that a violation of expectation is involved in the infants as in adults.

The Min Strategy

Productive development of number use begins much later, after language skills are present. As we have seen with studies of children learning to inhibit their actions (see chapter 4, this volume), physical strategies are quite common. At age 5 several strategies emerge during formal tuition (Siegler, 1996). If given the pair 5 + 2, children might raise fingers and count up from zero to the total. Sometimes they lift the fingers and give the overall total without any apparent overt count. Sometimes the child guesses rather than performs any overt action. The guess may be based, like the estimation condition in Figure 8.5, on more direct access to the number line. Another frequent strategy is to begin with the larger addend and add to it the smaller (the min strategy). When this strategy was used, there was a strong correlation between the size of the minimum and the overall solution time. This correlation dropped substantially when the responses appeared to be based on retrieval of the correct answer without any obvious counting (Siegler, 1996).

Even in adults for whom all these simple problems are probably based on a lookup rather than a calculation, longer RTs are found in verifying, for example, that $5 + 4 = 9$ than $5 + 2 = 7$, even though such pairs can be equally familiar. There seems to remain somewhere in adult processing a repeated operation that has some analogies to the min strategy used by 5-year-olds (Groen & Parkman, 1972). This highly serial result is coupled with elements of parallel processing. If one compares $4 + 3 = 12$ with $4 + 3 = 13$ (Winkelman & Schmidt, 1974), it takes longer to reject the former as wrong, presumably because it is actually a correct multiplication, and one's brain activates familiar solutions even when they are not related to the current goal.

Implications for Improving Number Education

Despite the strongly biological nature and the early appearance of knowledge of number, it is a long process to convert this primitive understanding to productive use of numbers in standard arithmetical operations. At least some students need to have their understanding of quantity strongly exercised before entry into elementary school instruction. Rightstart represents an effort to do that by the use of games that attach a quantity to each number.

SUMMARY

In this chapter we have examined information on the acquisition of number skills. One basic method was to use a model task determining whether a given number was above or below 5. This model task has been shown in adults to activate a network of areas related to the cognitive operations involved. Children as young as 5 seem to perform the model task in much the same way as adults but take much longer to provide an overt answer. It is possible this longer time reflects a difficulty in sending information from posterior to anterior brain areas involved in making the response. Processing quantity appears to be an automatic task in adults and can be made so in monkeys by training over many thousands of trials. However, some children appear to have difficulty in automatic access to the quantity operations.

Performance in elementary school arithmetic depends on an understanding of quantity in much the same way as performance in reading depends on an awareness of the structure of the spoken language (see

Phonemic Awareness section in chap. 7, this volume). As we noted in our discussion of Rightstart, children need to be taught to appreciate quantity. The number line underlying quantity appears to be in place in some children as early as 5 years of age, but other children may not have this information or may not be able to access it automatically. Children who are at risk for failure in elementary school arithmetic and who do not receive training in appreciation of quantity do not perform as well on various mathematical tasks as do those who have. Remedial work with children at risk for failure involves specific training in the use of quantity and appears to improve their prospects for success in school.

9

EXPERTISE

Reading and arithmetic are just two of the many skills children need to acquire in school. A more general approach to the study of skill acquisition in all domains of knowledge has been developed under the title *acquisition of expertise* (Chi, Glaser, & Farr, 1988; Ericsson & Smith, 1991). Literacy and numeracy are examples of fields in which there are many experts, and a basic tenet of the cognitive study of expertise has been the idea that experts differ from novices on the basis of the information they have stored in memory about their domain of interest.

Expertise depends on being able to access material stored in memory rapidly and automatically. The failure of these automatic routines in situations such as listening to a foreign language or reading technical material makes people aware of how dependent they are on these skills. Investigators have studied expert performance by asking experts to explain what they do or to speak aloud as they carry out their skill (Ericsson & Smith, 1991), but expertise also involves internal operations hidden from experts that thus cannot be reported by them. For example, in comprehending sentences, multiple meanings of ambiguous words may become active below the level of awareness and be suppressed by context (Gernsbacher & Robertson, 1995). The skill of the expert reader then depends heavily on the ability to suppress meanings inappropriate in the present context. As we have seen in chapter 7 (this volume), prime stimuli invisible to the subject may still bias the activation of the target.

Middle Game

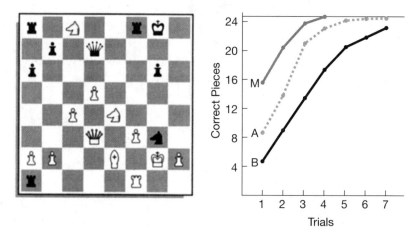

Random Middle Game

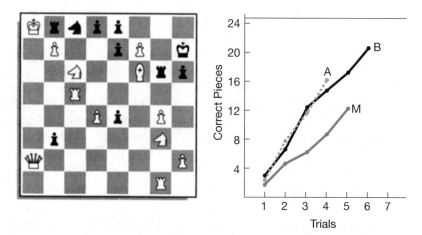

Figure 9.1. Studying performance in expert and novice chess players. On the top left is a master-level chess game and below it a random chessboard of about the same number of pieces. Data on reproduction of the board are shown on the right. Masters (M) are much better than others for the real game but no better than good players (A, B) for the random game. From "Perception in Chess," by W. G. Chase and H. A. Simon, 1973, *Cognitive Psychology, 4,* p. 60. Copyright 1973 by Elsevier. Reprinted with permission.

As described in chapter 1 (this volume), early work in the domain of expertise involved comparing the memory of chess masters to that of more ordinary players (Chase & Simon, 1973). Figure 9.1 shows the position of pieces from a master-level game. After a brief glance, the chess master could retain the position of all of the chess pieces on the board, provided they were in the orderly position expected from an actual game. An ordinary player could retain the position of only about 7 pieces. The reason for the difference was that the master was able to make a meaningful whole out of the disparate pieces. If the pieces were randomly placed, the master was little better than the ordinary player. Herbert Simon calculated that it might take 50,000 hours of practice to achieve the status of chess master.

Of course, few people become chess masters, but many people do acquire high-level skills in literacy and numeracy. A literate person has acquired expert-level performance in the visual recognition of words in his or her own language. Expertise is also clear from a person's ability to follow rapid speech in his or her native language. Speech appears to be divided into individual words, but in fact there are many pauses within as well as between words. High-level knowledge of the language imposes order for identifying words, in both speech and reading. Letters are chunked into words, and readers recognize every letter within a word better than if that letter had appeared in isolation.

In the previous two chapters, we reviewed literacy and numeracy, which are two school subjects that have strong biological bases in our species' ability to use language and number. Nonetheless, these skills require a long period of tuition before they reach adultlike levels. People in school also obtain an appreciation of areas of knowledge, such as history, science, or computers, that is based on learning new concepts and ideas. In this chapter, we emphasize some of the memory and conceptual systems required by this form of learning.

THE ROLE OF MEMORY IN EXPERTISE

When information is retrieved from semantic memory, it can be made available to consciousness through its temporary representation in working memory. Working memory is thought to be a buffer system that can temporarily hold information while it is related to other material. In this chapter, we first examine the structure of working memory as it has been revealed from imaging studies and consider how various forms of working memory are coordinated. Next, we turn to the acquisition of information and examine how the child learns to represent information in explicit form. The memory system is organized by the nature of the material that is stored. That is, the retrieval of facts about a domain such as animals or numbers temporarily improves the ability to activate associated material. As we have seen, this form of priming of related associations is an important feature of mental processes. Priming is a consequence of strong associations between material of similar semantic content. This form of semantic mapping has profound consequences on how memory is used throughout life. We examine how memory is organized and how this organization supports reasoning, imagery, concepts, and other thought processes.

Working memory is very closely associated with attention. Indeed, executive attention is a critical part of working memory. Items that have just recently been attended to tend to stay in an activated state called *activated state of working memory*. The executive attention network controls the reorganization and rehearsal within working memory.

Coding of Input

One of the best-known facts about memory is that the number of items that can be repeated back after a single presentation (memory span) is limited to about 7. Another is that the memory span develops over the early life of the child. Although both of these facts are true, they are highly misleading. As described in chapter 1 (this volume), a study involving 10 months of training of students at Carnegie Mellon University showed that their digit spans improved from the usual 7 to nearly 100 items (Ericsson & Chase, 1982). They had learned very specific coding rules relating input digits to highly specific track events, so that each set of 3 or 4 digits was given a unique and individual code. By developing a hierarchy of these scores, students were able to develop this unusual digit span. After days of reporting 100 digits, if the stimuli were shifted to letters, which were unrelated to their use of running time, their digit span fell again to 7. What had been learned was a method for chunking digits, not a general method of enlarging memory. In a similar way, much of the apparent development of memory in childhood is due to the child's increased familiarity with letters, digits, and other materials that make up memory tests (Chi, 1978).

Data from neuroimaging have provided a rich database for understanding the neural basis of working memory. Much of this work comes from positron emission tomography and functional magnetic resonance imaging (fMRI) studies of adults who are required to remember verbal material, nonverbal objects, or spatial locations (Smith, Jonides, Marshuetz, & Koeppe, 1998). The memory systems for isolated letters and digits are the most intensively studied. This focus is appropriate, because recoding incoming information into verbal form is probably the most commonly developed memory strategy in adults. Almost from birth, parents teach their children to recode events in the world in verbal form as a part of communication.

Studies of verbal memory over brief periods show strong areas of activity in the left frontal and parietal lobes. If subjects are asked to rehearse each item as it comes in but do not have to remember the items, the activity in the frontal area remains but activity in the more posterior area drops away. This finding suggests that the frontal area in and around classical Broca's area is involved in rehearsing the information (Awh & Jonides,

2001). In chapter 7 (this volume; see Figure 7.2), the frontal area was shown to involve articulatory coding. It appears that this same neural mechanism involved in speech and reading is also used in working memory. This finding fits well with the finding that the number of syllables contained in an utterance is an important basis for how much material can be stored in working memory.

The form of working memory that contrasts most strongly with the verbal system is memory for spatial location. Locations are very important for memory, even for verbal material. In fact, a frequently used method of remembering lists of verbal items is to associate each stored item with a particular location (the method of loci). The effectiveness of location as a method for improving memory presumably rests on the importance that finding one's way from place to place has had during the history of our species. When one has to remember exactly where a dot is located, there is frequently greater activity in the right hemisphere. As in the case of verbal memory, both frontal and posterior areas are active. However, rehearsal of spatial location involves mainly the posterior parietal site (Awh & Jonides, 2001), whereas storage appears to involve mainly frontal areas.

Components of Working Memory

It may seem odd that for verbal material, rehearsal mechanisms should be frontal, whereas for location they should be parietal (posterior). This fact probably represents a more general principle that methods for rehearsing material in memory build naturally on known output systems. In the case of verbal material, Broca's area is involved in the output of speech and in rehearsal by inner speech. In the case of location memory, rehearsal seems to involve the same parietal-based system involved in orienting to external objects. Because speech systems are left lateralized, and spatial attention often has a right bias (see chap. 3, this volume), the tendency for opposite lateralization of these two types of working memory is important in maintaining their separation.

The verbal and spatial working memory systems may overlap to some degree, and many tasks depend in part on both types of memory and thus activate both sets of brain areas. Thus, for example, there is less evidence for the strict separation of working memory for visual objects. This lack of evidence is likely due to the frequent use of the strategy of recoding objects into verbal form, which brings in the verbal working memory system in addition to the visual system.

Early views in cognitive psychology considered working memory as a single system for information processing and information storage that would serve as a gateway between sensory input and long-term memory (Atkinson & Shiffrin, 1968). This gateway view of a unitary system for working memory was challenged by data from dual-task experiments (Baddeley & Hitch, 1974) as well as by data from patients who showed normal long-term memory functions, despite impairments of working memory (Shallice & Warrington, 1970). Baddeley and Hitch (1974) originally proposed a multicomponent working memory. This model comprises three components. The central executive equivalent to what we have been calling executive attention provides coordination for two slave systems: a phonological loop and a visuospatial scratchpad. The phonological loop holds and manipulates verbal information and comprises a passive phonological store and an articulatory rehearsal process. The visuospatial scratchpad handles visual and spatial information. This view has been largely supported by the imaging results.

As we have indicated, there is evidence for the idea of separate brain areas in the working memory for verbal and spatial information, and some cognitive studies (Sanders & Schroots, 1968) have suggested that the memory span for mixtures of letters and locations is close to the sum of each taken individually. This conclusion fits with the separation between verbal and spatial rehearsal found in neuroimaging studies.

Both neural and cognitive evidence argue for separation of verbal and spatial information in working memory. Are these systems functionally separate? To test this idea, one needs to show that material is stored and retrieved either in one domain alone (e.g., verbal or spatial) or in the two together without causing interference in making the responses. The use of a full report method, as in memory span research, raises the problem of output interference of motor systems used for retrieval.

One test of the functional separation of visual and verbal working in our laboratory (Heidrich, 1990) examined the time it took to say whether a probe item was present in lists of either two or four stored locations or digits. In the pure blocks, the list was all of one kind (either locations or digits), but in the mixed blocks, there were either two or four pairs of items consisting of both a location and a digit. If the material were extracted and stored completely independently, one would expect exactly the same slope in the mixed blocks as in the pure blocks. However, if verbal and spatial information were in a common store, or if they interacted during retrieval, one would expect an increased slope. The results showed no significant slope increase in the mixed over the pure list. The lack of a general increase in slope between pure and mixed list for either locations or letters suggests that storage of the two materials is separate, and once the probe is properly classified, it is used to search only one of the two domains.

Individual Differences in Codes

There is also evidence that individuals differ in how they treat stimuli that can be coded in terms of visual representation or letter names. Within each individual, both types of codes are voluntarily available. According to the instruction or situation, a person may code a word or picture in verbal form or may retain the letters as a visual image. Imaging research has shown that attention to letter names activates brain areas related to storage and rehearsal of verbal information, whereas attention to the physical form of the letters activates visual areas. It would seem reasonable to equip the child with both types of coding, although in U.S. schools, verbal coding from visual input is stressed much more than is the reverse (Posner & Raichle, 1994).

Individuals differ greatly in their ability to carry out working memory tasks such as these. Working memory ability is a component of intelligence, and tests of working memory tend to be correlated with general intelligence test scores and with each other. A study of spatial working memory (Vogel & Machizawa, 2004) found a relatively pure measure of individual differences by recording lateralized electrical activity during the encoding and retrieval of spatial information. The information was presented to both visual fields, but persons were instructed to store and report only the information in one field. The number of elements in the visual field was systematically varied, and the amplitude of the lateralized activity increased with the number of items, reaching a maximum at the individual's working memory capacity (see Figure 9.2). Having an electrophysiological measure of working memory capacity not only allows increased ties to the underlying network involved but also gives the opportunity to examine genes that contribute to the differences among people. Because spatial working memory relies on rehearsal mechanisms related to the orienting attention network, genes involved in this network (see chap. 5, this volume) are good candidates.

Implicit Memory

Why does memory span improve with age? One reason is that the materials used (letters, digits, words) become more familiar and thus can be encoded and retrieved more easily than when they were novel. One does not have much recollection of how this kind of information is learned. It is acquired implicitly in the process of listening and reading.

The study of memory (Schacter, 1987; Squire, 1992) has identified two quite different forms of learning simple facts. Implicit learning occurs during the course of exposure to items and changes later encoding of related stimuli. We believe this form of learning is used to acquire the sequences of locations that infants can learn at 4 months (see chap. 3, this volume). Motor learning (e.g., learning to tie one's shoes or ride a bicycle) appears to rest on this form of learning. However, every type of memory probably has an implicit component. Explicit learning occurs through active conscious attention to the item and involves storage in a form that can be retrieved voluntarily by the subject in a variety of contexts.

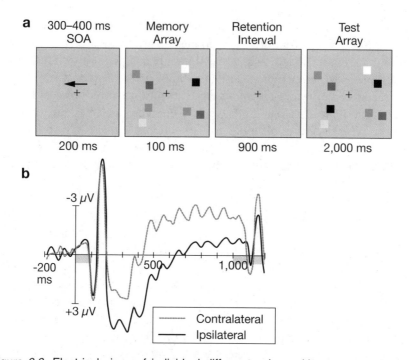

Figure 9.2. Electrical signs of individual differences in working memory. Panel *a* illustrates a working memory task in which people report as many items as possible from the array indicated by the arrow. The array size is varied over trials. Panel *b* shows the event-related potential from the two hemispheres. The hemisphere opposite the reported array shows more activity, and the amount of activity from this hemisphere is related to the size of the working memory span for that person. SOA = stimulus onset asynchrony (time between onset of one stimulus and onset of the next stimulus); µV = microvolts. From "Neural Activity Predicts Individual Differences in Visual Working Memory Capacity," by E. K. Vogel and M. G. Machizawa, 2004, *Nature, 428,* p. 748. Copyright 2004 by Macmillan Publishers Ltd. Reprinted with permission.

Imaging studies have identified important brain structures related to these forms of learning (Buckner et al., 1995; Squire et al., 1992). These studies have often used a form of cued recall. Subjects are first exposed to a list of words and are later asked to generate a response to a three-letter stem (stem completion). Stem completion can take place under implicit instructions to say the first word that comes to mind starting with the stem or under explicit instructions to generate a word from the prior list. During implicit generation, an area of the right posterior visual system appears reduced in blood flow for words that were presented previously, in comparison with words for which a new string has to be generated. Studies involving auditory presentation of the original word list find a similar alteration in blood flow for previously presented items within the auditory system. When explicit instructions are given, there is activation in both frontal and hippo-campal areas.

One intriguing result of the imaging studies was that priming reduced activation in right posterior visual areas when the original words were visually presented. This brain area has often been associated with the implicit storage of visual information. If less neuronal activity were needed in this area, it could indicate that, in this paradigm, the memory trace of the previously learned word was activated with greater efficiency by the three-letter cue. Improved efficiency would be indexed by a reduction in the neuronal activity needed to reactivate the visual code of the word stored from the prior exposure. However, because imaging studies did not provide a time course for the changed neuronal activity, it is also possible that the reduced blood flow merely means that when a word has been encountered before, less attention and effort are needed to generate a response to the three-letter cue. Less attention to the visual code of the primed word would also result in less blood flow than for unprimed items. In other words, the reduced activation of the right posterior area might either be automatic as the input came in or be generated later by differences in attention.

Scalp electrical recording is one method to determine which of these options is true (Badgaiyan & Posner, 1997). Badgaiyan and Posner's (1997) results suggest that the difference between primed and unprimed targets in this paradigm began by 100 milliseconds after the three-letter cue was presented. No difference between primed and unprimed targets was found in the last few hundred milliseconds before the response, where it would have been expected if it were due to the subjects working actively on the input string. Another important result of this study was that the right posterior reduction in blood flow was found irrespective of instructions. In this sense, the effect of the word on later string presentation was automatic regardless of the way the person was instructed. Such modification of early visual systems by new learning is likely the basis for the development of the visual word form system described in chapter 7 (this volume).

Other results from Badgaiyan and Posner's (1997) study suggest that the deliberate instruction to recall from the prior list differed from the priming instruction mainly in frontal areas that have been previously associated with semantic processing, and in the hippocampus, which has been linked with recall of previously learned events (see also Figure 9.3). When subjects were given implicit instructions and the word had been presented previously in the list, there was no frontal or hippocampal activation. These brain areas appear to be associated with volitional efforts to search the prior list or determine a related word.

These experiments used words, but there is clear evidence that any kind of information can be learned implicitly. No single network is involved in implicit memory; rather, the brain areas that code the information are altered so that the representation provides more efficient activation. We believe that all parts of the brain have the capacity to record information

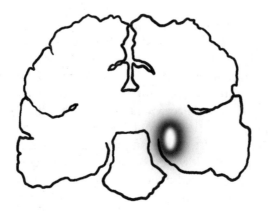

Figure 9.3. Hippocampal activation during a memory task. Instruction to report an item explicitly from memory is accompanied by activation in the hippocampus as shown by the oval (Buckner et al., 1995).

and alter their performance on the basis of experience. Thus implicit learning is a property of brain networks underlying all domains of human experience.

Explicit Memory

How is it that the child begins to develop the kinds of memory that can be retrieved at will as a particular learned episode? There is a great deal of evidence that adults cannot retrieve this form of explicit memory for events that occurred before about age 2. Efforts to get adults to recall information from their childhood usually reach a limit at around this age.

Neural Structures

The neural structures that have been most associated with the conscious recall of information lie within the temporal lobe and include areas in and around the hippocampus (see Figure 9.3 for an image of activation of this area). Damage to these brain areas can produce amnesia for explicit recall of information. These patients cannot bring to mind information learned after the injury, even after many exposures to the new information, such as meeting the same person each day. An amazing thing sometimes happens in amnesia induced by stroke, most often involving the hippocampus. A patient may have little conscious ability to recall items but still have the ability to show implicit retention of the same material. While denying any memory, they may still show high levels of performance based on the prior learning. This remarkable dissociation is important for school experiences. Children often acquire skills they have little explicit knowledge about. Much of what is called intuition probably rests on these unconscious skills.

When encouraged to guess about things they cannot remember, people may demonstrate a much better than chance performance.

Researchers have suggested that even infants and young children can demonstrate explicit memory when the method of imitation is used (Bauer, Wiebe, Carver, Waters, & Nelson, 2003). At birth, infants show a form of imitation that is illustrated by the protrusion of the tongue after the experimenter has carried out this gesture (Meltzoff & Borton, 1979). Imitation can be used to show a form of explicit memory in infants as young as 6 months of age because they seem able to reproduce a set of gestures previously shown to them. This memory seems to be limited to about 24 hours and only a single item. By 9 months, however, there is evidence that multiple items can be stored up to a month. By 20 months, these items can be retained for up to a year, and this is about the age from which adults can retrieve verbal memories.

Relation to Attention

In chapter 3 (this volume), we showed how the infants' eye movements could come to anticipate where a visual stimulus would be placed. At 4 months, there are real limitations in this process, because the attention system is not yet well developed enough to allow the resolution of conflict based on the context of the association. By about 2 years, attentional development is sufficient to allow context to have its influence. This form of learning may still be implicit, in that people may acquire the skill without being able to report anything about how it was learned. They have learned what location is coming next, but they do not yet know in any general sense what it is that they have learned.

In chapter 4 (this volume) we traced the development of higher level executive attention between 2 and 4 years of age and have used it to understand the acquisition of literacy and numeracy. It is also possible to see the slow gain in the ability to acquire explicit memories. One study examined improvements in reaction time (RT) for making key presses to a series of visual events that were presented in a repeating sequence (Thomas & Nelson, 2001). The subjects were instructed to respond as quickly as they could to each stimulus by pressing a key that was close to the stimulus. The responses of 4-, 7-, and 10-year-olds were compared with those of adults (see Figure 9.4). In one condition (implicit), the material was learned by exposure to the sequence alone. In most cases, the children showed very little verbal knowledge of the sequence or ability to predict where the next event would occur. In addition, their overall RTs showed little evidence of responses prior to the stimulus, which might have suggested anticipations. Subjects at all ages seemed to be processing the location of the stimulus and not anticipating it. Nonetheless, all groups showed clear evidence of having learned the sequence.

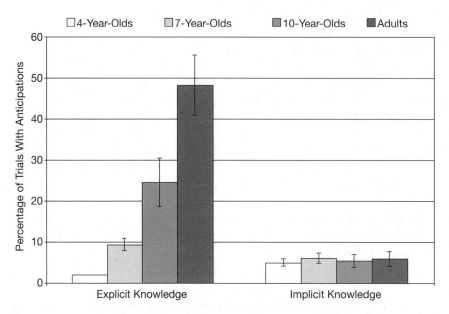

Figure 9.4. Development of sequence-learning skill. A regular sequence produces more explicit knowledge (as measured by higher levels of anticipation) in adults than in children. However, implicit knowledge of the same sequence results in similar levels of anticipation in adults and children (Thomas & Nelson, 2001).

Four-year-olds were much slower in overall RT and showed a slightly smaller percentage of improvement in the implicit condition, and all of the children made many more errors than did adults. An explicit condition was also examined in this study. In this condition, the subjects were given a demonstration of the sequence and clear verbal information about both what to expect next in the sequence and its nature. For adults, RTs dipped to close to 200 milliseconds, where many RTs were likely to be anticipations, that is, they were programmed before the presentation of the event. Many of the children, however, failed to generate or verbalize the sequence. As can be seen from Figure 9.4, there is little evidence that 4- and 7-year-old children benefited from the explicit information.

Some of the problem may be in children's learning and retaining the instruction, but we believe that children of this age also have difficulty in taking concepts present in one neural system (in this case the language system) and getting them to the appropriate brain system to implement them. Just as 5-year-olds can obtain the notion of quantity in the number line but have difficulty in getting the information to the motor system, 4-year-olds in this study might know the sequence information verbally but not be able to extend it so that it appropriately influences their responding. These data fit with findings in the same task in adults that explicit knowledge might be present in one system and still fail to influence responses in the implicit system.

The distinction between implicit and explicit knowledge is an important one for teachers to understand. Efforts with adults with amnesia to use their implicit knowledge to develop conscious recall have not generally proven successful. Thus it may prove difficult to develop curricula that can make explicit to the young the knowledge they may have gained implicitly. Exercises getting children to respond on the basis of feelings about what seems to them the correct answer might get children to reply on the basis of implicit knowledge. The success of Rightstart and word building in transferring training widely to number and reading tasks does provide some evidence that some forms of learning, even when they take place in preschool, have been shown to help children acquire school subjects more effectively.

EXPERT THOUGHT

People think in concepts. These concepts may not be precise, but they allow us to determine quickly if things are in the general neighborhood of what we have experienced before. When instructed to identify whether something is an animal, we will say yes quickly to a cow, but we need more time to agree that a salmon is an animal. A cow is a typical animal because it shares many properties with highly familiar animals, but a salmon does so to a much smaller degree. The distance effect for semantic categories is similar to the one we have encountered for number categories, and it probably has similar meaning. Just as numbers are stored in an analog number line, items similar in meaning tend to be stored closer together, where their connections are related to their degree of association. When one thinks about a category, one then tends to think about the central tendency or prototype of that category, rather than all of its members.

Although it is easy to impose a formal definition on the category "animal" that we might have learned in school, the memory system continues to reflect the more intuitive organization based on similarity of form, common elements, and other bases for shared relationships. Priming experiments give us a good way of seeing what items related to a given input are automatically activated when we think of a member of a category. Of course, we can also use our attention to overcome or restrict the boundary of activated items. In one experiment (Neely, 1977), people were taught to think "body part" when they saw the category name *animal*. When they did so, targets such as *arm* and *finger* were responded to more rapidly than were *dog* and *cat*. However, if the target was introduced very shortly after the prime, the person would still be fast to respond to the word *cow*, indicating that the animal category was automatically activated by the prime but became inhibited as attention was directed to the learned associations.

There is also a structure to categories. Categories such as *bird, chair,* or *ball* are basic categories, because their members are similar, have common parts, and tend to elicit the same response (Rosch, Mervis, Gray, Johnsen, & Boyes-Braem, 1976). Superordinate categories such as *animal, toy,* or *furniture* have diverse members with quite different forms. Unless one is an expert, subordinates of categories such as *robin* or *terrier* may not be well characterized. For nonexperts, the basic level is the easiest to use, but dog experts can find it easier to discriminate among types of terriers than to deal with the basic-level category of *dog* (Tanaka & Taylor, 1991).

Experts and Novices

Experts and novices use their memories in somewhat different ways. Work with children who are experts in dinosaurs and adults who are experts in physics (Chi & Koeske, 1983) has revealed the increased cohesiveness of their concepts in memory. Experts tend to use the relations among things in their thinking, whereas novices deal more with the surface features of individual instances. Experts use terms such as *because* and *if,* showing relationships, whereas novices tend to produce lists of features. In one study of students learning about psychology, investigators measured their ability to retrieve the names of well-known psychologists (Loftus & Fathi, 1985). Students with more experience tended to benefit from cues about the nature of the work the psychologists did or the field in which they made their contributions (e.g., behaviorists, cognitive psychologists), whereas beginning students tended to be helped most by a cue indicating the first letter of the name. It appeared that the organization of the material in the head was different depending on how much learning had taken place.

Mechanisms of Categories

We have presented a basis for understanding something about the neural systems that lie behind categories. Some categories are natural and can be used very early in development. An example of a natural category is *faces,* which can influence the infant's behavior at birth. It is believed that perception of faces in the first few months depends primarily on subcortical structures, but by 10 months there is clear evidence that infants are dealing with faces in a manner quite similar to adults (Johnson & Morton, 1991). For adults, faces activate an area of the posterior part of the fusiform gyrus, particularly on the right side, labeled the *fusiform face area.* This brain area probably has a role in organizing the features of the face into a whole so that the face can be recognized through processing of more anterior areas.

A more general function of this area has also been discovered, because experts in categories other than faces tend to show activation of this area for the material (e.g., dogs, birds, or automobiles) in which they are expert (Gautier, Tarr, Anderson, Skudlarsky, & Gore, 1999). This finding demonstrates how the function of a brain area initially associated with recognition of one category may, through training, come to be used by other categories.

A similar story underlies the visual word form area (see chap. 7, this volume). The word form area occupies a part of the fusiform gyrus that is mainly on the left and has been related to chunking visual letters into a unitary whole. However, there is evidence that visual objects involved in rapid naming tasks can use the same area. These findings suggest the importance of the operations performed on a particular brain area that may extend beyond any one kind of information. A particularly striking example of this plasticity is the use of the visual system in the recognition of Braille letters (Pascual-Leone & Hamilton, 2001). Although the visual system is specialized for visual stimuli, in this case, somatosensory information employed in the service of language can use visual mechanisms.

In general, expertise may involve the recruitment of posterior brain regions that can carry out crucial operations on input in an efficient way. Tanaka and Curran (2001) showed that experts in dogs and birds demonstrated changes in the event-related potentials often associated in infancy with the perception of faces. An early component of the event-related potential was associated with the recognition of familiar animals for dog and bird experts but not for novices. If this is a general neural mechanism, it provides a principle by which learning can develop an organization of posterior brain areas that can greatly improve the efficiency of handling concepts. This finding has significance for many areas of education in which expertise is a goal.

It has been possible to show that the amount of cortical tissue given over to an area of processing can reflect experience with that kind of processing. Merzenich and Jenkins (1995) studied the cortical representation of sensory information arising from a touch on the finger. They mapped out the brain area devoted to each finger within the somatosensory system of the monkey. They then trained the monkey for several months to make fine discriminations with one finger of the hand. After the training, the area of the cortex devoted to that finger expanded at the expense of surrounding fingers.

This same finding has been shown to apply to pianists and violinists who appear to have sensory and motor representations for the fine movements of their instruments that are far beyond those found in less involved areas (Elbert, Pantev, Wienbruch, Rockstroh, & Taub, 1995). In laboratory tests, a few hours of training with a particular sequence of movements was sufficient to increase the amount of the cortex activated by that sequence (Karni et al., 1998). This is an impressive achievement, because as in many situations, a few presentations actually decrease blood flow by shaping the neurons that will respond. This priming effect is rapid and ubiquitous and apparently gives way to a more structural change with long, sustained practice.

Semantic Maps

The reasons these learning results with monkeys and humans are so important is that there is evidence of some mapping of related items, at least for word and picture identification, within semantic areas of the left hemisphere (see Figure 7.2). When subjects were shown pictures of tools, animals, and so on, in an fMRI experiment, there was different activation within both frontal and posterior semantic processing areas for the different categories (Spitzer et al., 1998). It is still not fully known how many maps exist for different categories, and how similar maps for different kinds of categories might be. However, many observations suggest that brain lesions, particularly of the left posterior temporal lobe, can disrupt the ability to recognize specific categories of items, while leaving other categories completely intact.

Though the semantic priming, lesion, and neuroimaging data all suggest mapping of semantic areas by common features, there has always been some doubt about the underlying idea. However, maps of important features are very common in the visual, auditory, and motor systems, so it should not be too surprising that related items are stored in adjacent areas within semantic networks. Much work remains to be done to understand how this form of storage takes place and what form of organization might best foster high-level expertise.

Experience and Categorization

Some more or less direct evidence of the consequences of training in the natural environment is found in studies of processing letters and digits. We know that in most people, letters activate mainly left posterior sites (see chap. 7, this volume), whereas Arabic digits appear to have a strong bilateral activation (see chap. 8). A study comparing letters and digits directly confirmed that on the left, the letters produced far more activation than did the digits (Polk & Farah, 1998). Canadian postal workers are faced with stimuli that are mixtures of letters and digits (e.g., AF7 3UX) to an unusual degree compared with U.S. postal workers and other groups. Because of this intermixed experience, one might expect that brain areas set up for these two basic categories would be more alike than for control subjects (Polk et al., 2002). It was shown that it was easier for Canadian postal workers to find a digit among letters or a letter among digits than it was for those not used to dealing with mixed digits and letters. One interpretation is that letters and digits have a more mixed internal representation in the Canadian postal workers than in other groups not exposed to intermixed input. However, separation between digits and letters was found within a college population.

It is important for teachers to understand that they are shaping the way in which the brain will organize future information as they teach a given domain of knowledge. The basis of expertise is the organization of the memory system in the field of competence of the person. How does this organization support and direct our thought processes? It has been known since the earliest days of psychology that thought might be guided by associations between what is presently in front of the mind and related material stored in memory. Just as stimuli presented to the sense organs prime related items, so each item held in mind primes related thoughts. The research described earlier suggests an organization of material within semantic maps, so that once something is thought about in a particular way, it is more difficult to think about it in another way.

It is also important to keep in mind the finding that even sensory systems can be expanded in the amount of cortical space they occupy, with appropriate training. It would be expected that later developing maps based on semantic categories would be even stronger candidates for expansion and retraction with use. The idea of expanding semantic maps fits with subjective impressions of the frequency of intrusive thoughts or inappropriate interpretations of ambiguous stimuli and how strongly they are related to things people are working on consciously. When we were writing this book, ideas from imaging studies came to mind, often spontaneously and with little effort, but when we were on vacation, these thoughts did not occur.

It seems likely that a month decorating one's apartment would allow for more fluent generation in the naming of furniture, whereas a month spent at the zoo would have the same effect on interpreting animal pictures. Cortical tissue devoted to frequently experienced material expands. However, mere expansion of the cortical network is not enough. The information must also capture attention. The links between stored knowledge and attention capture form a topic of active research. It builds on the material in chapter 3 (this volume) to ask how knowledge stored in memory may influence current interests.

OTHER FORMS OF EXPERTISE

It is possible for humans to voluntarily take advantage of their sensory systems to create a representation, as is most clearly demonstrated by the ability to visually imagine a face, letter, word, or location. A major achievement of psychology has been the development of objective tests for sensory

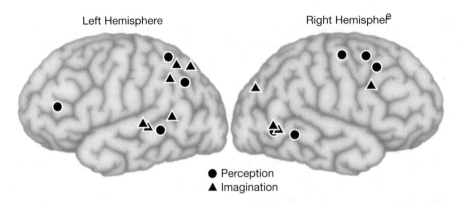

Left Hemisphere

Right Hemisphere

● Perception
▲ Imagination

Figure 9.5. Comparison of brain areas involved in perception and imagination. Imagined visual images (triangles) and actual visual perceptions (circles) of the same event produce activations in many of the same areas of the brain. From *Images of Mind* (p. 97), by M. I. Posner and M. E. Raichle, 1994, New York: Scientific American Books. Copyright 1994 by W. H. Freeman & Co. Adapted with permission.

representations created from memory (Kosslyn, 1980, 1996), such as having a subject imagine an uppercase letter at a particular angle of rotation and then observing the time it takes the subject to determine whether a target letter is correct or a mirror image (Cooper & Shepard, 1973). Some of these tests served as activation tasks for imaging studies and made it possible to work out the neural systems involved. Evidence (see Figure 9.5 for a summary) suggests that images take advantage of sensory systems. In the case of vision, the extrastriate cortex is involved, and in some cases, the primary visual cortex and the attention and language systems are involved (Kosslyn, Ganis, & Thompson, 2001).

Imagery

Images allow people to think in terms of concrete representations of the real or imagined world. This form of thought appears to be especially powerful in children, who often create imaginary companions and sometimes whole imaginary worlds and engage in play that takes advantage of this ability to imagine.

Imagery points to the importance of concrete representations as a support to thought processes. People, particularly children, tend to need sensory support for their more abstract thought processes. Just as there are differences among people in the acuity of their sensory systems, there are also vast individual differences in their awareness of images. Some people find that images intrude into their perception of the real world, whereas others are never consciously aware of having any visual representation that is not currently being presented to the sense organ. Imagery has proven particularly useful in helping long-term storage of information. In the method of loci, for example, people who image and store information of particular places along a familiar route acquire details that aid in later retrieval of the stored information.

Reasoning

A primary goal of schooling is to aid the child in the development of reasoning skills. As reviewed in chapter 1 (this volume), psychology has usually been seen as opposed to the idea that training in formal reasoning would automatically transfer to a broad range of subjects, but clearly the ability to form a reasoned discussion contributes in a wide variety of school subjects.

Although reasoning can involve a wide variety of skills, formal deduction provides a good model. One type of widely studied problem is the three-term syllogism. This problem can be stated in concrete or abstract form. The abstract form is in brackets; for example, all people are mortal [all X is Y]; I am a person [Z is an X]; therefore I am mortal [therefore Z is Y]. People do much better with the concrete than with the abstract form of the syllogism, particularly if the premises fit with knowledge they have of the real world. Imaging studies have indicated that concrete problems of this type engage mainly linguistic areas (Goel, Gold, Kapur, & Houle, 1998), but abstract problems may also involve spatial systems, possibly because solution of the problem draws on concrete images (Goel & Dolan, 2001).

Metaphor

More evidence of the importance of the concrete nature of human thought processes comes from the study of metaphor. Much of our reasoning involves the metaphorical use of concepts (Lakoff & Johnson, 1980). Our intuitive concepts tend to be organized around prototypical cases, making them very much more concrete than would be considered appropriate in formal logic. When we think of an animal, we often reason from a more specific instance such as a dog. Metaphors tend to map one semantic domain onto another. When we begin to learn new material, we may liken it to a journey and discuss how important it is to take the learning one step at a time, moving from one concept to another. We often liken memories to a picture. Understanding the new material involves "seeing" it. Or we think of our learning ability as a resource like gasoline for a car. If someone learns well, we say they will go a long way, but if they cannot express their new learning, they have "run out of ideas." Theories we encounter are often seen as buildings with foundations, and ideas that need support are too shaky to stand and will fall of their own weight.

In the view of Lakoff and Johnson (1980), adults do not have a choice as to whether to think metaphorically. These authors regard metaphorical maps as deeply embedded in the human brain, resting on the kind of graded concepts we described earlier in this chapter. Many metaphors are inevitably universal (e.g., life as a journey) because they depend on the nature of our common experience. Metaphors probably result from the common activation of language and concrete sensory and motor areas of the brain. An understanding of metaphorical thinking should be an important part of schooling, because it could help in both the construction and the understanding of arguments. It also teaches us to be aware of efforts to manipulate our thinking by others, who make metaphorical links that are appealing but that may lead to inappropriate reasoning.

SUMMARY

In this chapter we have attempted to go beyond literacy and numeracy to outline some general properties of all forms of human thought. Expertise depends on specific training of the domain in which it is sought. From studies of chess masters, we can infer that complex systems of human knowledge can require many years of acquisition. Much of this learning is implicit and may train the systems involved in solving problems of the domain of choice. In making this knowledge explicit in order to reason from it, attentional systems become engaged. Even when we carry out high-level abstract thinking, it is likely that sensory and motor areas of the brain give our thoughts concrete meaning. This form of conceptual representation may underlie the appeal of metaphorical arguments so common to discourse.

10

PREPARING FOR SCHOOL

In the overview of this book, we argued that

> it is our belief that the studies discussed in this volume provide a novel perspective on the acquisition of school subjects. The ability to learn literacy and numeracy appears to rest on specific brain networks involved in these subjects and also on attention networks, all of which are partly present prior to the start of formal schooling. Although in recent years parents and teachers have learned about the general importance of the first few years of life, they may not have realized the extent of specific learning about language, number, and attention that takes place. A combination of psychological and brain science studies have given us a window on the shaping of this knowledge early in life. (this volume, pp. 4–5)

This book gives primacy to the study of attentional networks because it is an important capacity that appears in infancy and early childhood and that is common to all people. Nonetheless, attentional networks vary in efficiency and can be shaped by experience. In this chapter, we summarize our argument for the importance of understanding and shaping brain networks, first for attention, then for language, and finally for numeracy. We further suggest that Web-based education can make the findings of brain science available to people everywhere.

ORIENTING OF ATTENTION

As discussed in chapter 3 (this volume), for the first few months infants are drawn to attend to novel objects by looking at them. During this period, not only their ability to see (visual acuity) but also their ability to orient attention improves week by week (see Figure 3.1). Infants also learn where they should put their eyes. In formal studies, infants exposed to visual objects at regular locations learn to anticipate these locations by moving their eyes even before the stimulus is presented (Clohessy, Posner, & Rothbart, 2001; Haith, Hazan, & Goodman, 1988). This laboratory skill is also important in their everyday life. Each culture has implicit rules about where one should place one's eyes during communication. Infants appear to learn these rules easily during this early period. Of course the eyes are not a perfect indicator of attention, because one can fixate at one location and attend at another, but they provide a fairly close indicator of where attention will be placed.

SELF-REGULATION

Whereas the orienting network develops most strongly in infancy, the executive attention network as outlined in chapter 4 (this volume) appears to develop from 2 to 7 years of age (Rueda, Fan, et al., 2004). Our training studies (chap. 5) suggest the possibility of improving the network in both 4- and 6-year-old children (Rueda, Rothbart, McCandliss, Saccamanno, & Posner, 2005). At both ages, 5 days of the training produced more adultlike performance than was found in the control group. Electroencephalogram recording data (see Figure 5.6) also indicated that activity in the anterior cingulate of the executive network was altered by the training. Generalization of the training to IQ test performance suggests that the training effects influence nontrained cognitive processes. The strength of this study is that the anatomy, neuromodulators, and genes involved in this network have been explored in prior studies, so it provides a model for viewing how experience with a particular network might improve its efficiency. It is not known if the improvement is confined to the period when the training took place or whether similar improvements might occur later in life.

Although parents and educators are quite familiar with the fact that self-regulation increases during childhood, they need to know that attention involves specific networks and can be improved by training. In the future we may use temperamental and even genetic differences among children to choose who might have the most difficulty with attention and who might benefit most from training. In addition, if attention training should prove useful in various forms of child psychopathology, it might provide a means of intervening early, before the pathological condition strongly influences the child's life.

As discussed in chapter 5 (this volume), the efficiency of brain networks related to attention has been related to specific genes. The orienting network develops in the 1st year of life (chap. 3). Studies using neuropharmacology in alert monkeys suggest that the network underlying orienting of attention is modulated by the cholinergic system (Marrocco & Davidson, 1998). Parasuraman, Greenwood, Kumar, and Fossella (2005) genotyped their subjects and examined performance in visual search tasks known to involve orienting of attention. They found alleles of two genes to be related to the efficiency of performance on these tasks. In a similar way, the later developing executive attention network is modulated by dopamine, and the efficiency of this network has been shown to be related to four dopamine genes (Fossella et al., 2002). Alleles of two of those genes were used in imaging studies done while the subjects performed the Attention Network Test (Fan, Fossella, Sommer, Wu, & Posner, 2003). The alleles were found to be related to differences in the strength of activation of the anterior cingulate, an important node of the executive attention network.

These genetic studies are based on the efficiency with which people with differing alleles activate the relevant attention network. It is likely that the same genes are important in building the networks that are common to all people. Thus it appears likely that there is genetic selection of brain areas recruited by skills such as reading and number processing, making it possible that we may eventually understand how different alleles influence the difficulty of acquiring these skills.

LANGUAGE

As discussed in chapter 7 (this volume), infants come into the world with the capability of discriminating among the units of language (phonemes) in all of the world's languages. That is, if one phoneme is sounded over and over again (e.g., *ba*) so that its novelty effects are reduced, a recovery occurs when a different phoneme is heard (e.g., *da*), which provides evidence of discrimination. The infant auditory system is capable of learning the phonemes to which it will be exposed, and in the period between 6 and 10 months there is a considerable shaping of this phonemic structure (P. K. Kuhl, 2000). Sounds to which the infant is exposed tend to solidify and form a unit around prototypical phonemes in the language, whereas the ability to discriminate unfamiliar sound units from familiar ones begins to disappear. Infants raised in English-speaking homes can maintain their ability to discriminate phonemes in a foreign language, such as Mandarin Chinese, if exposed to a speaker of those sounds during this 6- to 10-month period (P. K. Kuhl, Tsao, & Liu, 2003). However, learning unfortunately did not occur when the exposure was to a video rather than to an actual person. Current research is attempting to determine the most important aspects of the social interactions that shape language in hopes of determining whether a media presentation incorporating them could be designed. These findings and others like them show that the infants' auditory system is being trained by the speech patterns of their community.

Experiments with infants have also shown that the effectiveness of this training can be assayed by changes in scalp-recorded event-related potentials following a change from a frequent to an infrequent phoneme (Cheour et al., 1997; Guttorm et al., 2005; Molfese, 2000). The brain shows its discrimination between the two by responding differently when the novel phoneme occurs. Brain activity can be used to reveal whether or not the infant is making the discrimination between phonemes. This electrical difference serves as a measure of the efficiency of the brain in making the discrimination. Thus the effectiveness of caregivers in establishing the phonemic structure of their native and also of additional languages that they might desire to teach can be examined. It is also possible to predict later difficulties in spoken language and in reading from these recordings (Guttorm et al., 2005; Molfese, 2000). Recent methods for combining data from six electrode sites suggest that high accuracy can be obtained from infant recordings in predicting difficulties in acquisition of literacy (Kook, Gupta, Molfese, & Fadem, 2005). These methods make it possible to check for the development of a strong phonemic structure by use of electrical recording in early life, just as brain-stem event-related potentials are now widely used to allow early detection of hearing deficits in infants.

Numerous studies have shown that the skill of reading depends heavily on the child's success in having stored phonemes and being able to use them effectively (Stanovich, Cunningham, & Cramer, 1984). For example, studies of phonemic awareness have shown that the ability to segment auditory words serves as a predictor of future success in acquiring literacy. It would be useful to assess the success of parental instruction concerning phonemes without the need for expensive and time-consuming electrical recording. In fact, this assessment should be possible. If infants' attention is brought to a compelling visual stimulus to which they orient, they will turn their head in the direction of a novel auditory event (P. K. Kuhl, 2000). It should be possible to deliver these visual and auditory stimuli over the Web and allow the caregiver to assess the effectiveness of the child's learning. It seems likely that a clear and observable understanding of what the child is learning will motivate adults to provide a linguistic environment designed to shape the auditory system in a way that will prepare for future reading. We believe that the development of appropriate Web-based information on phonemic analysis, its role in reading, and methods to assess its effectiveness should have a high priority. This development would allow further parental understanding of the importance and effectiveness of their educational efforts.

NUMERACY

As suggested in chapter 8 (this volume) there is also evidence that areas of the brain involving an appreciation of number are carrying out number line functions during infancy (Berger, Tzur, & Posner, in press; Feigenson, Dehaene, & Spelke, 2004; Wynn, 1992). Infants appreciate the quantity of small numbers and can express their surprise at incorrect arithmetic operations in behavior (Wynn, 1992) and in brain activity (Berger et al., 2006).

Some children continue to have difficulty making the connection between a number stimulus and information about its quantity. These children are at risk for failure when they need to learn aspects of elementary school mathematics. The program Rightstart gave children at risk for failure in school a yearlong program of remediation that stressed the connection between numerical input and quantity (Griffin, Case, & Siegler, 1995). After the program, trained students were better able to succeed in elementary school math than were those who did not receive the training. A recent effort that trained students on quantity with a computerized program that will be made available on the Web also showed evidence of improvement following the training (Wilson, Dehaene, Rivkin, Cohen, & Cohen, 2006).

WEB-BASED EDUCATION

These discoveries have led a number of researchers under the leadership of the Center for Educational Research and Innovation of the Organisation for Economic Co-operation and Development to develop a Web site (http://www.teach-the-brain.org) to begin the process of developing educational experience based on brain research starting early in life. The Web site is a good start at using the Web to introduce different public audiences to brain-based research.

So far three programs have been developed for Web delivery: They address attention training (Rueda et al., 2005), literacy (McCandliss, Beck,

Sandak, & Perfetti, 2000), and numeracy (Wilson et al., 2006). Users need to access the Web site and then download the programs for use with their own computers. However, our goal is fully interactive programs that can simultaneously deliver services and collect relevant data on their use. In this way, the programs will be able to foster the research that can lead to updates and improvements.

Although some research shows that the use of these programs can lead to improvement and change aspects of brain function, there is as yet no reason to suppose that they are optimal. Rather, the site informs various public audiences about the research and the links between research and the programs that have been developed. In addition, many commercial programs of a somewhat similar nature are being sold to the public. We intend to include links to those programs with substantial research support as well as a discussion of the programs that have not been tested or have failed to live up to their commercial expectations.

Although many implications of brain research have been noted in this volume for very early education either before the start of formal schooling or in the early years of school, some findings can be related to the development of later skills (see chap. 9, this volume). For example, in chapter 7 we discuss research that has attempted to trace the development of the visual word form system from 4 years through 10 years of age (Posner & McCandliss, 1999). Findings suggest that the system starts to develop rather late, changing from a system mainly operating on familiar words to one that operates on the rules governing English orthography. This kind of study has relevance to the methodology that might be best followed for children acquiring genuine expertise in the skill of reading (see chap. 7). Other skills such as expert perception of visual objects also seem to show that they develop by gaining access to posterior systems that may have been used earlier for other stimuli (see chap. 9). Future research may help in the development of high levels of expertise for complex concepts. Brain imaging (chap. 2) may help by providing information necessary to determine how a given form of practice influences a particular part of the network underlying the skill.

A reasonable goal for the Web-based system would be to synthesize reading, attention, and numeracy exercises into children's development of improved comprehension of scientific documentation, including the weighing of evidence, the appreciation of graphs and charts and mathematical formulations, and the understanding of scientific communication. It is widely believed that such knowledge is important in the development of a global workforce appropriate for the 21st century and would be a worthy goal of a curriculum to aid children in all countries in obtaining this kind of knowledge.

FUTURE STUDIES

This chapter completes our story of human brain development in relation to attention and high-level skills. The future for this kind of investigation seems bright. In this final section we examine some of these hopes in the context of what has been accomplished so far.

The advent of neuroimaging has opened an important new window on brain development (chap. 2, this volume). Many of the benefits await the further exploitation of methods of pediatric neuroimaging. However, even with the relatively few studies involving children done so far, we are beginning to get a picture of important aspects of brain development.

Imaging affords the opportunity to examine functional activity and connectivity within the living human brain. Because of technological advances, structural imaging will increasingly allow us to see the size of individual brain areas as they change during development. Functional imaging will enable the tracing of changes in the pathways and the extent of activation in common tasks as they are learned in childhood. Diffusion tensor imaging will allow observation of the myelination of pathways connecting brain areas. Recording electrical activity from the scalp will show whether a pathway is producing correlated activity at remote locations indicative of the sharing of information. It is already known that the brains of children tend to shift in development from local computations to more global computations as the pathways connecting neural areas increase (Srinivasan, 1999).

It is possible to speculate on what might be found from the combination of the methodologies discussed earlier. Although the basic building blocks for reading (phonemic analysis) and for numeracy (the number line) are already present in the infant brain, the ability of the infant to learn to read or calculate is absent. These developments probably depend on two things: the maturation of more frontal areas allowing access to executive attention and connections between phonemic or number line areas and these frontal areas. Already Klingberg et al. (2000) have shown that in the brains of people with dyslexia, something about the connections between language areas is different. What is not yet known but can be found out is whether these problems are the cause of poor reading, or the result. Efforts to trace the development of these networks are just beginning (Nagy, Westerberg, & Klingberg, 2004). Nagy et al. (2004) showed that development of white-matter pathways underlying specific posterior areas is correlated with reading ability and working memory in children ages 8 to 18. If we can trace the development of these networks prior to reading and learn when they function correctly, we should be able to determine if they are the cause of reading difficulties and if instruction alters their development. In a similar way, we can ask if instruction about how numbers are related to quantity (see chap. 8, this volume) will improve the number line area itself or change the efficiency with which the number line area communicates with other crucial areas.

Whereas neuroimaging has provided an important perspective on the general development of the human brain, work on infant and child temperament (chaps. 2 and 6, this volume) has revealed important differences between children in their reaction to the sensory environment and in the ease with which they gain control of their emotions, thoughts, and behaviors. It is now possible to study the genetic and environmental contributions to these individual differences (chap. 5). The development of the networks underlying effortful control depends on specific genes, a few of which have already been identified. It has also been shown that specific training in cases of brain injury and psychiatric disorders and in normal children can alter attentional networks.

The mechanisms of effortful control also form the basis for the acquisition of subjects learned in school, such as literacy (chap. 7, this volume), numeracy (chap. 8), and the acquisition of expertise (chap. 9), in the many domains that form the basis of cultural knowledge. The future will bring a greater understanding of exactly what alterations of brain networks occur as the result of interventions at various ages. Such an understanding gives promise of being able to aid the growth of normal children and improve the prospects of a wide variety of developmental pathologies such as attention-deficit/hyperactivity disorder, autism, and personality disorders (Rothbart & Posner, 2006). Already, in the case of depression, convincing evidence shows that pharmacological and behavioral interventions both provide somewhat effective therapies but do so on very different networks (Goldapple et al., 2004). Imaging can shed light on what therapy to use on which people to achieve the best outcome.

As with therapy, the educational system can also benefit from an understanding of how various aspects of the curriculum, such as the acquisition of literacy and numeracy, influence brain networks. It seems likely that what are often viewed as opposing approaches to reading influence different parts of the network underlying the skill. In this book we have laid the foundation for considering the development of attention as a critical condition for the achievement of successful socialization in all of its emotional and cognitive aspects. There is much to learn in this domain, but the tools currently in place and certain to be developed will aid in the achievement of new knowledge in this area.

REFERENCES

Abdullaev, Y. G., & Posner, M. I. (1998). Event-related brain potential imaging of semantic encoding during processing single words. *NeuroImage, 7,* 1–13.

Adler, A. (1946). *Understanding human nature* (W. B. Wolfe, Trans.). New York: Greenberg.

Adolphs, R., Tranel, D., Hamann, S., Young, A. W., Calder, A. J., Phelps, E. A., et al. (1999). Recognition of facial emotion in nine individuals with bilateral amygdala damage. *Neuropsychologia, 37,* 1111–1117.

Ahadi, S. A., Rothbart, M. K., & Ye, R. (1993). Children's temperament in the U.S. and China: Similarities and differences. *European Journal of Personality, 7,* 359–378.

Anderson, A. K., & Phelps, E. A. (2001, May 17). Lesions of the human amygdala impair enhanced perception of emotionally salient events. *Nature, 411,* 305–309.

Ansari, D., Garcia, N., Lucas, E., Hamon, K., & Dhital, B. (2005). Neural correlates of number process in children and adults. *NeuroReport, 16,* 1769–1773.

Ashby, F. G., Isen, A. M., & Turken, U. A. (1999). Neuropsychological theory of positive affect and its influence on cognition. *Psychological Review, 106,* 529–550.

Assor, A., Roth, G., & Deci, E. L. (2004). The emotional costs of parents' conditional regard: A self-determination theory analysis. *Journal of Personality, 72,* 47–88.

Atkinson, R. C., & Shiffrin, R. M. (1968). Human memory: A proposed system and its control processes. In K. W. Spence & J. T. Spence (Eds.), *The psychology of learning and memory* (Vol. 2, pp. 89–195). New York: Academic Press.

Auerbach, J., Geller, V., Lezer, S., Shinwell, E., Belmaker, R. H., Levine, J., & Ebstein, R. P. (1999). Dopamine D4 receptor (D4DR) and serotonin transporter promoter (5-HTTLPR) polymorphisms in the determination of temperament in 2-month-old infants. *Molecular Psychiatry, 4,* 369–373.

Ausubel, D. P. (1996). *Ego development and psychopathology.* New Brunswick, NJ: Transaction Publishers.

Awh, E., & Jonides, J. (2001). Overlapping mechanisms of attention and spatial working memory. *Trends in Cognitive Sciences, 5,* 119–126.

Ayduk, O., Mendoza-Denton, R., Mischel, W., Downey, G., Peake, P. K., & Rodriguez, M. (2000). Regulating the interpersonal self: Strategic self-regulation for coping with rejection sensitivity. *Journal of Personality and Social Psychology, 79,* 776–792.

Baddeley, A., & Hitch, G. (1974). Working memory. In G. A. Bower (Ed.), *Recent advances in learning and motivation* (pp. 47–90). New York: Academic Press.

Badgaiyan, R., & Posner, M. I. (1997). Time course of cortical activations in implicit and explicit recall. *Journal of Neuroscience, 17*, 4904–4913.

Baldwin, D. A. (1991). Infant contribution to the achievement of joint reference. *Child Development, 62*, 875–890.

Bandura, A. (1989). Human agency in social cognitive theory. *American Psychologist, 44*, 1175–1184.

Bates, J. E., Pettit, G. S., & Dodge, K. A. (1995). Family and child factors in stability and change in children's aggressiveness in elementary school. In J. McCord (Ed.), *Coercion and punishment in long-term perspectives* (pp. 124–138). New York: Cambridge University Press.

Bauer, P. J., Wiebe, S. A., Carver, L. J., Waters, J. M., & Nelson, C. A. (2003). Developments in long-term explicit memory late in the first year of life: Behavioral and electrophysiological indices. *Psychological Science, 14*, 629–635.

Beauregard, M., Levesque, J., & Bourgouin, P. (2001). Neural correlates of conscious self-regulation of emotion. *Journal of Neuroscience, 21*, RC165.

Benes, F. (1995). A neurodevelopmental approach to the understanding of schizophrenia and other mental disorders. In D. Cichetti & D. J. Cohen (Eds.), *Developmental psychopathology: Vol. 1. Theory and methods* (pp. 227–253). New York: Wiley.

Benes, F. (1999). Model generation and testing to probe neural circuitry in the cingulate cortex of postmortem schizophrenic brains. *Schizophrenia Bulletin, 24*, 219–229.

Berger, A., Tzur, G., & Posner, M. I. (in press). Infant brains detect arithmetic errors. *Proceedings of the National Academy of Sciences of the USA*.

Blair, C. (2003). Behavioral inhibition and behavioral activation in young children: Relations with self-regulation and adaptation to preschool in children attending Head Start. *Developmental Psychobiology, 42*, 301–311.

Blair, R. J. R., Jones, L., Clark, F., & Smith, M. (1997). The psychopathic individual: A lack of responsiveness to distress cues? *Psychophysiology, 34*, 192–198.

Blanchard, D. C., & Takahashi, S. N. (1988). No change in intermale aggression after amygdala lesions which reduce freezing. *Physiology and Behavior, 42*, 613–616.

Blasi, G., Mattay, G. S., Bertolino, A., Elvevåg, B., Callicott, J. H., Das, S., et al. (2005). Effect of catechol-O-methyltransferase val[158]met genotype on attentional control. *Journal of Neuroscience, 25*, 5038–5045.

Block, J. H., & Block, J. (1980). The role of ego-control and ego-resiliency in the organization of behaviour. In W. A. Collins (Ed.), *Minnesota Symposia on Child Psychology: Vol. 13. Development of cognition, affect, and social relations* (pp. 39–101). Hillsdale, NJ: Erlbaum.

Bohart, A. C., & Stipek, D. J. (Eds.). (2001). *Constructive and destructive behavior: Implications for family, school, and society*. Washington, DC: American Psychological Association.

Botvinick, M. M., Braver, T. S., Barch, D. M., Carter, C. S., & Cohen, J. D. (2001). Conflict monitoring and cognitive control. *Psychological Review, 108*, 624–652.

Bowlby, J. (1969). *Attachment and loss* (Vol. 1). New York: Basic Books.

Boysen, S. T., & Berntson, G. G. (1996). Quantity-based interference and symbolic representation in chimpanzees (*Pan troglodytes*). *Journal of Experimental Psychology: Animal Behavior Processes, 22*, 76–86.

Bramlett, R. K., Scott, P. L., & Rowell, R. K. (2000). A comparison of temperament and social skills in predicting academic performance in first graders. *Special Services in Schools, 16*, 147–158.

Broadhurst, P. L. (1975). The Maudsley reactive and nonreactive strains of rats: A survey. *Behavioral Genetics, 5*, 299–319.

Broca, P. (1861). Perti de parole, remollissement chronique et destruction partielle du lobe anterieur gauche du cerveau [Loss of speech, chronic softening and partial destruction of the anterior lobe of the brain]. *Bulletin de la Societé Anthropologique Paris, 2*, 235–238.

Brown, J. R., Ye, H., Bronson, R. T., Dikkes, P., & Greenberg, M. (1996). A defect in nurturing in mice lacking the immediate early gene fosB. *Cell, 86*, 297–309.

Bruer, J. T. (1999). *The myth of the first three years of life.* New York: Free Press.

Bruner, J. S. (1960). *The process of education.* Cambridge, MA: Harvard University Press.

Brush, F. R., Gendron, C. M., & Isaacson, M. D. (1999). A selective genetic analysis of the Syracuse high- and low-avoidance (SHA/Bru and SLA/Bru) strains of rats (*Rattus norvegicus*). *Behavioral Brain Research, 106*, 1–11.

Buckner, R. L., Petersen, S. E., Ojemann, J. G., Meizin, F. M., Squire, L. R., & Raichle, M. E. (1995). Functional anatomic studies of explicit and implicit memory retrieval tasks. *Journal of Neuroscience, 15*, 12–29.

Bush, G., Frazier, J. A., Rauch, S. L., Seidman, L. J., Whalen, P. J., Rosen, B. R., & Biederman, J. (1999). Anterior cingulate cortex dysfunction in attention deficit/hyperactivity disorder revealed by fMRI and the counting Stroop. *Biological Psychiatry, 45*, 1542–1552.

Bush, G., Luu, P., & Posner, M. I. (2000). Cognitive and emotional influences in anterior cingulate cortex. *Trends in Cognitive Sciences, 4*, 215–222.

Buss, A. H., & Plomin, R. (1975). *A temperament theory of personality development.* New York: Wiley.

Buss, A. H., & Plomin, R. (1984). *Temperament: Early developing personality traits.* Hillsdale, NJ: Erlbaum.

Butcher, P. R., Kalverboer, A. F., & Geuze, R. H. (1999). Inhibition of return in very young infants: A longitudinal study. *Infant Behavior and Development, 22*, 303–319.

Butcher, P. R., Kalverboer, A. F., & Geuze, R. H. (2000). Infants' shifts of gaze from a central to a peripheral stimulus: A longitudinal study of development between 6 and 26 weeks. *Infant Behavior and Development, 23*, 3–21.

Calder, A. J., Lawrence, A. D., & Young, A. W. (2001). Neuropsychology of fear and loathing. *Nature Reviews: Neuroscience, 2,* 352–363.

Calkins, S., & Williford, A. (2003, April). Anger regulation in infancy: Consequences and correlates. In S. C. Crockenberg & E. M. Leerkes (Cochairs), *How infants regulate negative emotions: What is effective? What is adaptive?* Symposium presentation at the biennial meeting of the Society for Research in Child Development, Tampa, FL.

Canli, T., Zhao, Z., Desmond, J. E., Kang, E., Gross, J., & Gabrieli, J. D. E. (2001). An fMRI study of personality influences on brain reactivity to emotional stimuli. *Behavioral Neuroscience, 115,* 33–42.

Cantlon, J. F., Brannon, E. M., Carter, E. J., & Pelphrey, K. A. (2006). Functional imaging of numerical processing in adults and 4-year-old children. *Public Library of Science: Biology, 4,* 844–854.

Carlson, S. M., & Moses, L. J. (2001). Individual differences in inhibitory control and children's theory of mind. *Child Development, 72,* 1032–1053.

Carter, C. S., Botvinick, M. M., & Cohen, J. D. (1999). The contribution of the anterior cingulate cortex to executive processes in cognition. *Reviews in Neuroscience, 10,* 49–57.

Carter, C. S., Braver, T. S., Barch, D. M., Botvinick, M. M., Noll, D., & Cohen, J. D. (1998, May 1). Anterior cingulate cortex, error detection and on line monitoring of performance. *Science, 280,* 747–749.

Casey, B. J., Durston, S., & Fossella, J. (2001). Evidence for a mechanistic model of cognitive control. *Clinical Neuroscience Research, 4,* 267–282.

Casey, B. J., Trainor, R., Giedd, J., Vauss, Y., Vaituzis, C. K., Hamburger, S., et al. (1997). The role of the anterior cingulate in automatic and controlled processes: A developmental neuroanatomical study. *Developmental Psychobiology, 3,* 61–69.

Casey, B. J., Trainor, R. J., Orendi, J. L., Schubert, A. B., Nystrom, L. E., Giedd, J. N., et al. (1997). A developmental functional MRI study of prefrontal activation during performance of a go-no-go task. *Journal of Cognitive Neuroscience, 9,* 835–847.

Chase, W. G., & Simon, H. A. (1973). Perception in chess. *Cognitive Psychology, 4,* 55–81.

Cheatham, P. G., & White, C. T. (1954). Temporal numerosity III: Auditory perception of number. *Journal of Experimental Psychology, 47,* 425–428.

Cheour M., Alho, K., Sainio, K., Reinikainen, K., Renlund, M., Aaltonen, O., et al. (1997). The mismatch negativity to changes in speech sounds at the age of three months. *Developmental Neuropsychology, 13,* 167–174.

Chi, M. T. H. (1978). Knowledge structures and memory development. In R. S. Siegler (Ed.), *Children's thinking: What develops?* Hillsdale, NJ: Erlbaum.

Chi, M. T. H., Glaser, R., & Farr, M. J. (Eds.). (1988). *The nature of expertise.* Hillsdale, NJ: LEA.

Chi, M. T. H., & Koeske, R. D. (1983). Network representation of a child's dinosaur knowledge. *Developmental Psychology, 19*, 29–39.

Chochon, F., Cohen, L., van de Moortele, P. F., & Dehaene, S. (1999). Differential contributions of the left and right inferior parietal lobules to number processing. *Journal of Cognitive Neuroscience, 11*, 617–630.

Chua, H. F., Boland, J. E., & Nisbett, R. E. (2005). Cultural variation in eye movements during scene perception. *Proceedings of the National Academy of Sciences of the USA, 102*, 12629–12633.

Cicchetti, E., & Rogosch, F. A. (1996). Equifinality and multifinality in developmental psychopathology. *Development and Psychopathology, 8*, 597–600.

Clark, V. P., & Hillyard, S. A. (1996). Spatial selective attention affects only extrastriate but not striate components of the visual evoked potential. *Journal of Cognitive Neuroscience, 8*, 387–402.

Clifford, M. M. (1984). Thoughts on a theory of constructive failure. *Educational Psychologist, 2*, 108–120.

Clohessy, A. B., Posner, M. I., & Rothbart, M. K. (2001). Development of the functional visual field. *Acta Psychologica, 106*, 51–68.

Clohessy, A. B., Posner, M. I., Rothbart, M. K., & Vecera, S. P. (1991). The development of inhibition return in early infancy. *Journal of Cognitive Neuroscience, 3*, 345–350.

Cloninger, C. R. (1986). A unified biosocial theory of personality and its role in the development of anxiety states. *Psychiatric Developments, 3*, 167–226.

Cohen, L., Martinaud, O., Lemer, C., Lehericy, S., Samson, Y., Obadia, M., et al. (2003). Visual word recognition in the left and right hemispheres: Anatomical and functional correlates of peripheral alexias. *Cerebral Cortex, 13*, 1313–1333.

Connell, J. P., & Wellborn, J. G. (1991). Competence, autonomy, and relatedness: A motivational analysis of self-system processes. In M. R. Gunnar & L. A. Sroufe (Eds.), *Minnesota Symposia on Child Psychology* (Vol. 23, pp. 43–77). Hillsdale, NJ: Erlbaum.

Conturo, T. E., Lori, N. F., Cull, T. S., Akbudak, E., Snyder, A. Z., Shimony, J. S., et al. (1999). Tracking neuronal fiber pathways in the living human brain. *Proceedings of the National Academy of Sciences of the USA, 96*, 10422–10427.

Cooper, L. A., & Shepard, R. N. (1973). Mental rotation of letters. In W. G. Chase (Ed.), *Visual information processing*. New York: Academic Press.

Corbetta, M., & Shulman, G. L. (2002). Control of goal-directed and stimulus-driven attention in the brain. *Nature Reviews: Neuroscience, 3*, 201–215.

Covington, M. V. (1992). *Making the grade: A self worth perspective on motivation and school reform*. New York: Cambridge University Press.

Covington, M. V. (1998). *The will to learn: A guide for motivating young people*. New York: Cambridge University Press.

Crick, F. H. C., & Watson, J. D. (1954). The complementary structure of deoxyribonucleic acid. *Proceedings of the Royal Society of London. Series A, Mathematical and Physical Sciences, 223*, 80–96.

Crottaz-Herbett, S., & Mennon, V. (2006). Where and when the anterior cingulated cortex modulates attentional response: Combined fMRI and ERP evidence. *Journal of Cognitive Neuroscience, 18,* 766–780.

Damasio, A. (1994). *Descartes' error.* New York: Avon Books.

Davidson, M. C., & Marrocco, R. T. (2000). Local infusion of scopolamine into intraparietal cortex slows covert orienting in rhesus monkeys. *Journal of Neurophysiology, 83,* 1536–1549.

Davidson, R. J. (2000). Affective style, psychopathology and resilience: Brain mechanisms and plasticity. *American Psychologist, 55,* 1196–1214.

Davidson, R. J., Putnam, K. M., & Larson, C. L. (2000, November 10). Dysfunction in the neural circuitry of emotion regulation—A possible prelude to violence. *Science, 289,* 591–594.

Davis, M., Hitchcock, J. M., & Rosen, J. B. (1987). Anxiety and the amygdala: Pharmacological and anatomical analysis of the fear-potentiated startle paradigm. In G. Bower (Ed.), *The psychology of learning and motivation: Advances in research and theory* (Vol. 21, pp. 263–305). San Diego, CA: Academic Press.

Dehaene, S. (1996). The organization of brain activations in number comparison: Event-related potentials and the additive-factors method. *Journal of Cognitive Neuroscience, 8,* 47–68.

Dehaene, S. (1997). *The number sense.* New York: Oxford University Press.

Dehaene, S., Dupoux, E., & Mehler, J. (1990). Is numerical comparison digital? Analogical and symbolic effects in two-digit number comparison. *Journal of Experimental Psychology: Human Perception and Performance, 16,* 626–641.

Dehaene, S., Kerszberg, M., & Changeux, J.-P. (1998). A neuronal model of a global workspace in effortful cognitive tasks. *Proceedings of the National Academy of Sciences of the USA, 95,* 14529–14534.

Dehaene, S., Posner, M. I., & Tucker, D. M. (1994). Localization of a neural system for error detection and compensation. *Psychological Science, 5,* 303–305.

Dehaene, S., Spelke, E., Pinel, P., Stanescu, R., & Tsivkin, S. (1999, May 7). Sources of mathematical thinking: Behavioral and brain-imaging evidence. *Science, 284,* 970–974.

Dehaene-Lambertz, G., Dehaene, S., & Hertz-Pannier, L. (2002, December 6). Functional nueroimaging of speech perception in infants. *Science, 298,* 2013–2015.

Depue, R. A., & Iacono, W. G. (1989). Neurobehavioral aspects of affective disorders. In M. R. Rosenzweig & L. Y. Porter (Eds.), *Annual review of psychology* (Vol. 40, pp. 457–492). Palo Alto, CA: Annual Reviews.

Derryberry, D., & Reed, M. A. (1994a). Temperament and attention: Orienting toward and away from positive and negative signals. *Journal of Personality and Social Psychology, 66,* 1128–1139.

Derryberry, D., & Reed, M. A. (1994b). Temperament and the self-organization of personality. *Development and Psychopathology, 6,* 653–676.

Derryberry, D., & Reed, M. A. (1996). Regulatory processes and the development of cognitive representations. *Development and Psychopathology, 8,* 215–234.

Derryberry, D., & Rothbart, M. K. (1988). Arousal, affect, and attention as components of temperament. *Journal of Personality and Social Psychology, 55,* 958–966.

Diamond, A. (1991). Neuropsychological insights into the meaning of object concept development. In S. Carey & R. Gelman (Eds.), *The epigenesis of mind: Essays on biology and cognition* (pp. 67–110). Hillsdale, NJ: Erlbaum.

Diamond, A., Briand, L., Fossella, J., & Gehlbach, L. (2004). Genetic and neurochemical modulation of prefrontal cognitive functions in children. *American Journal of Psychiatry, 161,* 125–132.

Dienstbier, R. A. (1984). The role of emotion in moral socialization. In C. E. Izard, J. Kagan, & R. B. Zajonc (Eds.), *Emotions, cognition and behavior* (pp. 484–518). New York: Cambridge University Press.

Ding, Y. C., Chi, H. C., Grady, D. L., Morishima, A., Kidd, J. R., Kidd, K. K., et al. (2002). Evidence of positive selection acting at the human dopamine receptor D4 gene locus. *Proceedings of the National Academy of Sciences of the USA, 99,* 309–314.

Donders, F. C. (1868). On the speed of mental processes. *Acta Psychologia, 30,* 412–413.

Drevets, W. C., & Raichle, M. E. (1998). Reciprocal suppression of regional blood flow during emotional versus higher cognitive processes: Implications for interactions between emotion and cognition. *Cognition and Emotion, 12,* 353–385.

Dronkers, N. F. (1996, November 14). A new brain region for coordinating speech articulation. *Nature, 384,* 159–161.

Duda, R. O., & Shortliffe, E. H. (1983, April 15). Expert systems research. *Science, 220,* 261–268.

Duncan, J., Seitz, R. J., Kolodny, J., Bor, D., Herzog, H. Ahmed, A., et al. (2000, July 21). A neural basis for general intelligence. *Science, 289,* 457–460.

Dweck, C. (1991). Self-theories and goals: Their role in motivation, personality, and development. In R. A. Dienstbier (Ed.), *Nebraska Symposium on Motivation: Vol. 38. Perspectives on motivation* (pp. 199–236). Lincoln: University of Nebraska Press.

Dweck, C. S. (2000). *Self-theories: Their role in motivation, personality, and development. Essays in social psychology.* Philadelphia: Psychology Press.

Early, T. S., Posner, M. I., Reiman, E. M., & Raichle, M. E. (1989). Hyperactivity of the left striato-pallidal projection, Part I: Lower level theory. *Psychiatric Developments, 2,* 85–108.

Eccles, J. (1983). Expectancies, values, and academic behaviors. In J. T. Spence (Ed.), *Achievement and achievement motives: Psychological and sociological approaches* (pp. 75–146). San Francisco: Freeman.

Egan, M. F., Goldberg, T. E., Kolachana, B. S., Callicott, J. H., Mazzanti, C. M., Straub, R. E., et al. (2001). Effect of COMT Val108/158 Met genotype on frontal lobe function and risk for schizophrenia. *Proceedings of the National Academy of Sciences of the USA, 98,* 6917–6922.

Egan, M. F., Kojima, M., Callicott, J. H., Goldberg, T. E., Kolachana, B. S., Bertolino, A., et al. (2003). The BDNF val66met polymorphism affects activity-dependent secretion of BDNF and human memory and hippocampal function. *Cell, 112,* 257–269.

Eisenberg, N., Fabes, R. A., Guthrie, I. K., Murphy, B. C., Poulin, R., & Shepard, S. (1996). The relations of regulation and emotionality to problem behavior in elementary school children. *Development and Psychopathology, 8,* 141–162.

Eisenberg, N., Fabes, R. A., Nyman, M., Bernzweig, J., & Pinulas, A. (1994). The relations of emotionality and regulation to children's anger-related reactions. *Child Development, 65,* 109–128.

Eisenberg, N., Fabes, R. A., Shepard, S. A., Murphy, B. C., Guthrie, I. K., Jones, S., et al. (1997). Contemporaneous and longitudinal prediction of children's social functioning from regulation and emotionality. *Child Development, 68,* 642–664.

Eisenberg, N., & Okun, M. A. (1996). The relations of dispositional regulation and emotionality to elders' empathy-related responding and affect while volunteering. *Journal of Personality, 64,* 157–183.

Elbert, T., Pantev, C., Wienbruch, C., Rockstroh, B., & Taub, E. (1995, October 13). Increased cortical representation of the fingers of the left hand in string players. *Science, 270,* 305–307.

Elliot, A. J., & Harackiewicz, J. (1996). Approach and avoidance goals and intrinsic motivation: A mediational analysis. *Journal of Personality and Social Psychology, 70,* 461–475.

Emde, R. N., Gaensbauer, T. J., & Harmon, R. J. (1976). Emotional expression in infancy: A biobehavioral study. *Psychological Issues, 10*(1, Monograph No. 37). New York: International Universities Press.

Erez, A., & Isen, A. M. (2002). The influence of positive affect on the components of expectancy motivation. *Journal of Applied Psychology, 87,* 1055–1067.

Ericsson, K. A., & Chase, W. G. (1982). Exceptional memory. *American Scientist, 70,* 607–615.

Ericsson, K. A., & Smith, J. (Eds.). (1991). *Toward a general theory of expertise.* Cambridge, MA: Cambridge University Press.

Evans, D., & Rothbart, M. K. (2004). *A hierarchical model of temperament and the Big Five.* Manuscript submitted for publication.

Everatt, J. (Ed.) (1999). *Reading and dyslexia: Visual and attentional processes.* London: Routledge.

Fan, J., Flombaum, J. I., McCandliss, B. D., Thomas, K. M., & Posner, M. I. (2003). Cognitive and brain consequences of conflict. *NeuroImage, 18,* 42–57.

Fan, J., Fossella, J. A., Sommer, T., Wu, Y., & Posner, M. I. (2003). Mapping the genetic variation of executive attention onto brain activity. *Proceedings of the National Academy of Sciences of the USA, 100,* 7406–7411.

Fan, J., McCandliss, B. D., Fossella, J., Flombaum, J. I., & Posner, M. I. (2005). The activation of attentional networks. *NeuroImage, 26,* 471–479.

Fan, J., McCandliss, B. D., Sommer, T., Raz, M., & Posner, M. I. (2002). Testing the efficiency and independence of attentional networks. *Journal of Cognitive Neuroscience, 14,* 340–347.

Fan, J., Wu, Y., Fossella, J., & Posner, M. I. (2001). Assessing the heritability of attentional networks. *BMC Neuroscience, 2,* 14.

Feigenson, L., Dehaene, S., & Spelke, E. (2004). Core systems of number. *Trends in Cognitive Sciences, 8,* 307–314.

Ffytche, D. H., Guy, C. N., & Zeki, S. (1995). The parallel visual motion inputs into areas V1 and V5 of human cerebral cortex. *Brain, 118,* 1375–1394.

Filipek, P. A., Semrud-Clikeman, M., Steingard, R. J., Renshaw, P. F., Kennedy, D. N., & Biederman, J. (1997). Volumetric MRI analysis comparing subjects having attention-deficit hyperactivity disorder with normal controls. *Neurology, 48,* 589–601.

Flavell, J. H. (1963). *The developmental psychology of Jean Piaget.* Princeton, NJ: Van Nostrand.

Fossella, J., & Posner, M. I. (2004). Genes and the development of neural networks underlying cognitive processes In M. S. Gazzaniga (Ed.), *The cognitive neurosciences* (3rd ed., pp. 1255–1266). Cambridge, MA: MIT Press.

Fossella, J., Sommer T., Fan, J., Wu, Y., Swanson, J. M., Pfaff, D. W., & Posner, M. I. (2002). Assessing the molecular genetics of attention networks. *BMC Neuroscience, 3,* 14.

Friston, K. J., Holmes, A. P., Price, C. J., Buchel, C., & Worsley, K. J. (1999). Multisubject fMRI studies and conjunction analyses. *NeuroImage, 10,* 385–396.

Frith, U., & Frith, C. (2001). The biological basis of social interaction. *Current Directions in Psychological Science, 10,* 151–155.

Galton, F. (1907). *Inquiries into human faculty and its development.* London: J. M. Dent & Sons Ltd.

Gardner, H. (1983). *Frames of mind: The theory of multiple intelligences.* New York: Basic Books.

Gartstein, M. A., & Rothbart, M. K. (2003). Studying infant temperament via the Revised Infant Behavior Questionnaire. *Infant Behavior and Development, 26,* 64–86.

Gautier, I., Tarr, M. J., Anderson, A. W., Skudlarsky, P., & Gore, J. C. (1999). Activation of the middle fusiform gyrus "face area" with expertise in recognizing novel objects. *Nature Neuroscience, 2,* 568–573.

Gazzaniga, M. (1994). *Nature's mind.* New York: Basic Books.

Gerardi-Caulton, G. (2000). Sensitivity to spatial conflict and the development of self-regulation in children 24–36 months of age. *Developmental Science, 3/4,* 397–404.

Gerlai, R. (1996). Gene-targeting studies of mammalian behavior: Is it the mutation or the background genotype? *Trends in Neuroscience, 19,* 177–181.

Gernsbacher, M. A., & Robertson, R. R. W. (1995). Reading skill and suppression revisited. *Psychological Science, 6,* 165–169.

Gerstadt, C. L., Hong, Y. J., & Diamond, A. (1994). The relationship between cognition and action: Performance of children 3 1/2–7 years old on a Stroop-like day–night test. *Cognition, 53,* 129–153.

Gesell, A. (1928). *Infancy and human growth.* New York: Macmillan.

Giedd, J. N., Blumenthal, J., Jeffries, N. O., Castellanos, F. X., Liu, H., Zijdenbos, A., et al. (1999). Brain development during childhood and adolescence: A longitudinal MRI study. *Nature Neuroscience, 10,* 861–863.

Goel, V., & Dolan, R. J. (2001). Functional neuroanatomy of three-term relational reasoning. *Neuropsychologia, 39,* 901–909.

Goel, V., Gold, B., Kapur, S., & Houle, S. (1998). Neuroanatomical correlates of human reasoning. *Journal of Cognitive Neuroscience, 10,* 293–302.

Goldapple, K., Segal, Z., Garson, C., Lau, M., Bieling, P., Kennedy, S., & Mayberg, H. (2004). Modulation of cortical–limbic pathways in major depression. Treatment-specific effects of cognitive behavior therapy. *Archives of General Psychiatry, 61,* 34–41.

Grafton, S. T., Hazeltine, E., & Ivry, R. (1995). Functional mapping of sequence learning in normal humans. *Journal of Cognitive Neuroscience, 7,* 497–510.

Grandy, D. K., & Kruzich, P. J. (2004). A molecular genetic approach to the neurobiology of attention utilizing dopamine receptor-deficient mice. In M. I. Posner (Ed.), *Cognitive neuroscience of attention* (pp. 260–268). New York: Guilford.

Gray, J. A. (1971). *The psychology of fear and stress.* New York: McGraw-Hill.

Gray, J. A. (1982). *The neuropsychology of anxiety: An enquiry into the functions of the septo-hippocampal system.* London: Oxford University Press.

Gray, J. A. (1991). The neuropsychology of temperament. In J. Strelau & A. Angleitner (Eds.), *Explorations in temperament: International perspectives on theory and measurement* (pp. 105–128). New York: Plenum Press.

Graziano, W. G. (1994). The development of agreeableness as a dimension of personality. In C. F. Halverson, Jr., G. A. Kohnstamm, & R. P. Martin (Eds.), *The developing structure of temperament and personality from infancy to adulthood* (pp. 339–354). Hillsdale, NJ: Erlbaum.

Graziano, W. G., & Eisenberg, N. (1997). Agreeableness: A dimension of personality. In R. Hogan, J. A. Johnson, & S. R. Briggs (Eds.), *Handbook of personality psychology* (pp. 795–824). San Diego, CA: Academic Press.

Graziano, W. G., & Tobin, R. M. (2002). Agreeableness: Dimension of personality or social desirability artifact? *Journal of Personality, 70,* 695–727.

Green, C. S., & Bavelier, D. (2003, May 29). Action video game modifies selective attention. *Nature, 423,* 534–537.

Greenwood, P. M., Sunderland, T., Friz, J. L., & Parasuraman, R. (2000). Genetics and visual attention: Selective deficits in healthy adult carriers of the epsilon

4 allele of the apolipoprotein E gene. *Proceedings of the National Academy of Sciences of the USA, 97,* 11661–11666.

Griffin, S. A., Case, R., & Siegler, R. S. (1995). Rightstart: Providing the central conceptual prerequisites for first formal learning of arithmetic to students at risk for school failure. In K. McGilly (Ed.), *Classroom lessons: Integrating cognitive theory* (pp. 25–50). Cambridge, MA: MIT Press.

Groen, G. J., & Parkman, J. M. (1972). A chronometric analysis of simple addition. *Psychological Review, 79,* 329–343.

Guilford, J. P. (1967). *The nature of human intelligence.* New York: McGraw-Hill.

Gunderson, V. M., & Swartz, K. B. (1986). Effects of familiarization time on visual recognition memory in infant pigtailed macaques. *Developmental Psychology, 22,* 477–480.

Gusnard, D. A., Ollinger, J. M., Shulman, G. L., Cloninger, C. R., Price, J. L., Van Essen, D. C., & Raichle, M. E. (2003). Persistence and brain circuitry. *Proceedings of the National Academy of Sciences of the USA, 100,* 3479–3484.

Guttorm, T. K., Leppanen, P. H. T., Poikkeus, A. M., Eklund, K. M., Lyytinen, P., & Lyytinen, H. (2005). Brain event-related potentials (ERPs) measured at birth predict later language development in children with and without familial risk for dyslexia. *Cortex, 41,* 291–303.

Gwaizda, J., Bauer, J., & Held, R. (1989). From visual acuity to hyperacuity: A 10-year update. *Canadian Journal of Psychology, 43,* 109–120.

Habib, R., Nyberg, L., & Tulving, E. (2003). Hemispheric asymmetries of memory: The HERA model revisited. *Trends in Cognitive Sciences, 7,* 241–245.

Haith, M. M. (1980). *Rules that babies look by: The organization of newborn visual acuity.* Hillsdale, NJ: Erlbaum.

Haith, M. M., Hazan, C., & Goodman, G. S. (1988). Expectation and anticipation of dynamic visual events by 3.5-month-old babies. *Child Development, 59,* 467–469.

Harm, M. W., & Seidenberg, M. S. (2004). Computing the meanings of words in reading: Cooperative division of labor between visual and phonological processes. *Psychological Review, 111,* 662–720.

Harman, C., Posner, M. I., Rothbart, M. K., & Thomas-Thrapp, L. (1994). Development of orienting to objects and locations in human infants. *Canadian Journal of Experimental Psychology, 48,* 301–318.

Harman, C., Rothbart, M. K., & Posner, M. I. (1997). Distress and attention interactions in early infancy. *Motivation and Emotion, 21,* 27–43.

Harter, S. (1974). Pleasure derived by children from cognitive challenge and mastery. *Child Development, 45,* 661–669.

Harter, S. (1978). Effectance motivation reconsidered: Toward a developmental model. *Human Motivation, 21,* 34–64.

Harter, S. (1980). The development of competence motivation in the mastery of cognitive and physical skills: Is there still a place for joy? In D. M. Landers

(Ed.), *Psychology of motor behavior and sport* (pp. 3–20). Champaign, IL: Human Kinetics.

Harter, S. (1981). A new self-report scale of intrinsic versus extrinsic orientation in the classroom: Motivational and informational components. *Developmental Psychology, 17,* 300–312.

Harter, S. (1998). The development of self-representations. In W. Damon (Series Ed.) & N. Eisenberg (Vol. Ed.), *Handbook of child psychology: Vol. 3. Social, emotional, and personality development* (5th ed., pp. 553–617). New York: Wiley.

Harter, S. (1999). *The construction of the self: A developmental perspective.* New York: Guilford Press.

Hastings, N. B., Tanapat, P., & Gould, E. (2001). Neurogenesis in the adult mammalian brain. *Clinical Neuroscience Research, 1,* 175–182.

Hebb, D. O. (1949). *Organization of behavior.* New York: Wiley.

Heidrich, A. (1990). *Studies of working memory.* Unpublished manuscript, University of Oregon, Eugene.

Heinze, H. J., Mangun, G. R., Burchert, W., Hinrichs, H., Scholtz, M., Muntel, T. F., et al. (1994, December 8). Combined spatial and temporal imaging of brain activity during visual selective attention in humans. *Nature, 372,* 543–546.

Hubel, D. H., & Wiesel, T. (1977) Functional architecture of macque monkey visual cortex. *Proceedings of the Royal Society of London. Series B, Biological Sciences, 198,* 1–59.

Hugdahl, K., & Davidson, R. J. (Eds.). (2002). *The asymmetrical brain.* Cambridge, MA: MIT Press.

Hunt, J. M. (1961). *Intelligence and experience.* Oxford, England: Ronald Press.

Huttenlocher, P. R., & Dabholkar, A. S. (1997). Regional differences in synaptogenesis in human cerebral cortex. *Journal of Comparative Neurology, 387,* 167–178.

Hwang, J. (1999). *Affect and sustained engagement in infancy.* Unpublished master's thesis, University of Oregon, Eugene.

Insel, T. R. (2003). Is social attachment an addictive disorder? *Physiology and Behavior, 79,* 351–357.

Institute of Child Health and Human Development. (2000). *Report of the National Reading Panel: Teaching children to read: An evidence-based assessment of the scientific research literature on reading and its implications for reading instruction* (NIH Publication No. 00-4769). Washington, DC: U.S. Government Printing Office.

James, W. (1890). *Principles of psychology* (Vol. 1). New York: Holt.

Johnson, M. H. (2002). The development of visual attention: A cognitive neuroscience perspective. In M. H. Johnson, Y. Munakata, & R. O. Gilmore (Eds.), *Brain development and cognition: A reader* (2nd ed., pp. 134–150). Oxford, England: Blackwell.

Johnson, M. H., & Morton, J. (1991). *Biology and cognitive development: The case of face recognition.* Oxford, England: Blackwell.

Johnson, M. H., Posner, M. I., & Rothbart, M. K. (1991). Components of visual orienting in early infancy: Contingency learning, anticipatory looking and disengaging. *Journal of Cognitive Neuroscience, 3,* 335–344.

Jones, E. E. (1990). Constrained behavior and self-concept change. In J. M. Olson & M. P. Zanna (Eds.), *Self-inference processes: The Ontario Symposium* (pp. 69–86). Hillsdale, NJ: Erlbaum.

Jones, L., Rothbart, M. K., & Posner, M. I. (2003). Development of inhibitory control in preschool children. *Developmental Science, 6,* 498–504.

Kagan, J. (1994). *Galen's prophecy: Temperament in human nature.* Cambridge, MA: Harvard University Press.

Karni, A., Meyer, G., Rey-Hipolito, C., Jezzard, P., Adams, M. M., Turner, R., & Ungerleider, L. G. (1998). The acquisition of skilled motor performance: Fast and slow experience-driven changes in primary motor cortex. *Proceedings of the National Academy of Sciences of the USA, 95,* 861–868.

Kaufman, A. S., & Kaufman, N. L. (1990). *Kaufman Brief Intelligence Test manual.* Circle Pines, MN: American Guidance Service.

Keogh, B. K. (1982). Temperament: An individual difference of importance in intervention programs. *Topics in Early Childhood Special Education, 2,* 25–31.

Keogh, B. K. (1989). Applying temperament research to school. In G. Kohnstamm, J. Bates, & M. K. Rothbart (Eds.), *Temperament in childhood* (pp. 437–450). Chichester, England: Wiley.

Keogh, B. K. (2003). *Temperament in the classroom: Understanding individual differences.* Baltimore, MD: Paul H. Brookes.

Kieffer, B. L. (1999). Opioids: First lessons from knockout mice. *Trends in Pharmacological Sciences, 20,* 19–26.

Klein, R. M., & McMullen, P. (Eds.). (1999). *Converging methods for understanding reading and dyslexia* (pp. 305–337). Cambridge, MA: MIT Press.

Klingberg, T., Forssberg, H., & Westerberg, H. (2002). Training of working memory in children with ADHD. *Journal of Clinical and Experimental Neuropsychology, 24,* 781–791.

Klingberg, T., Hedehus, M., Temple, E., Salz, T., Gabrieli, J. D. E., Moseley, M. E., & Poldrack, R. A. (2000). Microstructure of temporo-parietal white matter as a basis for reading ability: Evidence from diffusion tensor magnetic resonance imaging. *Neuron, 25,* 493–500.

Kochanska, G. (1991). Socialization and temperament in the development of guilt and conscience. *Child Development, 62,* 1379–1392.

Kochanska, G. (1995). Children's temperament, mothers' discipline, and security of attachment: Multiple pathways to emerging internalization. *Child Development, 66,* 597–615.

Kochanska, G., & Knaack, A. (2003). Effortful control as a personality characteristic of young children: Antecedents, correlates, and consequences. *Journal of Personality, 71,* 1087–1112.

Kochanska, G., Murray, K. T., & Harlan, E. T. (2000). Effortful control in early childhood: Continuity and change, antecedents, and implications for social development. *Developmental Psychology, 36*, 220–232.

Kochanska, G., Murray, K., Jacques, T. Y., Koenig, A. L., & Vandegeest, K. A. (1996). Inhibitory control in young children and its role in emerging internalization. *Child Development, 67*, 490–507.

Koechlin, E., Naccache, L., Block, E., & Dehaene, S. (1999). Prime numbers: Exploring the modularity of numerical representations with masked and unmasked semantic priming. *Journal of Experimental Psychology: Human Perception and Performance, 25*, 1882–1905.

Kook, H., Gupta, L., Molfese, D., & Fadem, K. C. (2005). Multi-stimuli, multichannel data and decision fusion strategies for dyslexia prediction using neonatal ERPs. *Pattern Recognition, 38*, 2174–2184.

Kosslyn, S. M. (1980). *Image and mind.* Cambridge, MA: Harvard University Press.

Kosslyn, S. M. (1996). *Image and brain: The resolution of the imagery debate.* Cambridge, MA: Harvard University Press.

Kosslyn, S. M., Ganis, G., & Thompson, W. L. (2001). Neural foundations of imagery. *Nature Reviews: Neuroscience, 2*, 635–642.

Kosslyn, S. M., & Thompson, W. L. (2000). Shared mechanisms in visual imagery and visual perception: Insights from cognitive neuroscience. In M. S. Gazzaniga (Ed.), *The new cognitive neurosciences* (pp. 975–985). Cambridge, MA: MIT Press.

Kremen, A. M., & Block, J. (1998). The roots of ego-control in young adulthood: Links with parenting in early childhood. *Journal of Personality and Social Psychology, 75*, 1062–1075.

Krueger, R. F., Hicks, B. M., & McGue, M. (2001). Altruism and antisocial behavior: Independent tendencies, unique personality correlates, distinct etiologies. *Psychological Science, 12*, 397–402.

Kruglanski, A. W. (1978). Endogenous attribution and intrinsic motivation. In M. Lepper & D. Greene (Eds.), *The hidden costs of reward: New perspectives on the psychology of human motivation* (pp. 85–107). Hillsdale, NJ: Erlbaum.

Kuhl, J., & Kazen, M. (1999). Volitional facilitation of difficult intentions: Joint activation of intention memory and positive affect removes Stroop interference. *Journal of Experimental Psychology: General, 128*, 382–399.

Kuhl, P. K. (2000). A new view of language acquisition. *Proceedings of the National Academy of Sciences of the USA, 100*, 1185–1187.

Kuhl, P. K., Tsao, F. M., & Liu, H. M. (2003). Foreign-language experience in infancy: Effects of short-term exposure and social interaction on phonetic learning. *Proceedings of the National Academy of Sciences of the USA, 100*, 9096–9101.

Lakoff, G., & Johnson, M. (1980). *Metaphors we live by.* Chicago: University of Chicago Press.

Lane, R. D., Reiman, E. M., Axelrod, B., Yun, L. S., Holmes, A., & Schwartz, G. E. (1998). Neural correlates of levels of emotional awareness: Evidence of an interaction between emotion and attention in the anterior cingulate cortex. *Journal of Cognitive Neuroscience, 10*, 525–535.

Lashley, K. S. (1929). *Brain mechanisms and intelligence*. Chicago: University of Chicago Press.

Lawrence, A. D., & Calder, A. J. (2004). Homologizing human emotions. In D. Evans & P. Cruse (Eds.), *Emotions, evolution, and rationality* (pp. 15–47). Oxford, England: Oxford University Press.

Lawrence, A. D., Calder, A. J., McGowan, S. W., & Grasby, P. M. (2002). Selective disruption of the recognition of facial expressions of anger. *NeuroReport, 13*, 881–884.

LeDoux, J. E. (1987). Emotion. In F. Plum (Ed.), *Handbook of physiology. Section 1: The nervous system. Vol. V, Part 1: Higher functions of the brain* (pp. 419–460). Bethesda, MD: American Physiological Society.

LeDoux, J. E. (1989). Cognitive–emotional interactions in the brain. *Cognition and Emotion, 3*, 267–289.

Lepper, M. R., Greene, D., & Nisbett, R. E. (1973). Undermining children's intrinsic interest with extrinsic reward: A test of the "overjustification" hypothesis. *Journal of Personality and Social Psychology, 28*, 129–137.

Lillard, A. (2005). *Montessori: The science behind the genius*. New York: Oxford University Press.

Lobe, C. G., & Nagy, A. (1998). Conditional genome alteration in mice. *Bioessays, 20*, 200–208.

Loftus, E. F., & Fathi, D. C. (1985). Retrieving multiple autobiographical memories. *Social Cognition, 3*, 280–295.

Luu, P., Collins, P., & Tucker, D. M. (2000). Mood, personality, and self-monitoring: Negative affect and emotionality in relation to frontal lobe mechanisms of error monitoring. *Journal of Experimental Psychology: General, 129*, 43–60.

Marrocco, R. T., & Davidson, M. C. (1998). Neurochemistry of attention. In R. Parasuraman (Ed.), *The attentive brain* (pp. 35–50). Cambridge, MA: MIT Press.

Martin, R. P. (1989). Activity level, distractibility, and persistence: Critical characteristics in early schooling. In G. A. Kohnstamm, J. E. Bates, & M. K. Rothbart (Eds.), *Temperament in childhood* (pp. 451–462). Chichester, England: Wiley.

Maurer, D., & Lewis, T. L. (2001). Visual acuity: The role of visual input in inducing postnatal change. *Clinical Neuroscience Research, 1*, 239–247.

Maurer, D., & Maurer, C. (1988). *The world of the newborn*. New York: Basic Books.

McCandliss, B. D., Beck, I. L., Sandak, R., & Perfetti, C. (2000). Focusing attention on decoding for children with poor reading skill. *Scientific Studies of Reading, 7*, 75–104.

McCandliss, B. D., Cohen, L., & Dehaene, S. (2003). The visual word form area: Expertise for reading in the fusiform gyrus. *Trends in Cognitive Sciences, 7,* 293–299.

McCandliss, B. D., Posner, M. I., & Givon, T. (1997). Brain plasticity in learning visual words. *Cognitive Psychology, 33,* 88–110.

Meck, W. H., & Church, R. M. (1983). A mode control model of counting and timing processes. *Journal of Experimental Psychology: Animal Behavior Processes, 9,* 320–334.

Meltzoff, A. N., & Borton, R. W. (1979, November 26). Intermodal matching by human neonates. *Nature, 282,* 403–404.

Merzenich, M. M., & Jenkins, W. M. (1995). Cortical plasticity, learning, and learning dysfunction. In B. Julesz & I. Kovacs (Eds.), *Maturation windows and adult cortical plasticity* (pp. 247–272). New York: Addison Wesley.

Milberg, W., Blumstein, S., Katz, D., Gershberg, R., & Brown, T. (1995). Semantic facilitation in aphasia: Effects of time and expectancy. *Journal of Cognitive Neuroscience, 7,* 667–682.

Mills, D., & Mills, C. (2000). *Hungarian kindergarten curriculum translation.* London: Mills Production.

Mischel, W., Shoda, Y., & Peake, P. K. (1988). The nature of adolescent competencies predicted by preschool delay of gratification. *Journal of Personality and Social Psychology, 54,* 687–696.

Molfese, D. L. (2000). Predicting dyslexia at 8 years of age using neonatal brain responses. *Brain and Language, 72,* 238–245.

Montessori, M. (1965). *Spontaneous activity in education: The advanced Montessori method* (F. Simmonds, Trans.). New York: Schocken. (Original work published 1917)

Morgan, G. A., Harmon, R. J., & Maslin-Cole, P. M. (1990). Mastery motivation: Its definition and measurement. *Early Education and Development, 1,* 318–339.

Nagy, Z., Westerberg, H., & Klingberg, T. (2004). Maturation of white matter is associated with the development of cognitive functions during childhood. *Journal of Cognitive Neuroscience, 16,* 1227–1233.

Neely, J. H. (1977). Semantic priming and retrieval from lexical memory: Role of inhibitionless spreading activation and limited capacity attention. *Journal of Experimental Psychology: General, 106,* 226–254.

Neville, H. J. (1995). Developmental specificity in neurocognitive development in humans. In M. Gazzaniga (Ed.), *The cognitive neurosciences* (pp. 219–231). Cambridge, MA: MIT Press.

Newbury, D. F., Bishop, D. V. M., & Monaco, A. P. (2005). Genetic influences on language impairment and phonological short-term memory. *Trends in Cognitive Sciences, 9,* 528–534.

Newell, A., Shaw, J. C., & Simon, H. A. (1958). Elements of a theory of human problem solving. *Psychological Review, 65,* 151–166.

Nicholls, J. G. (1984). Conceptions of ability and achievement motivation. In R. E. Ames & C. Ames (Ed.), *Research on motivation in education: Vol. 1. Student motivation* (pp. 39–73). New York: Academic Press.

Nikolaev, A. R., Ivanitsky, G. A., Ivanitsky, A. M., Abdullaev, Y. G., & Posner, M. I. (2001). Short-term correlation between frontal and Wernicke's areas in word association. *Neuroscience Letters, 298*, 107–110.

Nimchinsky, E. A., Gilissen, E., Allman, J. M., Perl, D. P., Erwin, J. M., & Hof, P. R. (1999). A neuronal morphologic type unique to humans and great apes. *Proceedings of the National Academy of Sciences of the USA, 96*, 5268–5273.

Nishijo, H., Ono, T., & Nishino, H. (1988). Single neuron responses in amygdala of alert monkey during complex sensory stimulation with affective significance. *Journal of Neuroscience, 8*, 3570–3583.

Nobre, A. C., Allison, T., & McCarthy, G. (1994, November 17). Word recognition in the inferior temporal cortex. *Nature, 372*, 260–263.

Norman, D. A., & Shallice, T. (1986). Attention to action: Willed and automatic control of behavior. In R. J. Davidson, G. E. Schwartz, & D. Shapiro (Eds.), *Consciousness and self regulation*. New York: Plenum Press.

Ochsner, K. N., Bunge, S. A., Gross, J. J., & Gabrieli, J. D. E. (2002). Rethinking feelings: An fMRI study of the cognitive regulation of emotion. *Journal of Cognitive Neuroscience, 14*, 1215–1229.

Olesen, P. J., Westerberg, H., & Klingberg, T. (2004). Increased prefrontal and parietal activity after training of working memory. *Nature Neuroscience, 7*, 75–79.

Olson, S. L., Bates, J. E., Sandy, J. M., & Schilling, E. M. (2002). Early developmental precursors of impulsive and inattentive behavior: From infancy to middle childhood. *Journal of Child Psychology and Psychiatry and Allied Disciplines, 43*, 435–448.

Panksepp, J. (1982). Toward a general psychobiological theory of emotions. *Behavioral and Brain Sciences, 5*, 407–467.

Panksepp, J. (1986). The psychobiology of prosocial behaviors: Separation distress, play and altruism. In C. Zahn-Waxler, E. M. Cummings, & R. Iannotti (Eds.), *Altruism and aggression: Biological and social origins* (pp. 19–57). New York: Cambridge University Press.

Panksepp, J. (1993). Neurochemical control of moods and emotions: Amino acids to neuropeptides. In M. Lewis & J. M. Haviland (Eds.), *Handbook of emotions* (pp. 87–107). New York: Guilford Press.

Panksepp, J. (1998). *Affective neuroscience: The foundations of human and animal emotions*. New York: Oxford University Press.

Parasuraman, R., & Greenwood, P. M. (1998). Selective attention in aging and dementia. In R. Parasuraman (Ed.), *The attentive brain* (pp. 461–488). Cambridge, MA: MIT Press.

Parasuraman, R., Greenwood, P. M., Kumar, R. & Fossella, J. (2005). Beyond heritability: Neurotransmitter genes differentially modulate visuospatial attention and working memory. *Psychological Science, 16*, 200–207.

Parker, J. G., & Asher, S. R. (1987). Peer relations and later personal adjustment: Are low-accepted children at risk? *Psychological Bulletin, 102,* 357–389.

Pascual-Leone, A., & Hamilton, R. (2001). The metamodal organization of the brain. *Progress in Brain Research, 134,* 427–445.

Patterson, G. R. (1980). Mothers: The unacknowledged victims. *Monographs of the Society for Research in Child Development, 45*(5, Serial No. 186).

Paulesu, E., Demonet, J.-F., Fazio, F., McCrory, E., Chanoine, V., Brunswick, N., et al. (2001, March 16). Dyslexia: Cultural diversity and biological unity. *Science, 291,* 2165–2167.

Petersen, S. E., Fox, P. T., Posner, M. I., Mintun, M., & Raichle, M. E. (1989). Positron emission tomographic studies of the processing of single words. *Journal of Cognitive Neuroscience, 1,* 153–170.

Pfaff, D. W. (1999). *Drive: Neurobiological and molecular mechanisms of sexual motivation.* Cambridge, MA: MIT Press.

Piaget, J. (1952). *The origins of intelligence in children.* New York: International Universities Press. (Original work published 1936)

Piazza, M., Izard, V., Pinel, P., LeBihan, D., & Dehaene, S. (2004). Tuning curves for approximate numerosity in the human intraparietal sulcus. *Neuron, 44,* 547–555.

Pinel, P., Dehaene, S., Riviere, D., & LeBihan, D. (2001). Modulation of parietal activation by semantic distance in a number comparison task. *NeuroImage, 14,* 1013–1026.

Pintrich, P. R., Marx, R. W., & Boyle, R. A. (1993). Beyond cold conceptual change: The role of motivational beliefs and classroom contextual factors in the process of conceptual change. *Review of Educational Research, 63,* 167–199.

Pliszka, S. R. (1989). Effect of anxiety on cognition, behavior, and stimulant response in ADHD. *Journal of the American Academy of Child and Adolescent Psychiatry, 28,* 882–887.

Polk, T. A., & Farah, M. J. (1998). The neural development and organization of letter recognition, computation modeling and behavioral studies. *Proceedings of the National Academy of Sciences of the USA, 95,* 765–772.

Polk, T. A., Stallcup, M., Aguirre, G. K., Alsop, D. C., D'Esposito, M., Detre, J. A., & Farah, M. J. (2002). Neural specialization for letter recognition. *Journal of Cognitive Neuroscience, 14,* 145–159.

Posner, M. I. (1978). *Chronometric explorations of mind.* Hillsdale, NJ: Erlbaum.

Posner, M. I. (2003). Imaging a science of mind. *Trends in Cognitive Sciences, 7,* 450–453.

Posner, M. I. (2004). Neural systems and individual differences. *Teachers College Record, 106,* 24–30.

Posner, M. I., & Cohen, Y. (1984). Components of attention. In H. Bouma & D. Bowhuis (Eds.), *Attention and performance X: Control of language processes* (pp. 531–556). Hillsdale, NJ: Erlbaum.

Posner, M. I., & McCandliss, B. D. (1999). Brain circuitry during reading. In R. Klein & P. McMullen (Eds.), *Converging methods for understanding reading and dyslexia* (pp. 305–337). Cambridge: MIT Press.

Posner, M. I., & Pavese, A. (1998). Anatomy of word and sentence meaning. *Proceedings of the National Academy of Sciences of the USA, 95,* 899–905.

Posner, M. I., & Petersen, S. E. (1990). The attention system of the human brain. *Annual Review of Neuroscience, 13,* 25–42.

Posner, M. I., & Raichle, M. E. (1994). *Images of mind.* New York: Scientific American Books.

Posner, M. I., & Raichle, M. E. (Eds.). (1998). Overview: The neuroimaging of human brain function. *Proceedings of the National Academy of Sciences of the USA, 95,* 763–764.

Posner, M. I., & Rothbart, M. K. (1991). Attentional mechanisms and conscious experience. In M. Rugg & A. D. Milner (Eds.), *The neuropsychology of consciousness* (pp. 91–112). London: Academic Press.

Posner, M. I., & Rothbart, M. K. (1998). Attention, self regulation and consciousness. *Philosophical Transactions of the Royal Society of London. Series B, Biological Sciences, 353,* 1915–1927.

Posner, M. I., & Rothbart, M. K. (2000). Developing mechanisms of self-regulation. *Development and Psychopathology, 12,* 427–441.

Posner, M. I., Rothbart, M. K., & DiGirolamo, G. J. (1999). Development of brain networks for orienting to novelty. *Pavlov Journal of Higher Nervous Activity, 49,* 715–722.

Posner, M. I., Rothbart, M. K., Thomas-Thrapp, L., & Gerardi, G. (1998). Development of orienting to locations and objects. In R. Wright (Ed.), *Visual attention* (pp. 269–288). New York: Oxford University Press.

Premack, D., & Premack, A. (2003). *Original intelligence.* New York: McGraw Hill.

Price, C. J., Moore, C. J., & Friston, K. J. (1997). Subtractions, conjunctions, and interactions in experimental design of activation studies. *Human Brain Mapping, 4,* 264–267.

Price, C. J., Winterburn, D., Giraud, A. L., Moore, C. J., & Noppeney, U. (2003). Cortical localisation of the visual and auditory word form areas: A reconsideration of the evidence. *Brain and Language, 86,* 272–286.

Pullis, M. (1985). Students' temperament characteristics and their impact on decisions by resource and mainstream teachers. *Learning Disability Quarterly, 8,* 109–122.

Quartz, S., & Sejnowski, T. (2000). Constraining constructivism: Cortical and subcortical constraints on learning in development. *Behavioral and Brain Sciences, 23,* 785–792.

Rafal, R., Calabresi, P., Brennan, C., & Sciolto, T. (1989). Saccade preparation prohibits reorienting to recently attended locations. *Journal of Experimental Psychology: Human Perception and Performance, 15,* 673–685.

Raichle, M. E., Fiez, J. A., Videen, T. O., McCleod, A. M. K., Pardo, J. V., Fox, P. T., & Petersen, S. E. (1994). Practice-related changes in the human brain: Functional anatomy during nonmotor learning. *Cerebral Cortex, 4,* 8–26.

Rainville, P., Duncan, G. H., Price, D. D., Carrier, B., & Bushnell, M. C. (1997, August 15). Pain affect encoded in human anterior cingulate but not somatosensory cortex. *Science, 277,* 968–970.

Rakic, P., Bourgeois, J. P., Eckenhoff, M. F., Zecevic, N., & Goldman-Rakic, P. S. (1986, April 11). Concurrent overproduction of synapses in diverse regions of the primate cerebral cortex. *Science, 232,* 232–235.

Ravitch, D. (2000). *Left back: A century of failed school reforms.* New York: Simon & Schuster.

Rayner, K., & Pollatsek, A. (1989). *The psychology of reading.* Englewood Cliffs, NJ: Prentice Hall.

Reed, M. A., & Derryberry, D. (1995). Temperament and attention to positive and negative trait information. *Personality and Individual Differences, 18,* 135–147.

Reed, M., Pien, D., & Rothbart, M. K. (1984). Inhibitory self-control in preschool children. *Merrill-Palmer Quarterly, 30,* 131–148.

Reiss, A. L., Abrams, M. T., Singer, H. S., Ross, J. L., & Denckla, M. B. (1996). Brain development, gender and IQ in children. A volumetric imaging study. *Brain, 119,* 1763–1774.

Ro, T., Farné, A., & Chang, E. (2003). Inhibition of return and the human frontal eye fields. *Experimental Brain Research, 150,* 290–296.

Rosch, E., Mervis, C. B., Gray, W. D., Johnsen, D. M., & Boyes-Braem, P. (1976). Basic objects in natural categories. *Cognitive Psychology, 7,* 192–233.

Rothbart, M. K. (1988). Temperament and the development of inhibited approach. *Child Development, 59,* 1241–1250.

Rothbart, M. K. (1989a). Biological processes of temperament. In G. Kohnstamm, J. Bates, & M. K. Rothbart (Eds.), *Temperament in childhood* (pp. 77–110). Chichester, England: Wiley.

Rothbart, M. K. (1989b). Temperament and development. In G. A. Kohnstamm, J. E. Bates, & M. K. Rothbart (Eds.), *Temperament in childhood* (pp. 187–247). Chichester, England: Wiley.

Rothbart, M. K., Ahadi, S. A., & Hershey, K. L. (1994). Temperament and social behavior in childhood. *Merrill-Palmer Quarterly, 40,* 21–39.

Rothbart, M. K., Ahadi, S. A., Hershey, K. L., & Fisher, P. (2001). Investigations of temperament at three to seven years: The Children's Behavior Questionnaire. *Child Development, 72,* 1394–1408.

Rothbart, M. K., & Bates, J. E. (2006). Temperament in children's development. In W. Damon & R. Lerner (Series Eds.) & N. Eisenberg (Vol. Ed.), *Handbook of child psychology: Vol. 3. Social, emotional, and personality development* (6th ed., pp. 99–166). New York: Wiley.

Rothbart, M. K., & Derryberry, D. (1981). Development of individual differences in temperament. In M. E. Lamb & A. L. Brown (Eds.), *Advances in developmental psychology* (Vol. 1, pp. 37–86). Hillsdale, NJ: Erlbaum.

Rothbart, M. K., & Derryberry, D. (2002). Temperament in children. In C. von Hofsten & L. Bäckman (Eds.), *Psychology at the turn of the millennium: Vol. 2. Social, developmental, and clinical perspectives* (pp. 17–35). East Sussex, England: Psychology Press.

Rothbart, M. K., Derryberry, D., & Hershey, K. (2000). Stability of temperament in childhood: Laboratory infant assessment to parent report at seven years. In V. J. Molfese & D. L. Molfese (Eds.), *Temperament and personality development across the life span* (pp. 85–119). Hillsdale, NJ: Erlbaum.

Rothbart, M. K., Derryberry, D., & Posner, M. I. (1994). A psychobiological approach to the development of temperament. In J. E. Bates & T. D. Wachs (Eds.), *Temperament: Individual differences at the interface of biology and behavior* (pp. 83–116). Washington, DC: American Psychological Association.

Rothbart, M. K., Ellis, L. K., Rueda, M. R., & Posner, M. I. (2003). Developing mechanisms of effortful control. *Journal of Personality, 71*, 1113–1143.

Rothbart, M. K., Hershey, K., & Posner, M. I. (1995). Temperament, attention and developmental psychopathology. In D. Cicchetti & D. Cohen (Eds.), *Manual of developmental psychopathology* (pp. 315–340). New York: Wiley.

Rothbart, M. K., & Hwang, J. (2005). Temperament and the development of competence and motivation. In A. J. Elliot & C. S. Dweck (Eds.), *Handbook of competence and motivation* (pp. 167–184). New York: Guilford Press.

Rothbart, M. K., & Jones, L. B. (1998). Temperament, self regulation, and education. *School Psychology Review, 27*, 479–491.

Rothbart, M. K., & Jones, L. B. (1999). Temperament: Developmental perspectives. In R. Gallimore, C. Bernheimer, D. MacMillan, D. Speece, & S. Vaughn (Eds.), *Developmental perspectives on children with high incidence disabilities: Papers in honor of Barbara Keogh* (pp. 33–54). Hillsdale, NJ: Erlbaum.

Rothbart, M. K., & Mauro, J. A. (1990). Questionnaire approaches to the study of infant temperament. In J. W. Fagen & J. Colombo (Eds.), *Individual differences in infancy: Reliability, stability and prediction* (pp. 411–429). Hillsdale, NJ: Erlbaum.

Rothbart, M. K., & Posner, M. I. (2006). Temperament, attention and developmental psychopathology. In D. Cicchetti & D. J. Cohen (Eds.), *Handbook of developmental psychopathology* (pp. 465–500). New York: Wiley.

Rothbart, M. K., Posner, M. I., & Kieras, J. (2006). Temperament, attention, and the development of self-regulation. In K. McCartney & D. Phillips (Eds.), *The Blackwell handbook of early child development* (pp. 328–357). London: Blackwell Press.

Rothbart, M. K., & Rueda, M. R. (2005). The development of effortful control. In U. Mayr, E. Awh, & S. W. Keele (Eds.), *Developing individuality in the human brain: A tribute to Michael I. Posner* (pp. 167–188). Washington, DC: American Psychological Association.

Rothbart, M. K., & Sheese, B. (in press). Temperament and emotion regulation. In J. J. Gross (Ed.), *Handbook of emotion regulation*. New York: Guilford Press.

Rothbart, M. K., Ziaie, H., & O'Boyle, C. G. (1992). Self-regulation and emotion in infancy. *New Directions in Child Development, 55,* 7–23.

Rueda, M. R., Fan, J., Halparin, J., Gruber, D., Lercari, L. P., McCandliss, B. D., & Posner, M. I. (2004). Development of attention during childhood. *Neuropsychologia, 42,* 1029–1040.

Rueda, M. R., Posner, M. I., Rothbart, M. K., & Davis-Stober, C. P. (2004). Development of the time course for processing conflict: An event-related potentials study with 4 year olds and adults. *BMC Neuroscience, 5,* 39.

Rueda, M. R., Rothbart, M. K., McCandliss, B. D., Saccamanno, L., & Posner, M. I. (2005). Training, maturation, and genetic influences on the development of executive attention. *Proceedings of the National Academy of Sciences of the USA, 102,* 14931–14936.

Ruff, H. A., & Rothbart, M. K. (1996). *Attention in early development: Themes and variations.* New York: Oxford University Press.

Rumbaugh, D. M., & Washburn, D. A. (1995). Attention and memory in relation to learning: A comparative adaptation perspective. In G. R. Lyon & N. A. Krasnegor (Eds.), *Attention, memory and executive function* (pp. 199–219). Baltimore: Brookes Publishing.

Ryan, R. M., Connell, J. P., & Grolnick, W. S. (1992). When achievement is not intrinsically motivated: A theory of internalization and self-regulation in school. In A. K. Boggiano & T. S. Pittman (Eds.), *Achievement and motivation: A social-developmental perspective. Cambridge studies in social and emotional development* (pp. 167–188). New York: Cambridge University Press.

Sanders, A. F., & Schroots, J. J. F. (1968). Cognitive categories and memory span II: The effect of temporal vs. categorical recall. *Quarterly Journal of Experimental Psychology, 20,* 273–279.

Sapir, A., Soroker, N., Berger, A., & Henik, A. (1999). Inhibition of return in spatial attention: Direct evidence for collicular generation. *Nature Neuroscience, 2,* 1053–1054.

Schacter, D. (1987). Implicit memory: History and current status. *Journal of Experimental Psychology: Language, Memory and Cognition, 113,* 501–518.

Scherg, M., & Berg, P. (1993). Brain Electrical Source Analysis (Version 2.0) [Computer software]. Herndon, VA: Neuroscan.

Schiefele, A., Krapp, A., & Winteler, A. (1992). Interest as a predictor of academic achievement: A meta-analysis of research. In K. A. Renninger, S. Hidi, & A. Krapp (Eds.), *The role of interest in learning and development* (pp. 183–212). Hillsdale, NJ: Erlbaum.

Schumacher, E. H., Lauber, E., Awh, E., Jonides, J., Smith, E. E., & Koeppe, R. A. (1996). PET evidence for an amodal verbal working memory system. *NeuroImage, 3,* 79–88.

Seidenberg, M. S., & McClelland, J. L. (1989). A distributed, developmental model of word recognition and naming. *Psychological Review, 96*, 523–568.

Sethi, A., Mischel, W., Aber, L., Shoda, Y., & Rodriguez, M. (2000). The role of strategic attention development in development of self-regulation: Predicting preschoolers' delay of gratification from mother-toddler interactions. *Developmental Psychology, 36*, 767–777.

Shallice, T., & Warrington, E. K. (1970). Independent functioning of verbal memory stores: A neuropsychological study. *Quarterly Journal of Experimental Psychology, 22*, 261–273.

Shaywitz, B. A., Shaywitz, S. E., Blachman, B. A., Pugh, K. R., Fulbright, R. K., Skudlarski, P., et al. (2004). Development of left occipitotemporal systems for skilled reading in children after a phonologically-based intervention. *Biological Psychiatry, 55*, 926–933.

Shaywitz, S. E. (2003). *Overcoming dyslexia*. New York: Knopf.

Shiner, R. L. (1998). How shall we speak of children's personalities in middle childhood? A preliminary taxonomy. *Psychological Bulletin, 124*, 308–332.

Shiner, R. L. (2000). Linking childhood personality with adaptation: Evidence for continuity and change across time into late adolescence. *Journal of Personality and Social Psychology, 78*, 310–325.

Shiner, R., & Caspi, A. (2003). Personality differences in childhood and adolescence: Measurement, development, and consequences. *Journal of Child Psychology and Psychiatry and Allied Disciplines, 44*, 2–32.

Shirley, M. M. (1933). *The first two years: A study of 25 babies*. Minneapolis: University of Minnesota Press.

Shoda, Y., Mischel, W., & Peake, P. K. (1990). Predicting adolescent cognitive and self-regulatory competencies from preschool delay of gratification: Identifying diagnostic conditions. *Developmental Psychology, 26*, 978–986.

Siegler, R. S. (1996). *Emerging minds: The process of change in children's thinking*. New York: Oxford University Press.

Sieroff, E., & Posner, M. I. (1988). Cueing spatial attention during processing of words and letter strings in normals. *Cognitive Neuropsychology, 5*, 451–472.

Simon, H. A. (1969). *The sciences of the artificial*. Cambridge, MA: MIT Press.

Simon, T. J., Bish, J. P., Bearden, C. E., Ding, L., Ferrante, S., Nguyen, V., et al. (2005). A multi-level analysis of cognitive dysfunction and psychopathology associated with chromosome 22q11.2 deletion syndrome in children. *Development and Psychopathology, 17*, 753–784.

Skinner, B. F. (1968). *The technology of teaching*. New York: Appleton-Century-Crofts.

Slater, A. (1995). Individual differences in infancy and later IQ. *Journal of Child Psychology and Psychiatry and Allied Disciplines, 36*, 69–112.

Smeets, W. J. A. J., & González, A. (2000). Catecholamine systems in the brain of vertebrates: New perspectives through a comparative approach. *Brain Research Reviews, 33*, 308–379.

Smith, E. E., Jonides, J., Marshuetz, C., & Koeppe, R. A. (1998). Components of verbal working memory: Evidence from neuroimaging. *Proceedings of the National Academy of Sciences of the USA, 95*, 876–882.

Snyder, C. R., & Higgins, R. L. (1988). Excuses: Their effective role in the negotiation of reality. *Psychological Bulletin, 104*, 23–35.

Snyder, J. A. (1977). A reinforcement analysis of interaction in problem and nonproblem children. *Journal of Abnormal Psychology, 86*, 528–535.

Sobin, C., Kiley-Brabeck, K., Daniels, S., Blundell, M., Anyane-Yeboa, K., & Karayiorgou, M. (2004). Networks of attention in children with the 22q11 deletion syndrome. *Developmental Neuropsychology, 26*, 611–626.

Sohlberg, M. M., & Mateer, C. A. (1989). *Cognitive rehabilitation: Introduction to theory and practice.* New York: Guilford Press.

Sohlberg, M. M., McLaughlin, K. A., Pavese, A., Heidrich, A., & Posner, M. I. (2000). Evaluation of attention process therapy training in persons with acquired brain injury. *Journal of Clinical and Experimental Neuropsychology, 22*, 656–676.

Spangler, G. (1989). Toddlers' everyday experiences as related to preceding mental and emotional disposition and their relationship to subsequent mental and motivational development: A short-term longitudinal study. *International Journal of Behavioral Development, 12*, 285–303.

Spearman, C. E. (1904). General intelligence objectively determined and measured. *American Journal of Psychology, 15*, 201–293.

Spelke, E. (2004). Core knowledge. In N. Kanwisher & J. Duncan (Eds.), *Attention and performance XX: Functional neuroimaging of visual cognition* (pp. 29–56). Oxford, England: Oxford University Press.

Spitzer, M., Kischka, U., Guckel, F., Bellemann, M. E., Kammer, T., Seyyedi, S., et al. (1998). Functional magnetic resonance imaging of category-specific cortical activation: Evidence for semantic maps. *Cognitive Brain Research, 6*, 309–319.

Spoont, M. R. (1992). Modulatory role of serotonin in neural information processing: Implications for human psychopathology. *Psychological Bulletin, 112*, 330–350.

Sprengelmeyer, R., Young, A. W., Schroeder, U., Grossenbacher, P. G., Federlein, J., Buettner, T., & Pzuntek, H. (1999). Knowing no fear. *Proceedings of the Royal Society of London. Series B, Biological Sciences, 266*, 2451–2456.

Squire, L. R. (1992). Memory and the hippocampus: A synthesis from studies of rats, monkeys and humans. *Psychological Review, 99*, 195–231.

Squire, L. R., Ojemann, J. G., Miezin, F. M., Petersen, S. E., Videen, T. O., & Raichle, M. E. (1992). Activation of the hippocampus in normal humans: A functional anatomical study of memory. *Proceedings of the National Academy of Sciences of the USA, 89*, 1837–1841.

Srinivasan, R. (1999). Spatial structure of the human alpha rhythm: Global correlation in adults and local correlation in children. *Clinical Neurophysiology, 110*, 1351–1362.

Stanovich, K. E., Cunningham, A. E., & Cramer, B. (1984). Assessing phonological awareness in kindergarten children: Issues of task comparability. *Journal of Experimental Psychology, 38,* 175–190.

Sternberg, S. (1969). The discovery of processing stages. *Acta Psychologica, 30,* 276–315.

Sternberg, S. (2004). Separate modifiability and the search for processing modules. In N. Kanwisher & J. Duncan (Eds.), *Attention and performance XX: Functional brain imaging of visual cognition* (pp. 125–139). Oxford, England: Oxford University Press.

Stifter, C. A., & Braungart, J. M. (1995). The regulation of negative reactivity in infancy: Function and development. *Developmental Psychology, 31,* 448–455.

Swanson, J., Deutsch, C., Cantwell, D., Posner, M. I., Kennedy, J., Barr, C., et al. (2001). Genes and attention-deficit hyperactivity disorder. *Clinical Neuroscience Research, 1,* 207–216.

Swanson, J., Oosterlaan, J., Murias, M., Moyzis, R., Schuck, S., Mann, M., et al. (2000). ADHD children with 7-repeat allele of the DRD4 gene have extreme behavior but normal performance on critical neuropsychological tests of attention. *Proceedings of the National Academy of Sciences of the USA, 97,* 4754–4759.

Swanson, J. M., Posner, M. I., Potkin, S., Bonforte, S., Youpa, D., Cantwell, D., & Crinella, F. (1991). Activating tasks for the study of visual–spatial attention in ADHD children: A cognitive anatomical approach. *Journal of Child Neurology, 6,* S119–S127.

Tanaka, J. W., & Curran, T. (2001). A neural basis for expert object recognition. *Psychological Science, 12,* 43–47.

Tanaka, J. W., & Taylor, M. (1991). Object categories and expertise: Is the basic level in the eye of the beholder? *Cognitive Psychology, 23,* 457–482.

Tarkiainen, A., Helenius, P., Hansen, P. C., Cornelissen, P. L., & Salmelin, R. (1999). Dynamics of letter string perception in the human occipitotemporal cortex. *Brain, 122,* 2119–2132.

Teglasi, H., & Epstein, S. (1998). Temperament and personality theory: The perspective of cognitive–experiential self-theory. *School Psychology Review, 27,* 534–550.

Tellegen, A. (1985). Structures of mood and personality and their relevance to assessing anxiety, with an emphasis on self-report. In A. H. Tuma & J. D. Maser (Eds.), *Anxiety and the anxiety disorders* (pp. 681–706). Hillsdale, NJ: Erlbaum.

Temple, E., Deutsch, G. K., Poldrack, R. A., Miller, S. L., Tallal, P., Merzenich, M. M., & Gabrieli, J. D. E. (2003). Neural deficits in children with dyslexia ameliorated by behavioral remediation: Evidence from functional MRI. *Proceedings of the National Academy of Sciences of the USA, 100,* 2860–2865.

Temple, E., & Posner, M. I. (1998). Brain mechanisms of quantity are similar in 5-year-olds and adults. *Proceedings of the National Academy of Sciences of the USA, 95,* 7836–7841.

Terrace, H. S. (1963). Discrimination learning with and without "errors." *Journal of the Experimental Analysis of Behavior, 6*, 1–27.

Thomas, A., & Chess, S. (1977). *Temperament and development*. New York: Brunner/Mazel.

Thomas, A., Chess, S., Birch, H. G., Hertzig, M. E., & Korn, S. (1963). *Behavioral individuality in early childhood*. New York: New York University Press.

Thomas, K. M., & Nelson, C. A. (2001). Serial reaction time learning in preschool- and school-age children. *Journal of Experimental Child Psychology, 79*, 364–387.

Thorndike, E. L., & Woodworth, R. S. (1901). The influence of one mental function upon the efficiency of other functions. *Psychological Review, 8*, 247–261.

Thurstone, L. L. (1924). *The nature of intelligence*. New York: Harcourt Brace.

Toga, A. W., & Mazziotta, J. C. (Eds.). (1997). *Brain mapping: The methods*. New York: Academic Press.

Tyler, L. E. (1976). The intelligence test: An evolving concept. In L. Resnick (Ed.), *The nature of intelligence* (pp. 13–26). Hillsdale, NJ: Erlbaum.

Tzelgov, J., Meyer, J., & Henik, A. (1992). Automatic and intentional processing of numerical information. *Journal of Experimental Psychology: Learning, Memory and Cognition, 18*, 166–179.

Ungerleider, L. G. (1995, November 3). Functional brain imaging studies of cortical mechanisms for memory. *Science, 270*, 769–775.

Uttal, W. R. (2001). *The new phrenology*. Cambridge, MA: MIT Press.

Valenza, E., Simion, F., & Umilta, C. (1994). Inhibition of return in newborn infants. *Infant Behavior and Development, 17*, 293–302.

van Veen, V., & Carter, C. S. (2002). The timing of action-monitoring processes in the anterior cingulate cortex. *Journal of Cognitive Neuroscience, 14*, 593–602.

Vasey, M. W., Daleiden, E. L., Williams, L. L., & Brown, L. M. (1995). Biased attention in childhood anxiety disorders: A preliminary study. *Journal of Abnormal Child Psychology, 23*, 267–279.

Venter, J. C., Adams, M. D., Myers, E. W., Li, P. W., Mural, R. J., Sutton, G. G., et al. (2001, February 16). The sequence of the human genome. *Science, 291*, 1304–1335.

Vernon, P. E. (1961). Intelligence and attainment. New York: Philosophical Library.

Victor, J. B., Rothbart, M. K., & Baker, S. R. (2005). *Integrating child temperament and personality in the Child Temperament and Personality Questionnaire*. Manuscript submitted for publication.

Vogel, E. K., & Machizawa, M. G. (2004, April 15). Neural activity predicts individual differences in visual working memory capacity. *Nature, 428*, 748–751.

Voytko, M. L., Olton, D. S., Richardson, R. T., Gorman, L. K., Tobin, J. R., & Price, D. L. (1994). Basal forebrain lesions in monkeys disrupt attention but not learning and memory. *Journal of Neuroscience, 14*, 167–186.

Wahlsten, D. (1999). Single-gene influences on brain and behavior. *Annual Review of Psychology, 50,* 599–624.

Wang, K. J., Fan, J., Dong, Y., Wang, C., Lee, T. M. C., & Posner, M. I. (2005). Selective impairment of attentional networks of orienting and executive control in schizophrenia. *Schizophrenia Research, 78,* 235–241.

Washburn, D. A. (1994). Stroop-like effects for monkeys and humans: Processing speed or strength of association? *Journal of Psychological Science, 5,* 375–379.

Watson, D., & Clark, L. A. (1992). On traits and temperament: General and specific factors of emotional experience and their relation to the five-factor model. *Journal of Personality, 60,* 441–476.

Werker, J. F., & Yeung, H. H. (2005). Infant speech perception bootstraps word learning. *Trends in Cognitive Sciences, 9,* 519–527.

Whalen, J., Gallistel, C. R., & Gelman, R. (1999). Nonverbal counting in humans: The psychophysics of number representation. *Psychological Science, 10,* 130–137.

Wilson, A. J., Dehaene, S., Rivkin, S. K., Cohen, L., & Cohen, D. (2006). *Design and testing of adaptive remediation software for dyscalculia.* Manuscript submitted for publication.

Winkelman, J., & Schmidt, J. (1974). Associative confusions in mental arithmetic. *Journal of Experimental Psychology, 102,* 734–737.

Wurtz, R. H., Goldberg, E., & Robinson, D. L. (1980). Behavioral modulation of visual responses in the monkey: Stimulus selection for attention and movement. *Progress in Psychobiology and Physiological Psychology, 9,* 43–83.

Wynn, K. (1992, August 27). Addition and subtraction by human infants. *Nature, 358,* 749–750.

Young, L. J., Nilsen, R., Waymire, K. G., MacGregor, G. R., & Insel, T. R. (1999, August 19). Increased affiliative response to vasopressin in mice expressing the V(1A) receptor from a monogamous vole. *Nature, 400,* 766–768.

Zuckerman, M. (1984). Sensation seeking: A comparative approach to a human trait. *Behavioral and Brain Sciences, 7,* 413–471.

Zuckerman, M. (1991). *Psychobiology of personality.* New York: Cambridge University Press.

Zuckerman, M. (1995). Good and bad humors: Biochemical bases of personality and its disorders. *Psychological Science, 6,* 325–332.

AUTHOR INDEX

Abdullaev, Y. G., 39, 156, 159, 160, 162
Aber, L., 73
Abrams, M. T., 95
Adler, A., 144
Adolphs, R., 126
Ahadi, S. A., 23, 47, 94, 123, 129, 130,
    137–139
Akbudak, E., 40
Allison, T., 155
Anderson, A. K., 126
Anderson, A. W., 203
Ansar, D., 182
Ashby, F. G., 87
Asher, S. R., 124
Assor, A., 144
Atkinson, R. C., 193
Auerbach, J., 106
Ausubel, D. P., 144
Awh, E., 192, 193
Ayduk, O., 137

Baddeley, A., 194
Badgaiyan, R., 197
Baker, S. R., 134, 135
Baldwin, D. A., 64
Bandura, A., 23
Barch, D. M., 136
Bates, J. E., 20, 22, 47, 48, 121, 122, 129,
    136, 141
Bauer, J., 55, 56
Bauer, P. J., 199
Bavelier, D., 117
Beauregard, M., 86
Beck, I. L., 166, 167, 213
Benes, F., 103
Berg, P., 156
Berger, A., 65, 70, 185, 213
Berntson, G. G., 174
Bernzweig, J., 137
Birch, H. G., 21
Bishop, D. V., 152
Blair, C., 134
Blair, R. J. R., 124

Blanchard, D. C., 127
Blasi, G., 107
Block, E., 176
Block, J., 130, 133
Block, J. H., 130, 133
Blumstein, S., 154
Bohart, A. C., 135
Boland, J. E., 64
Borton, R. W., 199
Botvinick, M. M., 88, 136
Bourgeois, J. P., 41
Bourgouin, P., 86
Bowlby, J., 69
Boyes-Braem, P., 202
Boyle, R. A., 145
Boysen, S. T., 174
Bramlett, R. K., 139
Brannon, E. M., 182
Braungart, J. M., 73
Braver, T. S., 136
Brennan, C., 65
Briand, L., 107
Broadhurst, P. L., 50
Broca, P., 26
Bronson, R. T., 51
Brown, J. R., 51
Brown, L. M., 133
Brown, T., 154
Bruer, J. T., 41
Bruner, J. S., 12
Brush, F. R., 50
Buchel, C., 34
Buckner, R. L., 196, 198
Bunge, S. A., 87
Bush, G., 80, 82, 83, 87, 104, 124
Bushnell, M. C., 86
Buss, A. H., 22, 122
Butcher, P. R., 57, 65, 66

Calabresi, P., 65
Calder, A. J., 126, 127
Calkins, S., 73
Canli, T., 125

Cantlon, J. F., 182
Carlson, S. M., 138
Carrier, B., 86
Carter, C. S., 82, 85, 88, 115, 136
Carter, E. J., 182
Carver, L. J., 199
Case, R., 183, 213
Casey, B. J., 95, 96
Caspi, A., 135
Chang, E., 36
Changeux, J.-P., 88
Chase, W. G., 10, 15, 190, 192
Cheatham, P. G., 174
Cheour, M., 152, 212
Chess, S., 21
Chi, M. T. H., 15, 189, 192, 202
Chochon, F., 185
Chua, H. F., 64
Church, R. M., 174
Cicchetti, D., 21
Clark, F., 124
Clark, L. A., 131
Clark, V. P., 39
Clifford, M. M., 23
Clohessy, A. B., 74, 65, 210
Cloninger, C. R., 125
Cohen, D., 213
Cohen, J. D., 88, 136
Cohen, L., 151, 152, 185, 213
Cohen, Y., 65
Collins, P., 87, 141
Connell, J. P., 23, 140
Conturo, T. E., 40
Cooper, L. A., 206
Corbetta, M., 61, 62, 63
Cornelissen, P. L., 155
Covington, M. V., 143, 145, 146
Cramer, B., 152, 212
Crick, F. H. C., 7
Crottaz-Herbette, S., 124
Cull, T. S., 40
Cunningham, A. E., 152, 212
Curran, T., 203

Dabholkar, A. S., 41, 58
Daleiden, E. L., 133
Damasio, A., 22
Davidson, M. C., 101, 102, 211
Davidson, R. J., 23, 27, 128
Davis, M., 126

Davis-Stober, C. P., 84, 115
Deci, E. L., 144
Dehaene, S., 39, 85, 88, 151, 175–177,
    181, 182, 184, 185, 213
Dehaene-Lambertz, G., 42, 43
Denckla, M. B., 95
Depue, R. A., 134
Derryberry, D., 19, 46, 47, 73, 89, 121,
    124, 126, 127, 129, 130, 133–
    135, 139, 141
Dhital, B., 182
Diamond, A., 43, 89, 90, 107
Dienstbier, R. A., 138
DiGirolamo, G. J., 68
Dikkes, P., 51
Ding, Y. C., 107
Dodge, K. A., 129
Dolan, R. J., 207
Donders, F. C., 28
Drevets, W. C., 86
Dronkers, N. F., 34, 162
Duda, R. O., 14
Duncan, G. H., 86
Duncan, J., 155
Dupoux, E., 175
Durston, S., 96
Dweck, C. S., 23, 143, 145

Early, T. S., 103
Eccles, J., 23
Eckenhoff, M. F., 41
Egan, M. F., 107
Eisenberg, N., 135, 137, 140
Elbert, T., 45, 203
Elliot, A. J., 134
Ellis, L. K., 76
Embe, R. N., 58
Epstein, S., 141, 142
Erez, A., 132
Ericsson, K. A., 15, 189, 192
Evans, D., 132
Everatt, J., 149

Fabes, R. A., 137
Fadem, K. C., 153, 212
Fan, J., 49, 62, 83, 92, 94, 106, 107, 210,
    211
Farah, M. J., 204
Farné, A., 36
Farr, M. J., 15, 189

Fathi, D. C., 202
Feigenson, L., 213
Ffytche, D. H., 39
Fiez, J. A., 8
Filipek, P. A., 96
Fisher, P., 94, 123
Flavell, J. H., 12
Flombaum, J. I., 62, 83
Forssberg, H., 117
Fossella, J. A., 46, 62, 96, 103, 106–107, 211
Fox, P. T., 8, 153
Friston, K. J., 30, 34
Frith, C., 138
Frith, U., 138
Friz, J. L., 102

Gabrieli, J. D., 87
Gaensbauer, T. J., 58
Gallistel, C. R., 174
Galton, F., 17
Ganis, G., 206
Garcia, N., 182
Gardner, H., 19
Gartstein, M. A., 127
Gautier, I., 203
Gazzaniga, M., 10, 100
Gehlbach, L., 107
Gelman, R., 174
Gendron, C. M., 50
Gerardi, G., 67
Gerardi-Caulton, G., 84, 91, 94, 137
Gerlai, R., 50
Gernsbacher, M. A., 189
Gershberg, R., 154
Gerstadt, C. L., 90
Gesell, A., 20, 21
Geuze, R. H., 57, 66
Giedd, J. N., 45, 59, 95
Giraud, A. L., 151
Givon, T., 163
Glaser, R., 15, 189
Goel, V., 207
Gold, B., 207
Goldapple, K., 216
Goldberg, E., 62
Goldman-Rakic, P. S., 41
González, A., 127
Goodman, G. S., 74, 210
Gore, J. C., 203

Gould, E., 59
Grafton, S. T., 76
Grandy, D. K., 106
Grasby, P. M., 127
Gray, J. A., 122, 124, 126, 133
Gray, W. D., 202
Graziano, W. G., 135
Green, C. S., 117
Greenberg, M., 51
Greene, D., 145
Greenwood, P. M., 102, 103, 211
Griffin, S. A., 183, 213
Groen, G. J., 186
Grolnick, W. S., 140
Gross, J. J., 87
Guilford, J. P., 18
Gunderson, V. M., 67
Gupta, L., 153, 212
Gusnard, D. A., 125
Guttorm, T. K., 152, 212
Guy, C. N., 39
Gwaizda, J., 55, 56

Habib, R., 162
Haith, M. M., 68, 74, 210
Hamilton, R., 203
Hamon, K., 182
Hansen, P. C., 155
Harackiewicz, J., 134
Harlan, E. T., 136
Harm, M. W., 170
Harman, C., 66, 67, 71, 72
Harmon, R. J., 58, 131
Harter, S., 23, 132, 141, 143–145
Hastings, N. B., 59
Haxby, J. V., 9
Hazan, C., 74, 210
Hazeltine, E., 76
Hebb, D. O., 12, 60, 100
Heidrich, A., 109, 194
Heinze, H. J., 39
Held, R., 55, 56
Helenius, P., 155
Henik, A., 65, 175
Hershey, K. L., 23, 94, 96, 123, 129, 130, 134, 137, 138, 139
Hertzig, M. E., 21
Hertz-Pannier, L., 42
Hicks, B. M., 135
Higgins, R. L., 143

Hillyard, S. A., 39
Hitch, G., 194
Hitchcock, J. M., 126
Holmes, A. P., 34
Hong, Y. J., 90
Houle, S., 207
Hubel, D. H., 63
Hugdahl, K., 27
Hunt, J. M., 131
Huttenlocher, P. R., 41, 58
Hwang, J., 132

Iacono, W. G., 134
Insel, T. R., 50, 128
Institute of Child Health and Human
    Development, 166
Isaacson, M. D., 50
Isen, A. M., 87, 132
Ivanitsky, A. M., 159, 160
Ivanitsky, G. A., 159, 160
Ivry, R., 76

Jacques, T. Y., 139
James, W., 80
Jenkins, W. M., 42, 45, 203
Johnsen, D. M., 202
Johnson, M. H., 55, 58, 67, 69, 73, 74,
    202, 207
Jones, E. E., 143
Jones, L. B., 22, 23, 91, 124
Jonides, J., 34, 192, 193

Kagan, J., 127
Kalverboer, A. F., 57, 66
Kapur, S., 207
Karni, A., 203
Katz, D., 154
Kaufman, A. S., 114
Kaufman, N. L., 114
Kazen, M., 87
Keogh, B. K., 22, 140
Kerszberg, M., 88
Kieffer, B. L., 50
Kieras, J., 93
Klein, R. M., 149
Klingberg, T., 117, 215
Knaack, A., 47

Kochanska, G., 21, 47, 129, 136,
    139
Koechlin, E., 176
Koenig, A. L., 139
Koeppe, R. A., 34, 192
Koeske, R. D., 202
Kook, H., 153, 212
Korn, S., 21
Kosslyn, S. M., 157, 206
Krapp, A., 132
Kremen, A. M., 130, 133
Krueger, R. F., 135
Kruglanski, A. W., 145
Kruzich, P. J., 106
Kuhl, J., 87
Kuhl, P. K., 43, 152, 166, 211, 212
Kumar, R., 103, 211

Lakoff, G., 207
Lane, R. D., 86, 124
Larson, C. L., 128
Lashley, K. S., 26, 27
Lawrence, A. D., 126, 127
LeBihan, D., 176
LeDoux, J. E., 22, 123, 125
Lepper, M. R., 145
Levesque, J., 86
Lewis, T. L., 63
Lillard, A., 118
Liu, H. M., 43, 152, 212
Lobe, C. G., 51
Loftus, E. F, 202
Lori, N. F., 40
Lucas, E., 182
Luu, P., 80, 83, 87, 124, 141

MacGregor, G. R., 50
Machizawa, M. G., 195, 196
Marrocco, R. T., 101, 102, 211
Marshuetz, C., 34, 192
Martin, R. P., 22, 140
Marx, R. W., 145
Maslin-Cole, P. M., 131
Mateer, C. A., 109
Maurer, C., 42, 55
Maurer, D., 42, 55, 63
Mauro, J. A., 127
Mazziotta, J. C., xi, 30

McCandliss, B. D., 49, 62, 83, 112, 114,
    116, 151, 155, 163, 164, 166,
    167, 169, 171, 210, 213, 214
McCarthy, G., 155
McClelland, J. L., 149
McCleod, A. M. K., 8
McGowan, S. W., 127
McGue, M., 135
McLaughlin, K. A., 109
McMullen, P., 149
Meck, W. H., 174
Mehler, J., 175
Meltzoff, A. N., 199
Mennon, V., 124
Mervis, C. B., 202
Merzenich, M. M., 42, 45, 203
Meyer, J., 175
Milberg, W., 154
Mills, C., 117, 118
Mills, D., 117, 118
Mintun, M., 153
Mischel, W., 73, 137
Molfese, D. L., 152, 153, 212
Monaco, A. P., 152
Montessori, M., 118
Moore, C. J., 30, 151
Morgan, G. A., 131
Morton, J., 67, 202
Moses, L. J., 138
Murray, K. T., 136, 139

Naccache, L., 176
Nagy, A., 51
Nagy, Z., 215
Neely, J. H., 201
Nelson, C. A., 199, 200
Neville, H. J., 100
Newbury, D. F., 152
Newell, A., 14
Nicholls, J. G., 23
Nikolaev, A. R., 159, 160
Nilsen, R., 50
Nimchinsky, E. A., 93
Nisbett, R. E., 64, 145
Nishijo, H., 125
Nishino, H., 125
Nobre, A. C., 155
Noppeney, U., 151
Norman, D. A., 81, 82

Nyberg, L., 162
Nyman, M., 137

O'Boyle, C. G., 73
Ochsner, K. N., 87
Olesen, P. J., 117
Olson, S. L., 136
Ono, T., 125
Orendi, J. L., 96

Panksepp, J., 22, 124–126, 128, 135
Pantev, C., 45, 203
Parasuraman, R., 102, 103, 211
Pardo, J. V., 8
Parker, J. G., 124
Parkman, J. M., 186
Pascual-Leone, A., 203
Patterson, G. R., 130
Paulesu, M. I., 151
Pavese, A., 109, 156
Peake, P. K., 137
Pelphrey, K. A., 182
Perfetti, C., 166, 167, 214
Petersen, S. E., 8, 60, 124, 126, 153, 154
Pettit, G. S., 129
Pfaff, D. W., 51
Phelps, E. A., 126
Piaget, J., 130
Pien, D., 92
Pinel, P., 176, 178, 184
Pintrich, P. R., 145
Pinulas, A., 137
Pliszka, S. R., 129
Plomin, R., 22, 122
Polk, T. A., 204
Pollatsek, A., 159
Posner, M. I., xi, 7, 19, 22, 28, 30–33,
    36, 39, 46, 47, 49, 55, 60, 62, 66,
    67–74, 76, 80–85, 88, 91, 93, 96,
    103, 106, 107, 109, 112, 114–
    116, 124–127, 151, 153, 155–
    157, 159, 160, 162–164, 169,
    180, 182, 183, 185, 195, 197,
    206, 210, 211, 213, 214, 216
Premack, A., 43
Premack, D., 43
Price, C. J., 30, 34, 151
Price, D. D., 86

Pullis, M., 141
Putnam, K. M., 128

Quartz, S., 100

Rafal, R., 65
Raichle, M. E., xi, 7, 8, 30–36, 47, 62,
    68, 81, 82, 86, 88, 103, 153, 157,
    161, 162, 195, 206
Rainville, P., 86
Rakic, P., 41
Ravitch, D., 14
Rayner, K., 159
Raz, M., 49
Reed, M. A., 92, 124, 126, 133, 134,
    139, 141
Reiman, E. M., 103
Reiss, A. L., 95
Riviere, D., 176
Rivkin, S. K., 213
Ro, T., 36
Robertson, R. R. W., 189
Robinson, D. L., 62
Rockstroh, B., 45, 203
Rodriquez, M., 73
Rogosch, F. A., 21
Rosch, E., 202
Rosen, J. B., 126
Ross, J. L., 95
Roth, G., 144
Rothbart, M. K., 19, 20, 22, 23, 46–48,
    55, 57, 66, 67–69, 71–74, 76, 80,
    84, 89, 91–94, 96, 112, 114–116,
    121–127, 129–130, 132, 134–
    141, 210, 216
Rowell, R. K., 139
Rueda, M. R., 22, 76, 84, 92, 94, 107,
    112, 114–116, 125, 210, 213
Ruff, H. A., 57, 80
Rumbaugh, D. M., 110, 112
Ryan, R. M., 140

Saccamanno, L., 112, 114, 116, 210
Salmelin, R., 155
Sandak, R., 166, 167, 214
Sanders, A. F., 194
Sandy, J. M., 136
Sapir, A., 65

Schacter, D., 195
Scherg, M., 156
Schiefele, A., 132
Schilling, E. M., 136
Schmidt, J., 186
Schroots, J. J. F., 194
Schumacher, E. H., 180
Sciolto, T., 65
Scott, P. L., 139
Seidenberg, M. S., 149, 170
Sejnowski, T., 100
Sethi, A., 73
Shallice, T., 81, 82, 194
Shaw, J. C., 14
Shaywitz, B. A., 167, 169
Shaywitz, S. E., 35, 147, 150, 154, 167,
    168
Sheese, B., 122, 124, 140
Shepard, R. N., 206
Shiffrin, R. M., 193
Shimony, J. S., 40
Shiner, R. L., 131, 133, 135
Shirley, M. M., 20
Shoda, Y., 73, 137
Shortliffe, E. H., 14
Shulman, G. L., 61, 62, 63
Siegler, R. S., 183, 185, 213
Simion, F., 66
Simon, H. A., 10, 14, 190
Simon, T. J., 107
Singer, H. S., 95
Skinner, B. F., 11
Skudlarsky, P., 203
Slater, A., 70
Smeets, W. J. A. J., 127
Smith, E. E., 34, 192
Smith, J., 189
Smith, M., 124
Snyder, A. Z., 40
Snyder, C. R., 143
Snyder, J. A., 130
Sobin, C., 107
Sohlberg, M. M., 109
Sommer, T., 49, 107, 108, 211
Soroker, N., 65
Spangler, G., 132
Spearman, C. E., 18
Spelke, E., 43, 70, 184, 213
Spitzer, M., 204
Spoont, M. R., 127
Sprengelmeyer, R., 126

Squire, L. R., 195, 196
Srinivasan, R., 215
Stanescu, R., 184
Stanovich, K. E., 152, 212
Sternberg, S., 29–30, 35
Stifter, C. A., 73
Stipek, D. J., 135
Sunderland, T., 102
Swanson, J. M., 104, 106
Swartz, K. B., 67

Takahashi, S. N., 127
Tanaka, J. W., 202, 203
Tanapat, P., 59
Tarkiainen, A., 155
Tarr, M. J., 203
Taub, E., 45, 203
Taylor, M., 202
Teglasi, H., 141, 142
Tellegen, A., 131
Temple, E., 168, 180, 182, 183
Terrace, H. S., 12
Thomas, A., 21
Thomas, K. M., 83, 200
Thomas-Thrapp, L., 66, 67
Thompson, W. L., 157, 206
Thorndike, E. L., 11, 14
Thurstone, L. L., 18
Tobin, R. M., 135
Toga, A. W., xi, 30
Trainor, R. J., 95, 96
Tsao, F. M., 43, 152, 212
Tsivkin, S., 184
Tucker, D. M., 85, 87, 141
Tulving, E., 162
Turken, U. A., 87
Tyler, L. E., 17
Tzelgov, J., 175
Tzur, G., 70, 185, 213

Umilta, C., 66
Ungerleider, L. G., 9
Uttal, W. R., 26

Valenza, E., 66
Vandegeest, K. A., 139
van de Moortele, P. F., 185

van Veen, V., 85, 115
Vasey, M. W., 133
Venter, J. C., 7, 10, 99
Vernon, P. E., 18
Vicera, S. P., 65
Victor, J. B., 134, 135
Videen, T. O., 8
Vogel, E. K., 195, 196
Voytko, M. L., 102

Wahlsten, D., 50
Wang, K. J., 104, 105
Warrington, E. K., 194
Washburn, D. A., 94, 110, 112, 174
Waters, J. M., 199
Watson, D., 131
Watson, J. D., 7
Waymire, K. G., 50
Wellborn, J. G., 23
Werker, J. F., 152
Westerberg, H., 117, 215
Whalen, J., 174
White, C. T., 174
Wiebe, S. A., 199
Wienbruch, C., 45, 203
Wiesel, T., 63
Williams, L. L., 133
Williford, A., 73
Wilson, A. J., 213, 214
Winkelman, J., 186
Winteler, A., 132
Winterburn, D., 151
Woodworth, R. S., 11, 14
Worsley, K. J., 34
Wortz, R. H., 62
Wu, Y., 106
Wynn, K., 70, 185, 213

Ye, H., 51
Ye, R., 47, 123
Yeung, H. H., 152
Young, A. W., 126
Young, L. J., 50

Zecevic, N., 41
Zeki, S., 39
Ziaie, H., 73
Zuckerman, M., 125, 127, 128

SUBJECT INDEX

Activated state working memory, 192
Addition, 185
Additive factors approach, 29, 35, 178
ADHD. *See* Attention-deficit/
    hyperactivity disorder
Affiliativeness, 128, 135–136
Age equivalence, 17
Aggression
    defensive, 127
    and effortful control, 137
    and fear, 129
    and frustration, 126–127, 134–135
Aggressiveness, 111
Agreeableness, 135–136
Alerting network, 59, 60
    brain areas involved in, 36
    measuring efficiency of, 50, 51
    and norepinephrine, 101–102
Alzheimer's disease, 102
Amygdala
    and aggression, 126–127
    and fear/inhibition, 125–126
    and fear response, 48, 83
Animal studies, 110–112
"A not B" task, 43
ANT. *See* Attention Network Test
Anterior cingulate, 70
    evolution of, 93
    and executive attention, 81–83, 86
    and schizophrenia, 103, 104
    and training, 210
Anterior cingulate gyrus, 85
Anticipating targets, 74, 90
Anxiety
    and ADHD, 129
    and school motivation, 141
Apoliproprotein (APOE) gene, 102–103
Approach behavior
    brain function related to, 125
    and fear, 133
    and self-control, 135
Approximation, 184
APT. *See* Attention process therapy
Arabic digits, 174

Arithmetic, 183–186
Articulation, 149, 153
Artificial intelligence research, 14
Associationist view of learning, 11–12
Attention
    and education, 15–16
    executive. *See* Executive attention
    and explicit learning, 199–201
    imaging studies of, 9–10
    infant development of, xi
    orienting of, 210
    regulatory functions of, 128–130
    time-course data related to, 39
    visual, 63
    Web-based education for, 213
Attentional networks
    and child development, 9–10
    and education, 16
Attention-deficit/hyperactivity disorder
    (ADHD)
    and anxiety, 129
    and brain size, 96
    and dopamine-4 receptor, 93,
        103–106
    and training of attention, 117
Attention in Early Development (H. A.
    Ruff and M. K. Rothbart), 80
Attention Network Test (ANT), 48–50,
    52, 59, 62, 83, 84, 92–93, 211
Attention process therapy (APT),
    109–110
Attention system, 59–61
Auditory memory, 118
Auditory system, 211–212

Basal ganglia, 68, 76
BDNF gene, 107, 108
Bean bag game, 118
Behavioral Approach system, 20
Behavioral Inhibition System, 20, 134
Behavioral studies, 43, 106–107
Big Five personality factors, 48
Binet, Alfred, 16–18

Blood supply, 7
Braille letters, 203
Brain activity and areas
    for attentional networks, 60
    direct observation of, 7–8
    individual differences in, 44
    for perception/imagination, 206
    and quantity determination,
        176–177
    in reading, 155–161
    and reading training, 168
Brain development, 41–52
    behavioral/electrical recording
        studies of, 43
    early, 58–59
    and efficiency of neural networks,
        48–52
    and genetics, 45–46
    individual differences in, 44–48
    and intelligence/efficiency, 44–45
    longitudinal studies of, 42
    and marker tasks, 43–44
    morphometry of, 44
    synaptic exuberance/pruning in,
        41–42
    and temperament, 46–48
Brain imaging studies, design of, 33–35
Brain injury
    and attention deficit, 106
    concentration problems due to,
        108–109
    and explicit memory, 198
Brain networks, 9
    distributed, 36
    efficiency of, 48–52
    timing activity in, 36–38
Brain research
    and temperament, 22–23
    Web site about, xii
Brain size, 94–96
Broca's area, 192, 193
Bruner, Jerome, 12

Cajal, Santiago Ramon y, 7
Caregiver–infant relationship
    and attention, 64
    communication, 58
    and control of fixation, 69
    and soothing, 71–73
Carnegie Mellon University, 192

Cataracts, 63
Categorization
    and experience, 204–205
    mechanisms of, 202–204
CBQ (Children's Behavior
        Questionnaire), 123
CC. See Corpus callosum
Cells, 93–94
Center for Educational Research and
        Innovation, 213
Cerebral hemispheres, separated, 27
Checkerboard pattern, 68
Chemical modulators, 60
Chess, Stella, 21
Chess masters, 15, 190–191
Child development. See also
        Infants/infancy
    and attentional networks, 9–10
    and cognition, 12–13
    and eye movement, 57–58
    and temperament, 22
Children
    conflict-related tasks for, 83–85
    localization of number line in,
        181–183
    and Stroop tasks, 83
Children's Behavior Questionnaire
        (CBQ), 123
Child studies, 112, 113
Chinese culture, 64
Choleric temperament, 20
Cholinergic system, 102–103, 211
Chunking digits, 192
Chunking letters, 35
Ciccetti, D., 21
Cingulate, layer V of, 93
Cingulate gyrus, 81
Classical conditioning, 11
Clonidine, 101–102
Coding of input, 192–195
Cognition, 12–13
    control of emotion and, 80–81,
        86–89
    in reading, 149–155
Cognitive conflict, 82–85
Cognitive development, 11–13
Cognitive science, 14–15
Collicular system, 67
Color Stroop task, 85
Communication, 210
Competence, 134

Compulsory education, 17
Computations, 28
Computers, problem solving by, 14
COMT gene, 106–107
Conflict effect, 92
Conflict-related tasks, 84
Conflict resolution, 48
Conjunction designs, 34
Conscience, development of, 139
Constitution, 46
Constructivism, 10, 100–101
Content of mind's representation, 18–19
Control of fixation, developing, 68–71
Corpus callosum (CC), 40, 83
Cortex
    childhood thickening of, 42
    and control of fixation, 69
    development of, 41, 55
    and IOR, 65–67
    and orienting to sensory stimuli, 61
    and reading acquisition, 150
Counting, 185
Covington, M. V., 146
Cross-talk, 88
Cued recall, 196
Cultural differences
    in orienting, 64, 210
    and self-regulation, 47

DA. See Dopamine
DAT1 gene. See Dopamine Transporter
    gene
Defensive aggression, 127
Depression, 216
Developmental pathologies, 96
Diamond, Adele, 43
Diffusion tensor imaging, 40, 42, 215
Digits, memorization of, 15
Digit training, 174
Disengaging from stimuli, 69
Distance effect in number processing,
    175, 178, 179
Distraction, 71
Distress keeper, 71
Distributed brain networks, 36
DNA, discovery of, 7
Donders, F. C., 28, 29
Dopamine (DA)
    and ADHD, 93
    and cognitive processing, 87

and executive attention, 52,
    103–106, 211
and frustration, 127
genes related to, 107
and temperament, 125
twins studies related to, 106
Dopamine-4 receptor (DRD4) gene
    and ADHD, 52, 93, 105–106
    neuroimaging studies of, 107,
        108
    and sensation seeking, 48
Dopamine Transporter (DAT1) gene,
    107, 115
DRD4 gene. See Dopamine-4 receptor
    gene
Duda, R. O., 14–15
Dweck, Carol, 143
Dyslexia, 215

e4 allele, 102–103
Early core of personality, 20
Edges, preference for, 68
Education, 10–16
    and attention, 15–16
    brain-function, 109–110
    and cognitive development, 11–
        13
    and cognitive science, 14–15
    compulsory, 17
    selectionist vs. constructivist view
        of, 10
    and transfer of training/expertise,
        13–14
EEG. See Electroencephalogram
Efficiency
    and brain development, 44–45
    of brain networks, 48–52
Effortful control, 136–140
    and brain development, 46–47
    development of, 136–137
    and education, 139–140, 216
    and empathy/morals/social
        competence, 138–139
    individual differences in, 94
    and temperament, 22, 123
Ego development, 141–143
Einstein, Albert, 94–95
Electrodes, 36–40, 42
Electroencephalogram (EEG), 113,
    115–117

Emotion
  awareness and control of, 85–86
  control of cognition and, 80–81,
    86–89
  regulation of, 80
Empathy, learning, 138
English language, 151, 153
Environment, 13
ERP. *See* Event-related potential
Error
  correction, 179
  detection, 70
  response, 85
Error-related negativity, 87
Event-related potential (ERP), 36–39
Executive attention, 79–97
  anatomy of, 79–80
  and brain size, 94–96
  childhood testing of, 89–93
  of cognition/emotion, 80–81
  development of, 89–94
  and dopamine, 103–106
  individual differences in, 94
  measuring, 81–89
  and temperament, 22
Executive attention network
  brain areas involved in, 59–61
  functions of, 80–81
  and self-regulation, 210, 211
Experience, reading affected by, 161–
    166
Expertise, 189–208
  imagery, 206–207
  memory role in, 191–201
  metaphor, 207–208
  reasoning, 207
  thought, expert, 201–205
  and transfer of training, 13–14
Expert thought, 201–205
  categories used in, 201–204
  and novices, 202
Explicit learning, 80–81, 195
Explicit memory, 198–201
Extraversion
  and brain development, 46, 47
  and development, 133
  and fear, 21
  and 7-repeat allele, 106
Extrinsic motivation, 145
Eye contact exercises, 117
Eye movements, 57–58, 65

Eyes (as indicator of attention), 210
Eysenck, Hans, 20

Faces
  as natural categories, 202
  preference for, 67
Fast Forward program, 169
Fear
  and amygdala, 48
  brain systems involved in, 125–126
  and competence, 134
  and extraversion, 21
  and inhibition, 127
  and mastery motivation, 133
  and moral development, 129
  processing, 83
  and school motivation, 141
  and self-regulation, 47
  and sociability, 129
Fearfulness, 50, 51
Fear of failure, 143–144
Fixation, developing control of, 68–71
fMRI. *See* Functional magnetic resonance
    imaging
Formal educational disciplines, 13
4-repeat allele, 107
Frames of Mind (Howard Gardner), 19
Frustration, 126–127, 134–135
Functional imaging, 215
Functional magnetic resonance imaging
    (fMRI), 30, 32, 37–42
Fusiform gyrus, 39

g. See General factor
Galton, Francis, 17–18
Gardner, Howard, 19, 186
Gazzaniga, Michael, 10, 100
Gender differences, 144
Gene deletion, 51
General factor (*g*), 17–19
General Problem Solver, 14
Genes, 10
Genetics, 99–108
  and alerting–norepinephrine,
    101–102
  and attention, 211
  and behavioral studies, 106–107
  and brain development, 45–46
  and cholinergic system, 102–103

and dopamine, 103–106
and executive attention, 103–106
and heritability studies, 106
and neuroimaging studies, 107–108
and orienting, 102–103
selectionist/constructivist views of,
100–101
studies of human, 51–52
and temperament, 48
and 7-repeat allele of DRD4,
105–107
temperament and behavioral, 50, 51
and 22q11 deletion syndrome, 107
Geodesic sensor net, 36, 37
Gesell, A., 21
Go–no go task, 96
Gratification, delay of, 73, 137
Grating acuity, 56
Gray, Jeffrey, 20
Gray matter, 45
Guanfacine, 101–102
Guilford, J. P., 18

Habituation, 69–70
Harm avoidance, 130
Hebb, D. O., 12, 100
Helmholtz, Hermann von, 28
Heritability studies, 106
Hippocampus, 198
Human genome, 10
Hungary, 118
Hyperactivity, 52
Hypnotism, 87
Hypothalamic neuropeptide oxytocin,
128

Imagery, 206–207
Imaging of human brain function. See
also Neuroimaging technology
future uses for, 215
localized, 26
and therapy, 216
Imitation, 199
Implicit memory, 195–198
Inattention disorder, 52
Independent manipulation, 30
Individual differences, 16–23
in brain structure/function, 44–48
in executive attention, 94

in intelligence, 16–19
in temperament, 19–23
Infant habituation methods, 43
Infants/infancy
brain development in, 58–59
IOR development in, 65–67
soothing of, 71
visual attention in, 63
visual skills learned in, 55
Inferiority, feelings of, 143–144
Information representation, 80
Inhibition, behavioral
brain systems involved in, 125–126
and distress, 127
Inhibition of return (IOR), 63, 65–67
Input phonology, 149, 153
Instrumental conditioning, 11
Insula, 93
Intelligence(s), 16–19
approaches to thinking about, 145
and brain development, 44–45
general factor of, 17–19
and habituation, 70
interpersonal, 19
intrapersonal, 19
multiple, 19, 186
and prediction of school
performance, 16–17
Intelligence quotient (IQ), 17, 45
Internalization, 140
Intrinsic motivation, 23, 145
Intuition, 198
IOR. See Inhibition of return
IQ. See Intelligence quotient
Italian language, 153

James, William, 80

K-BIT, 114
Keki (artificial language), 163–165
Kinesthetic intelligence, 19
Kochanska, G., 21, 129, 136

Language
and arithmetic, 184–185
behavioral/electrical recording
studies of, 43
and counting, 185

Language, *continued*
  as localized function, 26
  and school preparation, 211–213
Lashley, K. S., 26
Lateral intraparietal (LIP) area, 62
Learning
  associationist view of, 11–12
  explicit, 80–81
  goals, 144–146
  principle (Hebb), 100
  social, 23
  and visual skill, 74–76
Left hemisphere, 27, 35, 62
Line of sight, 89
Linguistic intelligence, 19
LIP (lateral intraparietal) area, 62
Literacy, 147–172
  acquiring, 166–171
  experience effects on, 161–166
  implications for research on,
    171–172
  methods for studying, 148–161
  Web-based education for, 213
Localization of mental operations, 25–28,
    35
  history of study, 26
  and number line development,
    181–183
  and split-brains, 27–28
Location
  conflicts with, 83–85
  and memory, 193
  novel object vs., 67–68
Locus coeruleus, 60
Longitudinal MRI studies, 42
Long-term memory, 107

Magnetic resonance image (MRI), 31,
    32, 44, 45
MAOA gene, 107, 108
Marker tasks, 43–44
Mastery motivation, 131–136
  definitions of, 131
  developmental changes in, 132–136
  and fear, 133
  and positive affect, 132
MAT (matrix task), 114
Mathematics, 19, 213
Matrix task (MAT), 114
Melancholic temperament, 20

Memory
  auditory, 118
  and coding of input, 192–193
  expertise and role of, 191–201
  explicit, 198–201
  and explicit learning, 80–81
  implicit, 195–198
  long-term, 107
  working. *See* Working memory
Memory span, 192
Mental chronometry, 28
Mental operations
  localization of, 25–28
  speed of, 28–30
Metaphor, 207–208
Methylphenidate, 104
Microscope, 7
Min strategy, 185–186
Molecular genetics research, 101
Montessori tradition, 118
Moral development, 129, 139
Morphometry, 44
Motivation, 23
  learning goals fostering, 144–146
  for school subjects, 141
Motor effect, 179
Motor learning, 195
MRI. *See* Magnetic resonance image
Mueller, Johannes, 28
Multifinality, principle of, 21
Multiple intelligences, 19, 186
Music sessions, 118
Myelin sheath, 42, 59

Nasal field stimuli, 65
National Institutes of Health, 95
National Reading Panel, 166
Natural categories, 202
Nature's Mind (Michael Gazzaniga), 10
Negative affect
  and cognition, 86–87
  and guilt, 138–139
  and soothing, 73
  and temperament, 46, 47, 123
Negative emotionality, 127–128
Neuroimaging, 30–41
  of brain networks, 9
  and design of brain imaging studies,
    33–35
  of distributed brain networks, 36

and effect of practice on brain
   activity, 35
electrical imaging and functional,
   37–41
fMRI, 32
PET, 31–32
of practiced activity, 8
of timing activity in brain networks,
   36–38
Neuroimaging studies, 107–108
Neuroimaging technology, 7–9
New York Longitudinal Study (NYLS),
   21–22
Nimchinsky, E. A., 93
Norepinephrine
   and alerting, 60, 101–102
   and MAOA gene, 107
Norman, Donald, 81, 82
Notation effect, 179
Noun use, 88
Novelty
   detecting, 64
   and IOR, 65–67
   of objects vs. locations, 67–68
   preference for, 71
Nucleus basalis of Meynert, 102
Number line, 174–180
   and arithmetic, 183–186
   and counting, 185
   definition of, 176
   development of, 180–186
   implications for improving
      education, 186
   and localization in children,
      181–183
   and min strategy, 185–186
   training in, 183
Numeracy, 173–187
   and brain, 176–177
   development of, 180–186, 215
   interaction of other skills and,
      186–187
   order of operations in, 177–180
   quantity, understanding of, 173–174
   and school preparation, 213
   and training, 216
   Web-based education for, 214
Numerical Stroop effect, 174, 175
Numerical Stroop task, 110–111
NYLS. See New York Longitudinal Study

Object, novel locations vs., 67–68
Obligatory looking, 68–69
OECD. See Organisation for Economic
   Co-operation and Development
Organisation for Economic Co-operation
   and Development (OECD), xii,
   213
Orienting
   and cholinergic system, 102–103
   detecting novel events, 64
   development of, 92
   functions of, 63–68
   measuring efficiency of, 50, 51
   and school preparation, 210, 211
   soothing by, 71–72
Orienting network, 59–63
Output phonology, 149, 153

Pain perception, 87
Panksepp, J., 124
Parasuraman, R., 103
Parietal lobe, 61, 62, 69
Parietal structures, 76
Parietal systems, 70
Passive viewing of words, 33
Pavlov, I. P., 11, 20
Peripheral vision, 57
Perseveration, 91, 96
Persistence, 125
Personality
   early core of, 20
   and ego development, 141–143
PET. See Positron emission tomography
Phoneme awareness, 43, 166–169,
   211–213
Phoneme discrimination, 70
Phonological processing, 152–154
Phrenology, 26
Piaget, Jean, 12, 130
Polymorphisms, 10
Positive affect
   and cognition, 87
   and dopamine, 125
   and sustained engagement, 132
Positron emission tomography (PET),
   30–32, 39, 42
Positrons, 31
Postal workers, 204–205

Practiced activity, 8
    effect of, 35
    and reading, 161–163
    and rehabilitation of attention, 109
Prefrontal cortex, 44
Preschool children, 112, 113
Primate vocalization, 93
Priming, 191, 197
Problem of pure insertion, 33
Problem solving, 14–15, 87
Product of mind's representation, 19
Puberty, 41, 42, 58
Punishments, 23, 130

Quantity, understanding, 173–174

Ravitch, Diane, 14
Reaching task, 43–44, 89–90
Reaction-time studies, 33
Reactivity, 19, 46, 121
Reading. *See also* Literacy
    model of operations involved in,
        149
    network of cortical areas involved
        in, 34, 35
    order of operations in, 157–160
    and Stroop task, 83
    timing of brain activation in,
        155–161
    and training, 167–169
    visual processing involved in,
        150–152
Reading aloud, 88, 159
Reading skill
    development of, 215
    and phoneme awareness, 212
    and training, 216
    and visual word form system
        development, 214
Reasoning, 207
Reflex response, 11
Rehabilitation of attention, 109–110
Representation of information, 80
Responsivity, 22
Reward(s)
    in animal studies, 110
    and instrumental learning, 141
    and motivation for learning, 23
    problems with use of, 145

B. F. Skinner's study of use of, 11,
    13
    and temperament, 130
Rhyming, 153
Right hemisphere, 27, 60
Rightstart, 183, 186, 213
Rothbart, M. K., 80
Ruff, H. A., 80

Saccades, 64, 148
Sanguine temperament, 20
Scalp electrodes, 42
Scalp-recorded electrical activity, 36–40,
    43, 215
Scalp signature, 38
Schizophrenia, 103–105, 107
School environment
    attention training in, 117–118
    control of cognition/emotions in, 81
    and effortful control, 139–140
    and temperament, 124, 140–146
    temperament applied to, 22
School performance prediction, 16–17
School preparation, 209–216
    future studies on, 215–216
    and language, 211–213
    and numeracy, 213
    and orienting of attention, 210
    and self-regulation, 210–211
    Web-based education for, 213–214
School-related self-concepts, 23
Scopolamine, 102
Selectionism, 10, 100–101
Self-differentiation, 144–145
Self-regulation, 85
    and approach behavior, 135
    and brain development, 46, 47
    and school preparation, 210–211
    and temperament, 19–20, 22
Self-soothing, 73
Self-worth, 143–144
Semantic activations, 156–157
Semantic analysis, 154–155
Semantic maps, 204
Sensation seeking, 48, 106, 107, 125
Sequence learning, 74–76
Sequential eye movement task, 91
Shallice, Tim, 81, 82
Shifting operation, 36
Shirley, M. M., 20

Shortliffe, E. H., 14–15
Simon, Herbert, 10, 13, 15, 100, 191
Simon Says (game), 91–92
Skinner, B. F., 11–13, 141
Sleep, 60
Sociability, 111
Social development
    and self-regulation, 140
    and temperament, 139
Social learning, 23
Soothing, 71–73
Spatial conflict task, 85, 90–91
Spatial intelligence, 19
Spatial location, 193
Spatial Stroop conflict task, 138
Spearman, C. E., 18
Speed of mental operations, 28–30
Sperry, Roger, 27
Split-brain research, 27–28, 151–152
Stem completion, 196
Stop–go games, 117–118
"Streams of thought," 80
Stripes, 68
Stroop effect, 61, 82–83
Stroop-like tasks, 90
Structural imaging, 215
Structural MRI, 32
Subroutines, 28
Subtractive method, 28–29, 33, 34, 39
Superior coliculus, 65, 66, 68
Superior parietal lobe, 36, 62
Surgency–extraversion, 123, 131, 132
Sustained engagement, 132
Synapses
    exuberance/pruning of, 41, 42
    proliferation/pruning of, 215
Synaptic density, 58–59

teach-the-brain.org (Web site), xii
Temperament, 19–23, 121–146
    affiliativeness, 128
    alternatives to, 23
    approach/inhibition/mastery
        motivation in, 130–140
    and behavioral genetics, 50, 51
    and brain development, 46–48
    and brain research, 22–23
    definition of, 121
    development of, 22, 122–130
    dimensions of, 21–23

and effortful control, 22, 123
emotional aspects of, 123–124
history of study, 20–21
negative emotionality, 127–128
neural models for, 124–127
regulatory functions of attention,
    128–130
and reward/punishment, 130
and school environment, 22,
    140–146
Temperamental reactivity, 121
Temporal visual stimuli, 65
Theory-of-mind tasks, 138
Thick-letter task, 157–158
Thomas, Alexander, 21
Thorndike, Edward, 11, 13–14
Thought(s)
    expert, 201–205
    generating new, 162–163
Thurstone, L. L., 18
Time-course data, 39, 40
Timing activity, 36–38
TMS (transcranial magnetic stimulation),
    36
Tonic alertness, 60
Training
    and cognitive science, 14–15
    and expertise, 13–14
    numeracy, 183
    self-regulation, 210
Training of attention, 108–118
    animal studies of, 110–112
    child studies of, 112, 113
    developmental interventions for,
        110–117
    EEG data regarding, 115–117
    effects of, 112–115
    in rehabilitation, 109–110
    in schools, 117–118
Transcranial magnetic stimulation
    (TMS), 36
Transmitter systems, 101
Twins studies, 106
Tyler, Leona, 17

Vasopressin receptors, 50
Verbal coding, 194–195
Verbal conflict, 90
Verbal systems, 192–193
Vernon, P. E., 18

Video games, 117
Visual activations, 155–156
Visual acuity, 55, 56
Visual attention, 63
Visual coding, 194–195
Visual object perception, 214
Visual processing (in reading), 150–152
Visual skill, 55–77
    acuity, 56
    attention in infancy, 63
    attention system of human brain,
        59–61
    early brain development, 58–59
    eye movements in children, 57–58
    fixation control development, 68–71
    and learning, 74–76
    orienting functions, 63–68
    orienting network, 62–63
    soothing, 71–73
Visual system mapping, 39
Visual word form area, 149, 151
Visual word form system development,
    214
Vocabulary, learning, 163–166
Vocalization, 93

Voluntary control. *See* Executive
    attention

Warning signal, 60, 92, 101–102
Web-based education, 213–214
Wernicke's aphasia, 154
Wernicke's area, 154
White matter, 40–42, 45, 59
Wisconsin card sort task, 90
Word form area, 203
Word form systems, development of,
    169–171
Word forms, developing, 164–165
Word meaning, 165–166
Word output, 162
Word processing, 148
Word production, 80, 88
Word retrieval, 162
Working memory
    activated state, 192
    brain areas involved in, 80, 88
    components of, 193–194
    and expertise, 191–192
    future studies of, 215
    training of, 112, 117

ABOUT THE AUTHORS

Michael I. Posner, PhD, is currently professor emeritus at the University of Oregon, Eugene, and adjunct professor of psychology in psychiatry at the Weill Medical College of Cornell University, Ithaca, New York, where he served as founding director of the Sackler Institute. Dr. Posner is best known for his work with Marcus E. Raichle on imaging the human brain during cognitive tasks. He has worked on the anatomy, circuitry, development, and genetics of three attentional networks underlying maintaining alertness, orienting to sensory events, and voluntary control of thoughts and ideas. His methods for measuring these networks have been applied to a wide range of neurological, psychiatric, and developmental disorders. Since 1980, he has worked with Mary K. Rothbart to understand the interaction of specific experience and genes in the development and efficiency of attentional networks.

Mary K. Rothbart, PhD, is a distinguished professor emerita at the University of Oregon, Eugene. She studies temperament and emotional and social development, and for the last 25 years she has worked with Michael I. Posner studying the development of attention and its relation to temperamental effortful control. She coedited the book *Temperament in Childhood* and coauthored, with Holly Ruff, the book *Attention in Early Development*. She has also made contributions to the education and support of new parents through the Birth to Three organization in Eugene, Oregon. This year, the group honored her as a "Champion for Children."